PHILOSOPHY 101

PHILOSOPHY 101

AN ESSENTIAL GUIDE TO THE STUDY OF GREAT IDEAS

PETER GIBSON

ARCTURUS

This edition published in 2024 by Arcturus Publishing Limited
26/27 Bickels Yard, 151–153 Bermondsey Street,
London SE1 3HA

Copyright © Arcturus Holdings Limited

All rights reserved. No part of this publication may be reproduced, stored in a retrieval system, or transmitted, in any form or by any means, electronic, mechanical, photocopying, recording or otherwise, without prior written permission in accordance with the provisions of the Copyright Act 1956 (as amended). Any person or persons who do any unauthorised act in relation to this publication may be liable to criminal prosecution and civil claims for damages.

ISBN: 978-1-3988-3438-5
AD011591US

Printed in China

CONTENTS

Introduction..........................6

Chapter 1
What is Philosophy?..................7

Chapter 2
Truth..........................23

Chapter 3
Reasoning........................35

Chapter 4
Existence........................49

Chapter 5
Knowledge........................61

Chapter 6
Mind..........................79

Chapter 7
Persons........................93

Chapter 8
Thought........................107

Chapter 9
Language........................121

Chapter 10
Values........................139

Chapter 11
Ethics........................151

Chapter 12
Society........................169

Chapter 13
Nature........................187

Chapter 14
Transcendence....................205

Glossary..........................217

Suggested Reading..................219

Index..........................221

Picture Credits....................224

INTRODUCTION

Philosophy is a very enjoyable subject. It asks difficult questions, and at first, some of these may seem impossible to answer. But once the methods of breaking down the problem are learned, the pleasure is in the thrill of a chase. One idea leads to another, and exciting moments of revelation follow. As well as providing the challenge of solving puzzles, philosophy touches on everything that really matters. Most students of the subject become fascinated by one or two particular areas, but it is essential also to keep a broad view, and that is what this book offers.

The following pages provide a comprehensive account of philosophy in a single volume. We cover all of the major topics of Western philosophy, with a slight emphasis on the English-speaking tradition when it comes to the thinkers of the modern day. Each chapter focuses on a single topic. The book begins with general and theoretical subjects, then moves on to examine issues concerned with human beings and their behavior, and it ends by looking at nature and transcendence. The chapters can be read in any order, and each section within can be read separately. Technical terms are explained where relevant and can also be found in the glossary at the end.

Philosophy studies a particular set of problems in a particular way. The problems are nothing less than the deepest and most important issues that philosophers have been able to identify. They cover the essential nature of human beings, the way we think, the nature of reality, and our ability to know that reality, and this interconnected family of problems is covered systematically as the book progresses.

The techniques for studying these problems form a carefully refined set of tools for reasoning. These methods are used in every area of human thought, but philosophers have identified them more precisely and clearly than is normal in other disciplines. One benefit of studying philosophy, therefore, is that it offers us a toolkit for thinking, which is then applicable to other areas of life. As you read this book, you should gradually absorb these thinking strategies.

Chapter One
WHAT IS PHILOSOPHY?

Defining Philosophy—Methods of Study—The Critics—Philosophy and Real Life

- PHILOSOPHY
  - IDEAS
  - METHODS OF STUDY
  - CONTINENTAL VS ANALYTIC
  - JARGON
- DEVELOPMENTS
  - CLASSICAL GREECE
  - RISE OF SCIENCE
  - ENLIGHTENMENT
  - ROMANTICISM
  - MEDIEVAL
  - MODERN PHILOSOPHY
  - FEMINISM
  - LOGIC
- THE CRITICS
  - PRECISION
  - PROGRESS
  - EVIDENCE
  - SCIENCE
  - RELIGION
  - THE ARTS

CHAPTER 1

DEFINING PHILOSOPHY

If you sit quietly at the back of a philosophy class you will hear people expressing views about fairly abstract matters. They are not, however, merely swapping opinions. Not only do their listeners demand reasons for opinions, but the speakers themselves focus more on their reasons than on their opinions, and may even offer objections to their own views. The study of reasons for opinions is at the center of philosophy.

When swapping opinions in class, budding philosophers offer reasons for, or even objections to, their own opinions.

Of course, a rational discussion of law or gardening is also interested in the reasons given for opinions, but philosophy also has a distinctive subject matter. Philosophers try to understand the world. However, many other disciplines—such as physics, chemistry, statistics, biology, literature, geography, and history—seek the same thing.

Philosopher's Questions

Philosophers step back from these studies, and ask more general questions:

- What is an object?
- a law?
- a number?
- a life?
- a person?
- a society?
- a story?
- an event?

Each of these concepts is taken for granted by ordinary speakers, until we wonder *exactly* what each of them means—and that is where the puzzles, ambiguities, and vagueness begin. Other disciplines must take such normal terminology for granted, but philosophy tries to take nothing for granted.

> **Continental vs Analytic Philosophy**
>
> About two hundred years ago, Western philosophy divided into two camps. The **continental school**, flourishing most notably in Germany and France, sees philosophy as closely allied to literature and psychology, and focuses on major concepts that offer broad insights. The **analytic school**, predominant in the United Kingdom and the United States, pays more attention to the physical sciences and to logic, and seeks precision and clarity by means of definitions and proofs.

CHAPTER 1

Ideas

Philosophers focus on the key concepts that are the basis of our thinking. Philosophy does not simply study the problematic nature of ordinary ideas. Ideas are in our minds, but they refer to the outside world, and the aim is to think more clearly in order to understand the world more clearly. Philosophy aims for clarity, but its key feature is its highly-generalized nature. Specialists investigate the physical world, or the past, or how to improve our practical lives, but philosophy aims to get the framework of our understanding right. We all want to do the right thing, and to be good people, but what makes something "right" or "good"? We want to live in a just society, but what is "justice"?

We might therefore define philosophy as *trying to understand reality and human life in very general terms, by studying key ideas in our thinking, to form a picture guided by good reasons*. Most of the famous works of philosophy fit that description, apart from a few misfits. Philosophers are inclined to question everything, even the nature of their own subject.

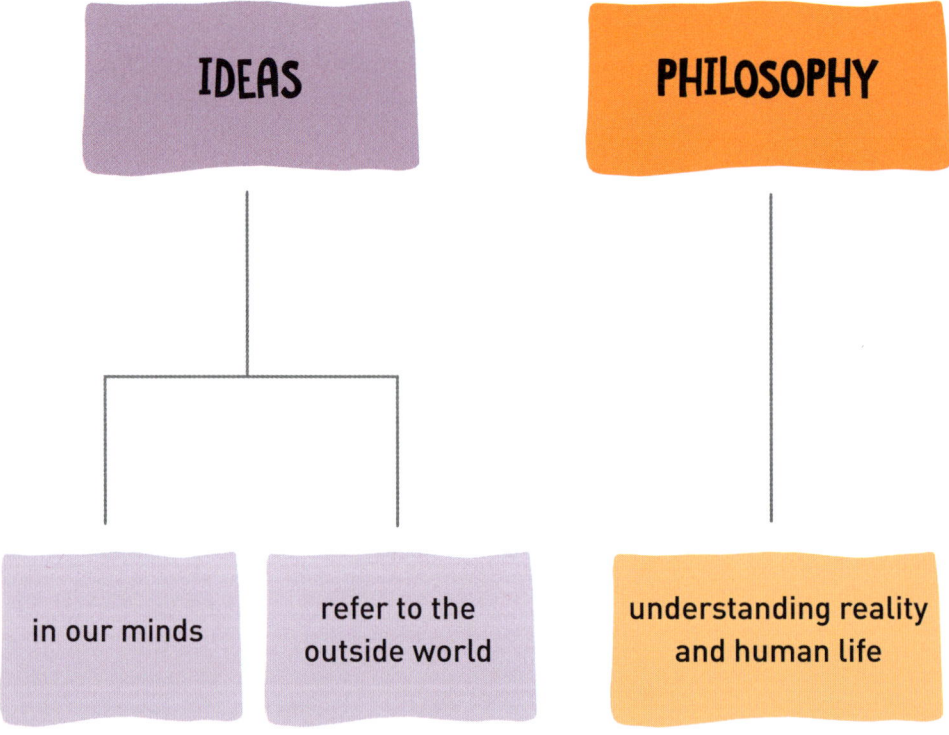

Enlightenment

The years 1620 to 1800 were the period of the European Enlightenment, sometimes called the Age of Reason. It was an age of classicism in architecture, and a new mechanical inventiveness in industry. Though some philosophers such as David Hume were pessimistic about the power of reason, the dominant view was that our understanding and way of life could become much more rational (see page 14). Isaac Newton had explained the movement of the solar system in one short equation, and a rational account of all of reality seemed attainable. In the 1780s, Immanuel Kant made a notable contribution by offering a theory of morality, built on nothing more than consistency and rationality in our principles of behavior.

Philosophy acquired great prestige in the Age of Reason. When philosophy allied itself with the new science, it looked like a winning team which could finally make human life a rational affair.

Romanticism

But just as rational and scientific philosophy was poised for victory, rebellions arose, mainly among artists and writers. The cold classicism and the logical mode of life seemed to neglect the most important part of our lives—our feelings. In the early nineteenth century, important philosophers continued to flourish, but in a more cautious vein than their bolder Enlightenment predecessors.

With the discoveries of Isaac Newton, it seemed that everything could now be explained in rational terms.

CHAPTER 1

Philosophers of the Enlightenment

Britain

Thomas Hobbes
(1588–1679)

George Berkeley
(1685–1753)

France

René Descartes
(1596–1650)

Germany

Gottfried Leibniz
(1646–1716)

John Locke
(1632–1704)

David Hume
(1711–1776)

Jean-Jacques Rousseau
(1712–1778)

Immanuel Kant
(1724–1804)

The Women of Philosophy

The history of philosophy is, without doubt, dominated by men. Hypatia of Alexandria was a notable female philosopher in the ancient world, and in the Enlightenment a number of women engaged in high-level philosophical correspondence and wrote significant books. The idea that women should have full equality as citizens began to emerge in the nineteenth century, and women wrote forcefully on that topic. It is only, though, when women gained the right to study at universities that they became major contributors to philosophy. Nowadays women have, at least in formal terms, full access to all areas of philosophical activity.

The University

In modern universities there is less emphasis on taking wider views of knowledge, because specialists are investigating smaller parts of the project, but every philosopher is motivated by interests wider than their own narrow specialism, and always bear these in mind. Philosophy can even be seen as a way of life, rather than an academic subject, but the aim is still to place one's life within a bigger picture.

Hypatia of Alexandria (c. AD 350–415) was a leading philosopher in the ancient world.

CHAPTER 1

METHODS OF STUDY

Most philosophers agree on the need for rationality, clear concepts, general truths, and a big picture—but they disagree about the appropriate methods.

In ancient Greece, philosophy was mostly studied through conversation in the famous schools, with books as occasional by-products.

In medieval Europe, the main focus was on explaining the famous surviving ancient texts, especially those by Aristotle. With the arrival of printing, it became possible to give new books a wide circulation, and philosophy centered on written debate between leading scholars, who often lived in isolation from one another.

The rise of science divided philosophers: some of them embracing the new physical discoveries as an expansion of traditional philosophy, while others asserted its separateness, and its concern with thought, abstractions, and eternal truths.

In medieval Europe, philosophers focused their attention on surviving ancient texts.

The emergence of many new universities in the nineteenth century greatly changed the practice of philosophy, and today leading philosophers mostly spend their careers within university departments. The modern university seminar resembles the conversations in ancient schools, but there are also innumerable papers published in journals, with critical responses from colleagues, and regular international conferences which focus on the specialist topics within philosophy.

The final strand in the changing methods of philosophy is the modern emergence of formal logic. Aristotle invented formal logic, but that skill remained on the margins of philosophy until the twentieth century. Once the formal languages had become more expressive and powerful, philosophers in the *Analytic tradition* saw them as tools for extending rational thought into new territory, while also adding the sort of precision that was usually confined to mathematics.

WHAT IS PHILOSOPHY?

THE CRITICS
Western philosophy has a two-and-a-half-thousand-year tradition, and it continues to flourish. The subject has, however, always had its critics, and their doubts are a good focus for what philosophers are trying to achieve. Typical doubts about philosophy come from theologians, poets, scientists, feminists, interested laymen, and practical people.

Theologians fear that continual questioning undermines the well-established doctrines on which a religion has to be founded.

Scientists believe that modern physical research has left philosophy behind, because armchair thinking can never demonstrate the facts.

Poets fear that the icy precision of philosophical thinking stunts our deep feelings, and prevents us from living a fulfilled life.

Feminists are suspicious of the way in which philosophy embodies the typical interests of men, neglecting the somewhat different priorities of women.

Laymen frequently become frustrated by those elements typically found in philosophy—the jargon, long sentences, obscure claims, and lack of physical examples—and suspect it of being an elitist conspiracy.

Practical people rail against the infuriating detachment of philosophers, who withdraw to schools and universities when their intellects could be put to much better practical use.

CHAPTER 1

Religious Dilemmas
The major religions have conducted a love-hate relationship with philosophy. Once a religion becomes established in its main beliefs and has attracted a widespread following, it usually seeks a consistent and comprehensive theological system to answer all of its believers' questions. This is precisely what philosophy offers, with techniques for eliminating contradictions and finding a secure framework of concepts. A typical issue is whether the remote rational God of the philosophers can be reconciled with the personal God of a religion, who intervenes in human life. The main problem, of course, is that philosophy has no rule saying skeptical questioning should stop when it becomes uncomfortable.

Faith and Philosophy
Ninth-century Islam took a keen interest in Greek philosophy, but by the twelfth century this movement had died out and loyalty to the sacred texts once again predominated. Christian thinkers became excited when they first read Aristotle in the twelfth century, and several generations of outstanding scholars sought to reconcile Greek systems of metaphysics and ethics with the teachings of the New Testament. New doctrines became increasingly independent and challenging, until the church leaders abruptly (in 1347) put a stop to it, and the scholars were persecuted and dispersed. The emphasis on pure faith became even stronger with the Protestant Reformation (beginning in 1517), though the Roman Catholic Church retained a great interest in the reconciliations achieved by medieval thinkers such as Thomas Aquinas. Judaism, too, has had great philosophical theologians, such as Maimonides in the twelfth century, and maintains an active interest in reconciling philosophical issues with the laws laid down in early texts.

The reconciliations between philosophy and theology made by Saint Thomas Aquinas formed the foundations for the doctrine of the Catholic Church.

PHILOSOPHY AND THEOLOGY'S INTERACTIONS

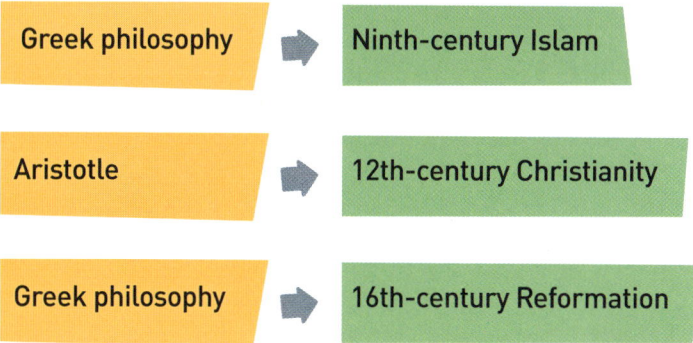

Theology and Science

However, the gap between theology and philosophy has become steadily wider since the seventeenth century, when the rise of modern science and renewed interest in ancient skepticism led to ever more challenging fundamental questions. The emergence of explicit atheism in the eighteenth century seemed to create an unbridgeable gulf, but new approaches to religion (from the existentialist Kierkegaard, for example) kept theological issues alive within philosophy, and the philosophy of religion is nowadays a flourishing topic in most philosophy departments.

Modern theologians remain concerned with the formal arguments for God's existence, and whether the objections to them adavanced by skeptics are valid. The problem of evil must be addressed, because it is often cited as a reason for atheism. The most common focus of modern theology, though, concerns the nature of God, often seen as an aspect of the Self and the way it relates to the world, rather than as a supreme person. From the religious perspective, modern materialism seems soulless and lacking purpose.

Maimonides (c. 1135–1204) was a leading Jewish philosopher.

CHAPTER 1

The Attack from Science

For a long time, science was called "natural philosophy," and the two subjects were inseparable. But when Francis Bacon helped to launch modern experimental science (around 1610), he linked it to an attack on traditional metaphysics, which was like an inert statue which never went anywhere. This led to three new criticisms of philosophy:
- it fails to make progress
- it lacks precision
- it pays too little attention to evidence.

In recent times, the huge progress of science in so many areas has suggested that it might eventually solve all the genuine philosophical problems. *Scientism* is the label used by philosophers for this strong claim.

Some philosophers accept this idea, and have become pessimistic about their own subject. To understand the mind and its thinking, human behavior, matter, space, and time, and how we gain knowledge, it may be more important to keep up with modern research than to sit speculating.

Francis Bacon helped to launch experimental science.

Optimists
- Believe science and philosophy remain part of a single enterprise (with philosophers specializing in the most generalized and conceptual part).

- See science as irrelevant to philosophy. The workings of the physical world are seen as minor details, with more important problems residing at an entirely different level of thought.

Pessimists
- Believe philosophy is a self-inflicted conceptual confusion, which must first be clarified and then abandoned.

- Believe that to better understand the world, we should keep up with modern research rather than just sit and speculate.

Progress

It is a common charge that philosophy fails to make progress, since it has wrestled with the same problems for many centuries, and failed to solve any of them. In reply, it can either be said that some problems have been solved (although the correct solution may not have been fully appreciated), or that the aim never was to solve the problems. This second view sees the problems as permanent puzzles that will always face the human race:

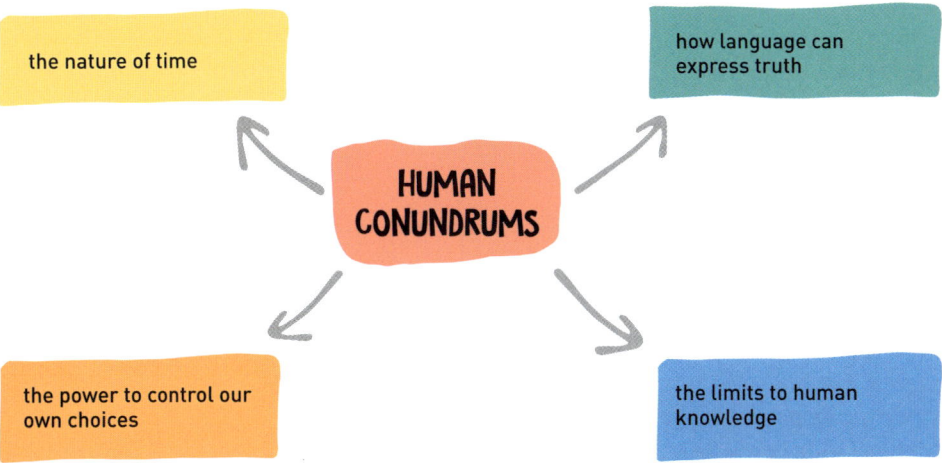

The aim is to fully understand the puzzles and map out the possible arguments and counter-arguments, which philosophers are doing very successfully.

Precision

The charge that philosophy is imprecise is met by the use of logic as a tool of enquiry. This certainly gives precision and strict proof, but there is disagreement about whether such an exact tool is appropriate for such difficult and imprecise problems.

Evidence

The charge that philosophy does not respect the evidence is usually met by philosophers accepting that they must learn about science. It is now normal for philosophers to have a good working knowledge of quantum and relativity theory, brain biology, the standard model of physical matter, and evolutionary theory. Such knowledge does not replace philosophical thinking, but respect for established facts is indispensable.

The Poet's Objection

A new form of objection to philosophy emerged, which preferred dramatic music and emotional poetry to the cool analysis of rational thought. This romantic view is still with us, in a preference for intense personal experiences rather than the detached pursuit of wisdom.

Modern philosophers have responded by acknowledging the importance of emotion within their theories of the mind, and of ethics. Modern neuroscience endorses the idea that pure rational thought is a myth, because emotions are entangled in even our most logical mental activity. The lack of emotional motivation is a large gap in many ethical theories—we can formulate impressive rules for behaving well, but why should we bother to follow the rules? Accounts of the good life now pay far more attention to the role of love and selfish desires.

Feminism

Feminist thinkers have several concerns. Two thousand years of thoroughly masculine philosophy have left their mark on the subject (as in other areas of society), and explicitly feminist philosophers are now engaged in deconstructing those ideas and theories. An obvious example is the philosophy of morality, in which modern masculine discussions have been very legalistic in character, seeking precise rules for guiding and evaluating behavior. Women have been at the forefront of the revival of the place of virtue in ethics, seeing the upbringing of children (which is barely mentioned in earlier discussions) as central to moral life. There is also some suspicion of the male love of precise logic and awe-inspiringly grand concepts, which sweep aside the subtleties of ordinary life.

Women are nowadays major players in all the standard areas of philosophy, contributing important work to the philosophies of logic, mathematics, and science, as well as to the more human aspects of the subject. There seems no reason why philosophy in the near future should not become gender-blind.

Romantics valued passion over rational analysis.

Bewildered by Jargon

Outsiders to philosophy are often appalled by its apparent obscurity. Not only are there very long trains of thought and many technical words, but there is often a sustained focus on minute issues that normal people wouldn't waste their time on.

An obvious response is to say that all subjects—take chemistry, for example—are obscure, full of jargon, and concerned over details, whenever they are studied to a high level, so why should philosophy be different? The critic might respond that philosophy largely concerns normal human experience, with which we might all hope to engage. Philosophers can persist in claiming that jargon and minutiae remain essential, even when discussing what is ordinary, but they should probably concede some of the criticisms.

Philosophy has always been difficult, because it asks people to think much harder about everything. The philosophy texts of the ancient Greeks are certainly more challenging than their histories and literature. However, from the time of Kant onward (about 1790), the style of expression used in philosophy books becomes notably more difficult, and the specialist jargon greatly increases. Part of this is inevitable, because the explorations of past philosophers accumulate, and new students must be familiar with the concepts, theories, and famous illustrations of their predecessors. But many modern philosophers are concerned about the exclusive and elitist image which the subject has developed. The fight for clarity is vital in every academic subject, but especially important in philosophy, because it is too easy to introduce technical vocabulary which is not anchored in the physical world.

Philosophers like Martha Nussbaum seek to question traditional masculine wisdom.

Philosophy texts, from the Greeks onward, have become increasingly filled with jargon.

CHAPTER 1

Socrates discussed the merits of rhetoric and philosophy in Gorgias.

Impracticality

In Plato's dialogue *Gorgias*, Socrates engages in a discussion about the relative merits of persuasive rhetoric and true philosophy. During the discussion, Plato introduces a character called Callicles, who despises philosophers and their subject. What particularly annoys him is the withdrawal of philosophers from practical life. They idealize notions of goodness and virtue, while real life is just a power struggle, full of winners and losers. Philosophers are cowardly, irresponsible, and irrelevant. There is no easy answer to an onslaught like that, but since most academics have indeed withdrawn from the practical world (in a very responsible manner), it is the charge of irrelevance which is most in need of an answer.

PHILOSOPHY AND REAL LIFE

So what is the relevance of philosophy to real life? Most philosophers accept that the more abstract parts of the subject have little immediate relevance, and even the more practical discussions of ethics and theoretical politics have no direct link to how we live now, but they still believe that in the long term philosophy is of enormous importance. This conviction is very hard to justify, but if we examine the underlying beliefs shaping modern society, and ask where they came from, we realize that those beliefs developed as a mixture of responses to practical situations in the world and to the influence of dominant thinkers from previous generations. The principles of our justice system, the values of liberal democracy, and the topics and cultures taught in schools are not the result of mere chance. The history of such ideas leads us back to powerful general insights from the past. Many of those come from warriors, economists, charismatic leaders, and imaginative writers, but the philosophers may well have had the greatest influence. Philosophers can effect huge changes in the world—but very, very slowly.

Chapter Two
TRUTH

Aiming at Truth—Relativism—Correspondence—Practical Truth—The Linguistic Approach—Truthmakers

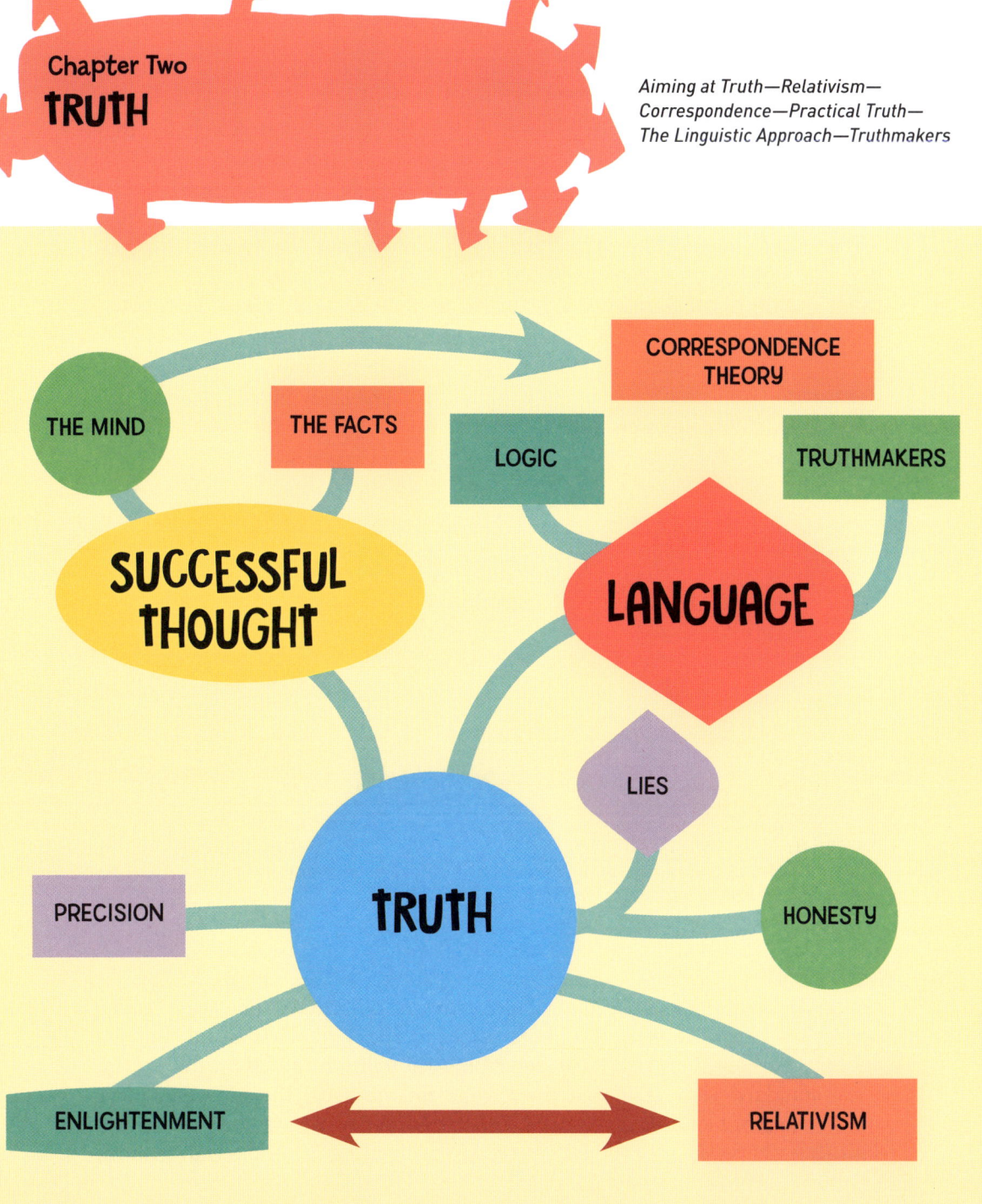

CHAPTER 2

AIMING AT TRUTH

Truth is at the center of human life, and at the center of philosophy. Philosophy only makes sense if its thinkers are trying to avoid what is false. Truth may even be the supreme value of philosophy, if we believe Plato's remark that *"Truth heads the list of all things good, for gods and men alike."*

Animals, too, have a sense of "getting it wrong," as when a cat misjudges a leap, or a dog is confused about the location of a ball. Their behavior in these situations only makes sense if they realize they have got things right or wrong. They may not have a concept of truth, but that human concept refers to the success or failure of judgments, and larger animals certainly make judgments.

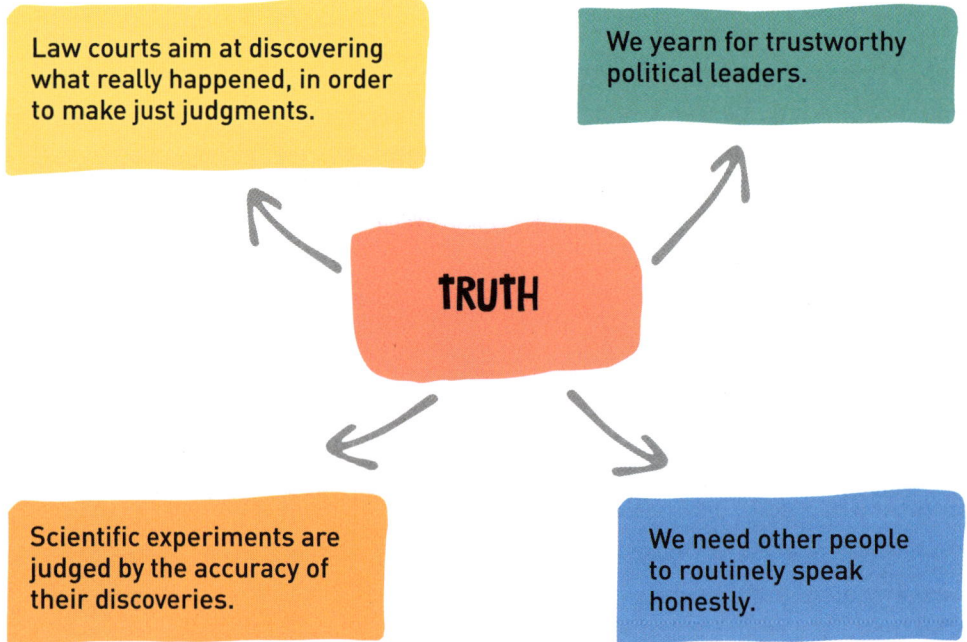

What is Truth?

In everyday conversation, we say "the truth is out there" or "we need to discover the truth," but philosophers prefer to speak of what is out there as "the facts," reserving "true" for describing thoughts rather than the world. So the standard view is that if there were no minds in the universe, there would be lots of facts—but no truth. Truth, in other words, is understood as a relationship between a mind and the facts (the "getting it right" relationship).

TRUTH

TRUTH ▶ *A relationship between a mind and the facts.*

THE UNIVERSE / Facts — **TRUTH** — **MINDS** / Thoughts

Truth might be captured in a sentence, and we may say that some sentence of Plato's remains true, even though the mind of Plato is no longer with us. Hence modern discussions often focus on language, but there is no truth if a mind is not involved somewhere in the process.

Given, then, that successful thinking is true thinking, and that in simple cases it is obvious whether our judgments have been successful, the concept, and its role in philosophy, should be fairly simple and self-evident. Sadly, this is not the case. For every philosopher who has endorsed Plato's optimistic valuation, there has usually been another who was not so sure. At the two extremes, there have been philosophers who have sacrificed everything for the pursuit of truth (Socrates and Spinoza, for example), but also philosophers (such as Protagoras and Nietzsche) who have doubted its value, or even its very existence.

Plato held truth to be the greatest of all virtues.

RELATIVISM

Truth is successful thought, but if there is no such thing as genuine "success" in thought, then there is no such thing as truth. The earliest doubts took exactly this form. Early philosophers asserted all sorts of claims, but disagreement is the driving force of philosophy, and for every new theory of nature or morality there quickly appeared objections.

The crisis came when Protagoras (one of the sophists, or so-called "wise men") observed that these continual arguments and counter-arguments cancel one another out. Seneca reports Protagoras as saying that "it is possible to argue

CHAPTER 2

either side of any question with equal force, even the question whether or not one can equally argue either side of any question!" If the opposing sides of every argument are indeed equal in force, then knowledge of the correct answer will always be out of reach, and truth can be abandoned. All that remains are the rival arguments, each representing someone's point of view—expressed in the slogan "man is the measure of all things." This social doctrine (of extreme *relativism*) means that both social life and philosophy are merely battles for supremacy between rival doctrines, with emotional powers of persuasion dominating the battle, rather than objectivity and reason.

Protagoras, a sophist, believed that equally powerful arguments are found on both sides, making it impossible to discover what is the true answer.

EXTREME RELATIVISM ▶ Both social life and philosophy are merely battles for supremacy between rival doctrines, with emotional powers of persuasion dominating the battle, rather than objectivity and reason.

Defenders of the Truth

The relativism of Protagoras remained, however, a minority view. A common response was to **turn the tables**, and say that if there is no truth in any theory, then that means there is no truth in relativism either, so we can ignore it. With the early successes of modern science, the status of truth rose to new heights, and achieved its pinnacle during the Enlightenment.

Enlightenment Philosophers on Truth

John Locke—"Nothing [is] so beautiful to the eye as truth is to the mind."

Spinoza—"Men necessarily always agree with one another in so far as they live according to the guidance of reason."

Optimism about the truth and optimism about the prospects of rational agreement have always gone hand in hand, and still inspire many thinkers. But the challenges were far from over.

Relativism in the Age of Science

The age of science brought a reverential attitude to truth, but in the 1880s Friedrich Nietzsche wondered why it had acquired this sacred aura:

- After all, animals live successfully without worrying about it.
- Many human cultures are built on mythologies and strange fantasies which are clearly false.
- Powerful people in a society don't need to worry much about truth, so championing The Truth began to look like a slogan favored by the downtrodden, rather than a neutral target of thought.

Such suggestions began a modern attitude that sees truth as less of an absolute ideal sought by everyone, and more of a dream subtly woven into modern cultures. Sociology and cultural studies have developed this view, which is much closer to Protagorean relativism than to the ideals of Plato and Spinoza. Relativism may also have become popular because it seems to encourage tolerance, but this is a misunderstanding, because consistent relativism requires that intolerance must also be tolerated.

COHERENCE THEORY ▶ *Truth is nothing more than fitting into a conceptual scheme, like a piece in a jigsaw.*

Friedrich Nietzsche challenged the reverential aura around truth.

Philosophers offer the *Coherence Theory* of truth to support the relativist approach, by saying that it is nothing more than fitting into a conceptual scheme, like a piece in a jigsaw. To say that truth is just a matter of fitting neatly has some plausibility in a large, detailed, and successful conceptual scheme such as modern chemistry, but seems wrong when the scheme of thought is very restricted, such as fitting well with claims that the Earth is flat, or with fictional worlds, such as the Sherlock Holmes stories.

CORRESPONDENCE

Defenders of truth needed a clearer theory of its nature, and the idea of *correspondence* was developed. It proposed a precise correspondence between the ingredients of a truthful thought or sentence, and the ingredients of the fact which it asserts.

> **CORRESPONDENCE THEORY ▶**
> *There is a precise correspondence between the ingredients of a truthful thought or sentence, and the ingredients of the fact which it asserts.*

In 1912, Bertrand Russell suggested that the nouns and verbs of a true sentence are precisely aligned with the objects and actions of an event being described, so that they match—like two congruent triangles, or a map and the landscape it depicts. This *Correspondence Theory* remains the most popular with those who see truth as a robust concept, despite subsequent problems with the theory.

Just like a map corresponds to the landscape it represents, so the words of a sentence correspond to objects and actions in the real world.

If the meaning of a simple true sentence corresponds to a fact, how should we understand "meaning," "correspond" and "fact?" If these concepts are being used in the definition of truth, then the definitions of the concepts had better not involve truth, or the whole theory would be hopelessly circular.

Meaning
If the meaning of a true sentence corresponds to the facts, what is "meaning?" The most popular theory says the meaning of a sentence is its "truth conditions"—how things would be if the sentence were true. But how can we pick out the situation truly described by the sentence if we don't yet understand "true?" Hence this definition of truth is circular, and needs the concept of meaning to have nothing to do with truth, which seems unlikely.

Correspond
We can see how points on a triangle or a map correspond with points located elsewhere, but the correspondence between words or concepts and the situations they describe is much more obscure, because they are entirely different types of things (it's like asking how music corresponds to architecture). Similarly, it is hard to define *correspondence* without suggesting that the match-up should be accurate—which seems to involve truth. If we don't add such a restriction, a map of France can be shown to correspond to Germany.

Fact
It is impossible to specify the corresponding fact without expressing it in a sentence—but that fact will probably already be the sentence under discussion. Thus, if "The cat is on the mat" is true, it is held to match a fact. But what is the fact? That "The feline is on the small door carpet?" It is more sensible to state the fact as "The cat is on the mat." If, when we try to express facts in this way, they turn out merely to be true sentences, then the correspondence theory tells us nothing.

To give a robust view of truth, we need a robust view of facts, which needs a strong commitment to the existence of an external world that is independent of what we say about it.

PRACTICAL TRUTH

Given the difficulties with defining "true," it seemed tempting to just say how the concept affects our behavior, or how the word is used in language. The *American Pragmatist* movement (of the late nineteenth century) adopted the first approach. If truth is an abstract ideal, then it seems remote, perplexing, and indefinable, so the aim of pragmatists is to drag it back into real life.

Explaining the problem through our ordinary experience is obviously attractive, but the pragmatists can't deny that success in action may not always imply truth, because some very deluded people can still get through life quite successfully. Pragmatism offers a useful view of truth, but at the expense of making it a lot less robust than the correspondence theory, and taking it much closer to relativism.

THE LINGUISTIC APPROACH

The linguistic approach started with Frank Ramsey's challenge in the 1920s—that the word "true," when examined in practice, appears to be meaningless.

This **Redundancy Theory** points out that there is no significant difference between saying:
- "Brutus murdered Caesar."
- "It is true that Brutus murdered Caesar."

The second sentence merely repeats the first, or says it louder. With the correspondence view unable to give a sharp definition of truth, pragmatists absorbing it into daily life, and the redundancy theory's demolition, truth was in crisis. "Truth" as a precise concept was either going to disappear, or be absorbed into historical and cultural studies.

The Redundancy Theory states that there is no difference between saying "Brutus murdered Caesar" and "It is true that Brutus murdered Caesar."

The final nail in the coffin came in the 1930s, when Alfred Tarski pondered the statement "this sentence is false" (which is false if it is true, and true if it is false!), and proved that it is logically impossible to define the concept of truth from within a precise language. The good news was that you could still give a precise account of truth by stepping outside of the language, into a *meta-language*—a separate language used to describe the language you are interested in. You can't use ordinary English to say that some English sentence is true. You have to step up into a separate level of English, the one used by linguistics experts to discuss languages. From this higher viewpoint, you can specify which sentences in the **object language** are true. Thus, we arrive at the slightly bewildering pronouncement that: *"snow is white" is true if and only if snow is white*.

It is a little clearer if we say: *"la neige est blanche" is true if and only if snow is white*, where the meta-language (English) is used to show that the French sentence is true—as long as it is permissible to say that snow is white in English.

CHAPTER 2

Truth and Logic
On the basis of this simple idea, a theoretical catalog of all the permissible sentences in the object language can be compiled, amounting to a fat book defining truth for that language. For the logician, the importance was that "true" was now precise enough to show how it is transmitted in logical proofs.

We can say that if A is true, and A implies B, then B is true.

Simply attaching a "T" to the statement "Paris is the capital of France" is not sufficient when it comes to language and logic.

Without concepts of true and false, logic is just a meaningless game with symbols, but now it was possible to connect logic to the world, by means of the symbols "T" and "F."

This was great news for the logicians, but you may have doubts about whether we now understand any better what "true" and "false" mean (since they are taken for granted in the meta-language). "T" and "F" can now be assigned to sentences in logic, rather in the way that we might assign a "1" or a "0" to formulae in a computer.

You can't know that Paris is the capital of Spain, because it isn't true.

This enables some interesting calculations that may produce spectacular results (in a physics laboratory, for example), but to say that "true" can be expressed as "1" in a computer isn't what Plato had in mind when he praised it as an ideal. Tarski himself conceded that he was showing only how we could use "true," and was not telling us what it means. For some modern philosophers, the implications of Tarski's account are sufficient, and the more robust theories can be dropped in favor of a **Minimalist** or **Deflationary Theory** of truth. "True" is not actually redundant, because it is useful when you refer to sentences without expressing them, as in "what you said yesterday is true," or "every sentence in this sacred text is true." However, this only reinforces Tarski's discovery that *you have to step back from the language in order to say which truths it contains.*

The reason why this important account of truth is not sufficient for philosophy is seen when we come to examine language and logic. In language, we are looking for accounts of how the parts of a sentence can "refer" to real entities in the world, and then accurately attach "predicates" (or properties) to them—which implies the sort of success or failure which probably needs a robust concept of truth. In knowledge, one of the most basic assumptions is that you can never be said to know something that is not true. No one knows that Paris is the capital of Spain, even if they have piles of evidence for it, because Paris just isn't the capital of Spain. This point cannot be expressed properly if we say no more than that the letter "T" can be attached to the sentence "Paris is the capital of France."

TRUTHMAKERS

An interesting modern idea that employs a robust notion of "true" is the claim that every true sentence must have a *truthmaker*—something which makes it true. This suggestion seems thoroughly plausible for simple statements about physical facts. "The cat is on the mat" is true if the cat is indeed on the mat, and if I whisk the mat away from under the cat, that immediately makes the sentence false. The truth of the sentence is directly responsive to the actual situation, and that particular "fact" is what makes the sentence true—so the sentence has a truthmaker. The bold and controversial suggestion is that all true sentences are like that. If every truth does indeed have a truthmaker, this would delight defenders of the robust theories, because truthmakers are substantial facts or states of affairs, and not mere affirmations made in a meta-language.

Inevitably, there are tricky cases where the truthmaker claim is not so obvious:

- "Cats tend to sit on mats"—we can try to specify the truthmaker for each instance, but it will no longer be a neat state of affairs.
- "Cats are mammals"—all the current cats will act as truthmakers, but the statement even refers to future cats, which don't exist yet—rather less robust than a real situation.
- "There is no cat on my mat"—where it is clear that the mat is empty, but it is unclear why that fact has anything to do with cats.

Defenders of the truthmaker idea are currently hard at work trying to account for these tricky cases, in ways that can retain a strong idea of truth as a successful relationship between mind and reality.

The cat sitting on the mat is the truthmaker for the sentence, "The cat is on the mat." If the cat were to be removed, it would no longer be true.

Chapter Three
REASONING

Enquiry Through Conversation—Logic—Scientific Reasoning—Philosophical Reasoning

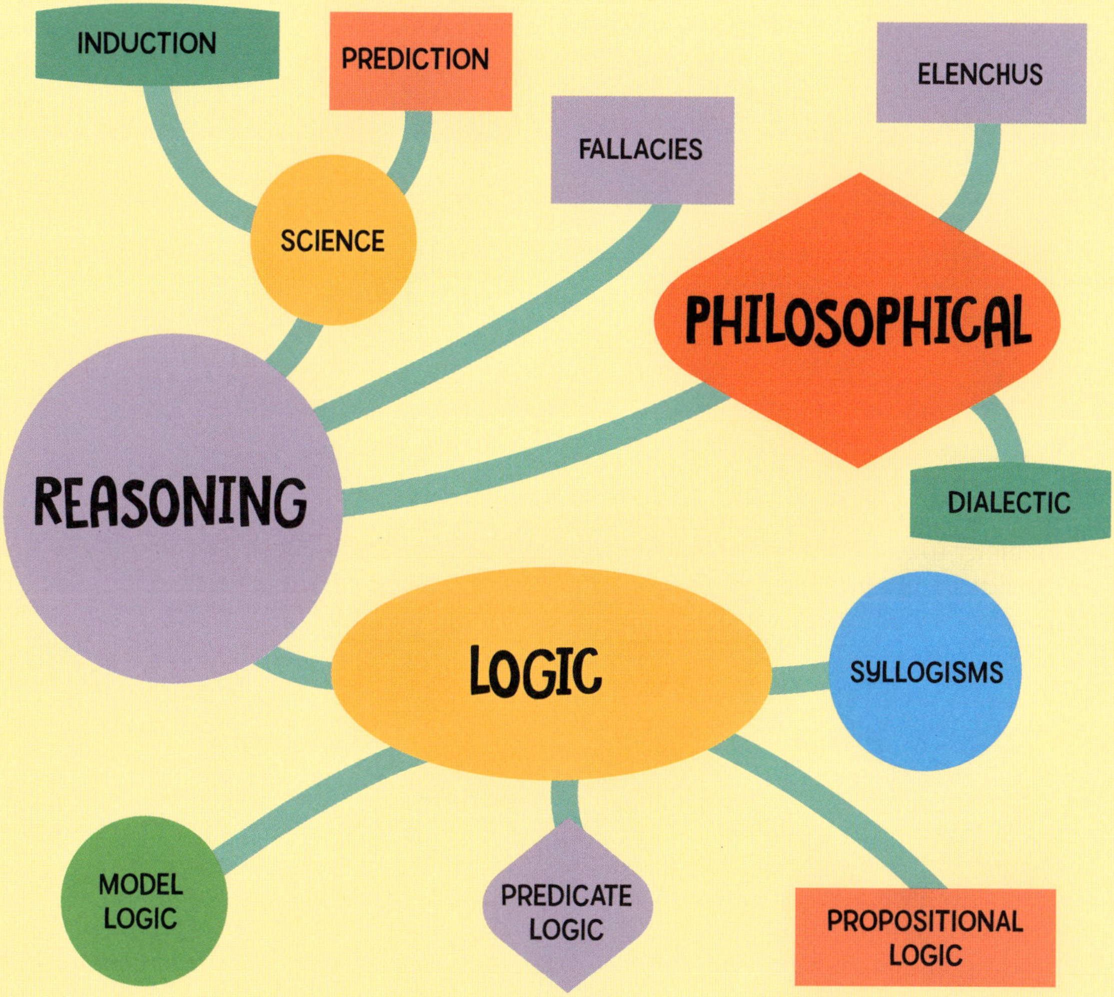

CHAPTER 3

ENQUIRY THROUGH CONVERSATION

The greatest aspiration of philosophy is to be fully rational. In its earliest stages, enquiry was mainly by means of conversation, so discussion techniques were investigated. The vital first step was the right to challenge vague or dubious assertions, and it became obvious that contradiction is at the center of rationality. No law of thought is more basic than *non-contradiction*: we cannot simultaneously say that a proposition is both true and false.

If I say "P," and you say "Not P," we can't both be right.

If both parties to a conversation accept this principle, and have enough humility to concede a point, then progress can be made by a repeated exchange of views and objections. With practice, this procedure—called dialectic—can enormously advance our philosophical understanding.

DIALECTIC ▶ *Progress through a repeated exchange of views and objections.*

To begin with, dialectic meant no more than "conversation," but it gradually increased in importance. What matters is good conversation, and that must be interesting and focused, and lead somewhere. Great conversations lead to wisdom, which needs people to be engaged in reasoning, rather than just exchanging views.

Socrates used the mechanism of the dialectic to advance philosophical understanding.

The Elenchus

But where do you start? Socrates (as reported by his pupil, Plato) saw that we must start from what people actually believe, and he developed a method of interrogation (the *elenchus*) that built on the exchanges of dialectic. Ask someone their opinions about an important concept—such as justice, courage, the law, knowledge, friendship, or beauty—and then invite them to define it. Offer them examples which don't fit their definition, and ask them to re-define it. Eventually, they will reach a point where they have contradicted themselves, and must thus return to their presuppositions and dig deeper.

The usual result of these famous dialogues of Plato is a deeper understanding of the issue, often combined with some confusion that cannot be resolved.

The Dialogues of Plato

Plato wrote about 30 dialogues featuring the elenchus method, most of which feature Socrates. The most famous of these include:

- Apology
- Gorgias
- Phaedo
- The Republic
- Symposium
- Timaeus

ELENCHUS ▶ *A method of interrogation which involves asking someone to define an important concept, and then providing examples that don't fit the definition, forcing them to make a new definition.*

CHAPTER 3

In the elenchus, *a person is interrogated about their definition of an idea, pushing them toward truth.*

Aristotle (384–322 BC) arrived from northern Greece as a teenager, to study at Plato's Academy in Athens. He studied there for 20 years before leaving to start his own school of philosophy, the Lyceum. Over the course of his life, he had a major influence on fields as varied as biology, rhetoric, politics, ethics, theology, and psychology.

Aristotle, a pupil of Plato, went much further in analyzing the workings of rational thought. At Plato's academy, he listened very carefully to the ongoing arguments, noting down patterns of successful and unsuccessful reasoning. His brilliant insight was to see that you could leave out the details and just describe the patterns, mainly by assigning letters to their ingredients, just as we do in algebra. He spotted the simple rules used by reasoners, and then explored the many ways in which the rules could be used to connect and transform the patterns. He thus single-handedly invented formal logic.

REASONING

LOGIC

The basis of Aristotle's logic is the *syllogism*, which presents a pair of statements and then infers some third statement from them. Thus, if we consider the two statements:

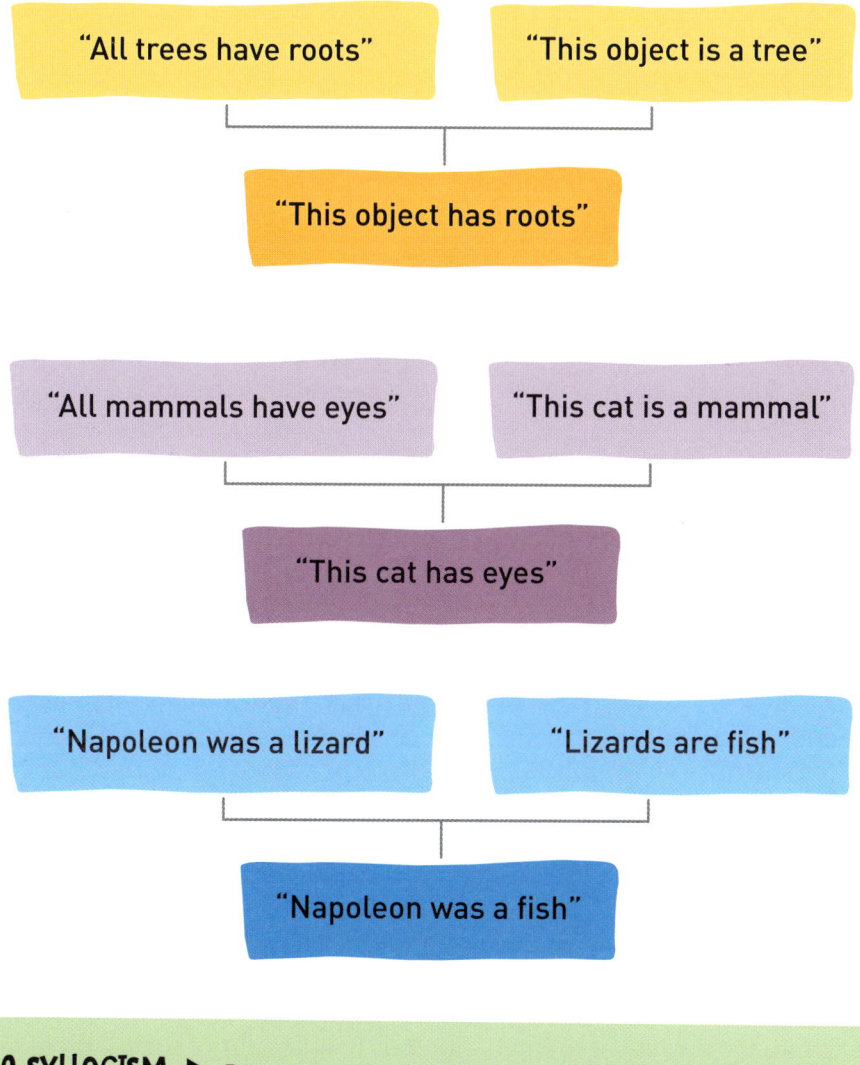

A SYLLOGISM ▶ *Presents a pair of statements and then infers a third statement from them.*

CHAPTER 3

We see that all three syllogisms have the same pattern. Notice that in the last example, we must conclude that Napoleon was a fish (which he wasn't). All three of these syllogisms are *valid*, because the steps in the reasoning are good. In the third case, however, the first two statements (the *premises* of the argument) are false, and so is the conclusion. Notice also that if our premises are:

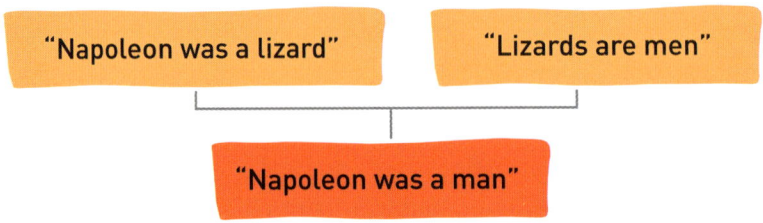

From this, we can validly infer the truth that Napoleon was a man (despite starting with two falsehoods). We must therefore distinguish clearly between statements which are true and arguments which are valid. If you believe nonsense, you can validly infer either truth or nonsense from it.

> **VALID ARGUMENTS** ▶ *Well-reasoned statements in which true premises will always produce a true conclusion.*

Truth and *validity* are quite different concepts, but we can use truth to define validity. An argument pattern is valid if true premises always imply a true conclusion. An argument is clearly invalid if true premises can produce a false conclusion. Liars and scoundrels can argue validly, but if they start from falsehoods we cannot tell whether their conclusions are true or false.

What interests philosophers is that if you are sure your premises are true, and you then apply a pattern of argument which is known to be valid, this guarantees the truth of the new conclusion, even if you had never thought of it before. Aristotle identified 256 patterns of syllogism, and decided that just 19 of them were valid.

Modern logicians have modified some of his findings, but his basic discovery remains unchanged—that a huge variety of human reasoning can be reduced to a few patterns, and we can show whether or not they are valid without delving into the details. Computers can thus handle a lot of logical thought (as long as the patterns are precise), and the method of syllogisms was an excellent fit. Thus, Aristotle created a powerful new tool of reasoning to add to the methods of dialectic and elenchus.

Propositional Logic

Aristotle's syllogisms analyze the relationships between the two components (or terms) of simple sentences, having the form "a is Y" (e.g. "trees have roots"). But we also reason about complete sentences, about relationships, and about possibilities. The ancient Stoics investigated the relationship between complete sentences. Much of their work is lost, but the whole system (called propositional or sentential logic) was improved and clarified by George Boole in the nineteenth century.

> **PROPOSITIONAL LOGIC** ▶ *The logical system of relationships between complete sentences.*

Truth Tables

The logical connections between sentences were reduced to a very small group (by seeing that "but," for example, has the same logical meaning as "and" and "not"), and then these connectives were given precise definitions. If we start with two sentences, P and Q, then:

- P-*and*-Q is true only if they are both true.
- P-*or*-Q is true if at least one of them is true.
- *not*-P is true if P is false.
- if-P-*then*-Q is true if a true P can never imply a false Q.

If we add **T** and **F** for "true" and "false," we can set out the definitions in a ***truth table***.

George Boole clarified the system of propositional logic by providing precise definitions for a variety of logical operators.

The formal symbols for the *connectives* are:
. for and
∨ for or
¬ for not
→ for if . . . then.

	P	Q	P-and-Q P.Q	P-or-Q PvQ	not-P ¬P	if-P-then-Q P→Q	
inputs	T T F F	T F T F	T F F F	T T T F	F F T T	T F T T	outputs

This gives us the language of propositional logic, which is the easiest logic to understand. It is used in electronics, where "1" and "0" are used instead of "T" and "F," to automatically switch circuits on or off. Once these connectives are defined, it is possible to prove a combination of statements, built up from simple truths. You can prove a statement is true in logic by showing that if you assume it is false you will end up with a contradiction. Thus if you assume "humans are fish," this implies we have fins—but we know we don't have fins, so you made a false assumption.

Predicate Logic

With a good logic of sentences in place, a logic was still needed to describe mathematical reasoning. Gottlob Frege provided it, in 1879. Numbers and other entities were treated as *objects*, which had various properties (or linguistic *predicates*). Letters are used to represent these.

"a, b, c . . ." represent *fixed* objects,
"x, y, z . . ." represent *variable objects*.
"F, G, H . . ." represent the properties of objects.

(The supply of letters can continue indefinitely, with $a_1, a_2, a_3 \ldots$ and $x_1, x_2, x_3 \ldots$) If we write "Ga," this means that the object a has the property G. If we write "Gx" this means that some object x has the property G.

The connectives of propositional logic are included in the new system. Hence, if we write Gx→¬Hy, this says "if x is G, then y is not H" (e.g. "if the door is shut, the room is not cold").

A *domain* of objects is either specified or assumed (such as the doors in the building, or the prime numbers). Two further symbols are added, to say whether a statement refers to all of the domain, or just part of it.

- The symbol ∀ is the ***universal quantifier***, and "∀x" is read as "for all x . . ."
- The symbol ∃ is the ***existential quantifier***, and "∃x" is read as "there is at least one x such that . . ."

Using this language you might encounter, in more technical philosophical writing, a formula like this:

$$\forall x \exists y((Fx.Gx) \rightarrow Hy)$$

which reads as "for all the x's, there is at least one y such that if the x's are both F and G, then y is H." For example, "if the whole team is fit and healthy, then at least one of the fans is happy" (where x is a team member, and y is a fan).

Mastering the Symbols

For newcomers this symbolic language looks daunting, but it is needed for the more precise aspects of analytic philosophy. One must first master the symbols, and then learn to translate between this symbolic language and everyday language. To become more advanced you do the proofs, and discover where these proofs can take you. Few philosophers, though, spend their time doing proofs. Predicate logic is mainly used to express statements with precision, and disentangle ambiguities.

Once predicate logic settled down, it became so useful and reliable that it is now referred to as "classical logic," and it is even defended as the only correct system for logical thinking. It relies on treating the world as a set of objects with properties, and (crucially) it relies on every proposition being either true or false. In normal talk, though, this is wrong, because some objects and predicates are vague, and it may be unclear whether some perfectly good proposition is true or false (and occasionally a proposition might even be both). Rival variants of classical logic have been created to try to deal with such problems.

Modal Logic

There are good logics for sentences, and for objects with properties, but other areas of logical thought remain to be formalized. Relations between objects can be added to predicate logic, by allowing a term like "Lxy," which can mean "x is to the left of y," so that we can write "Lxy→Ryx" ("… so y is to the right of x").

An important area of philosophical thought is *modality*—ideas concerning what is possible, impossible, or necessary. For this, ***modal logic*** was created by introducing symbols for "necessary" and "possible":

> □ means "necessary," ◊ means "possible."

"Necessarily true" is the same as "not possibly false," and "possibly true" is the same as "not necessarily false," so ◊ and □ can be defined in terms of one another, and "impossible" is the same as "not possibly true." These symbols can be attached to simple terms, such as ◊Gx, meaning "something might be G," or to whole sentences, such as ∃x(Gx.Hx), meaning "there must exist an x which is both G and H." Using these new symbols, precise translations of modal sentences, and proofs concerning them, can proceed just as they do in predicate logic.

An important aspect of modal logic is its interpretation in terms of possible worlds. Every system of logic has a formal language, and semantics, which is the way in which T and F are applied to the language. The truth tables on page 42 give the normal semantics for propositional logic.

- If we say: "It is possible that donkeys might talk," the standard expression of this is: "There is a possible world where donkeys talk."
- If we say: "Squares must have four corners," we are saying: "Squares have four corners in all possible worlds."

The relationships between the possible worlds can be defined in various ways, leading to different systems of modal logic, each with different strengths, suited to reasoning about different topics, such as time or obligations. Though the framework of possible worlds is obviously excellent for logic, it is controversial in philosophy. Nonetheless, it is undeniably useful when trying to clarify talk of what is necessary or possible.

SCIENTIFIC REASONING

There is a lot more to rationality than mere logic. Most important is the evaluation of evidence. Even animals evaluate evidence, when seeking a home and food, or avoiding dangers. Great detectives are experts at evaluating tiny details in the evidence, and this is highly rational even if they struggle to put it into words ("there is something not right here"). Our greatest achievements in the rational evaluation of evidence are the natural sciences.

The evaluation of evidence is highly rational, but it is not the same as logic.

Induction and Nature

For scientists, the main evidence is patterns of activity in the natural world. A single event may only be a coincidence (when a dog meets a cat), and a feature of one object may just be an accident (a five-legged spider). It is the repetition of certain types of event, or a feature common to all objects of one type, or regular resemblances between events or features, which can tell us most about nature. If we decide that some repetition in nature points to a general or universal truth, such reasoning is called *induction*. We can say "gravity pulls toward the center of the Earth," and "lightning strikes from stormy skies," both claims deriving from many observations over a long period of time. After innumerable cases of lightning emerging from clouds, reason says this is always the case, and that may even be a sort of logic.

If we think of induction as just "learning from experience," it is eminently sensible. It would be good for science if induction were more precise, like logic, but this leads to well-known problems. Why it is that "we can draw an inference from a thousand objects which we couldn't draw from one?" (asked David Hume in 1748). No precise logic can tell us how many lightning flashes we must see before we can accept the general rule. Even after a thousand observations, we may still be wrong, since we may be failing to see the bigger picture.

Observing many instances of lightning can tell us that it always comes from stormy skies.

The Power of Prediction

A useful addition to induction is therefore the power of *prediction*. If we can predict when lightning will strike (or earthquakes occur), that is more impressive than a mere accumulation of observations. However, this still is not as precise as logic, because we can predict something if we are just in the habit of expecting it—as when a local walker regularly passes your window. The impressive predictions are the complex and surprising ones, because this implies genuine understanding, rather than habit derived from repetition. To predict the passing of Halley's Comet (every 76 years) is easy—but predicting the next earthquake would be a great triumph of reasoning from evidence.

CHAPTER 3

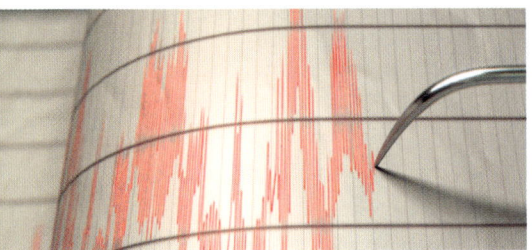

It is much more difficult to predict the next earthquake than it is to predict the passing of Halley's Comet.

To understand earthquakes takes more than recording the pattern over time of their occurrences. We now have a successful theory of plate tectonics, more information about the geology of the Earth, and mathematical theories of mechanics. The achievements of science result from wide connections, and so the exact logic of induction now seems a minor difficulty. Explanation is what matters, rather than mere repetition, and finding a story which fits a wide pattern of diverse information is the real target. Good predictions are a useful by-product, and a way of testing the theory.

PHILOSOPHICAL REASONING

Evidence is important to philosophers for knowledge of reality, and logic is important for precision. However, philosophers have developed their own styles of reasoning, starting with the conversational techniques of *dialectic* and *elenchus*.

Which grain creates the heap?

Paradoxes

Paradoxes are breakdowns in reasoning, which stimulate new thinking. The paradox of **The Liar** concerns the truth of the sentence "this sentence is false." A little thought shows that if it is true, then it must be false—but if it is false, it must be true. This was an odd puzzle for two thousand years, and then stimulated Alfred Tarski (see page 31) to produce his new theory of truth. The paradox of **The Heap** says that one grain of wheat is not a heap, and neither are two, but if you keep adding grains you must arrive at a heap—but which grain triggered its arrival? Thinking about vague objects like clouds and bald heads tends to focus on this paradox. The paradox of *The Lottery* says if you are one of millions of people who buy a lottery ticket, you have overwhelming evidence that you won't win the lottery, but you still don't know that you won't win it. Students of justification in knowledge find that one intriguing.

Philosophers regularly ask: "what would we think if . . . ," followed by a situation involving a pet theory. This is a *thought experiment*, many of which are famous.

- How would you behave if a ring of invisibility enabled you to get away with crimes?
- What would you think if an illiterate pauper suddenly acquired the knowledgeable mind of a prince?
- What would you do if you could guide a runaway trolley to kill one person, in order to save five other people?

Each case is constructed to test a particular view of morality, or personal identity. Details can be adjusted, as in a physics experiment, to see how this affects your conclusions.

THOUGHT EXPERIMENT ▶ **Considers a potential scenario and thinks through the consequences.**

Perhaps the commonest device in philosophical argument is the *counterexample*, which undermines some claimed general truth. If I defend the moral Golden Rule ("treat others as you would like to be treated"), you might suggest giving me for Christmas something you would like, rather than something I would like. When philosophers of language told Hilary Putnam that all meanings occur in his mind, he said he used the words "elm tree" without knowing their exact meaning, which he left to tree experts. The spotting of such problem cases is an important skill in philosophy.

THE COUNTEREXAMPLE ▶ **Used to undermine so-called *"general truths."***

CHAPTER 3

FALLACIES IN REASONING

- If your explanation always requires some further explanation, that is an ***infinite regress***.
- If your explanation takes for granted the very thing being explained, you are ***begging the question***.
- If you use B to explain A, and later use A to explain B, you are guilty of ***circularity***.
- If you attack my views by attacking my character, this is the ***ad hominem fallacy***.
- If you ask where the happiness is located at a wedding, you are probably guilty of a ***category mistake***.

You can use the phrase "elm tree" without knowing its precise meaning, which only experts in trees know.

Chapter Four
EXISTENCE

Ontology—Objects—Change—Realism vs Anti-Realism

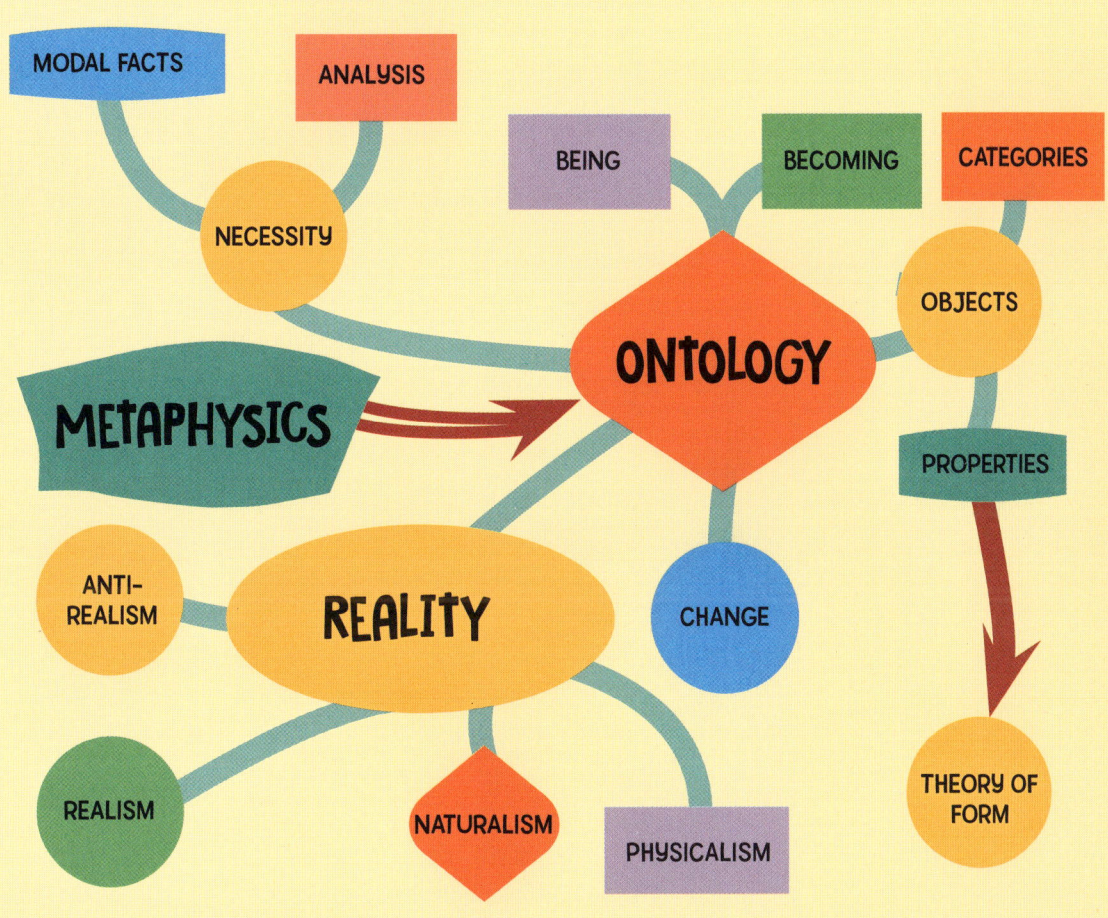

ONTOLOGY

Philosophy concerns general truths, and **Metaphysics** focuses on the most general aspects of our understanding. Metaphysics covers the presuppositions of physics, such as time, space, objects, and laws; the presuppositions of human affairs, such as minds, persons, and values; our beliefs about the supernatural; and any ultimate purposes in existence.

> **METAPHYSICS** ▶ Covers the presuppositions of physics, such as time, space, objects, and laws; the presuppositions of human affairs, such as minds, persons, and values; our beliefs about the supernatural; and any ultimate purposes in existence.

A narrower but still vast topic is **Ontology**, which is the study of existence itself. The sheer fact that anything at all exists is either so obvious as to not require comment, or so weird that it induces panic. Philosophers don't expect to explain existence, but aim to investigate the topic until we reach the limits of what can be said about it.

Parmenides made the first serious attempt to address the problem of existence, in a poem which only survives as fragments. The first half, which explains the true nature of reality, is fairly complete, but the second part, on the illusions of experience, survives only in fragments.

Parmenides' philosophy only survives as a series of fragments of a poem.

Being

Being is the essence of what it is to exist. Parmenides was struck by the contrast with non-Being; by the necessity that something has to exist; by the unchanging aspect of Being that contrasts with Becoming; and by the unity that Being seems to have, behind its surface variety. Plato added the thought that Being must surely be active, because otherwise we would be unaware of it.

This ultimate question of Being made little further progress in ancient times, but Leibniz (in 1697) thought it worth asking, "Why there is something rather than nothing?" His answer involved God, but modern physical cosmologists also find the question worth investigating. The question of Being itself resurfaced in the continental school of philosophy after 1800. Heidegger, in 1927, gave the topic of Being a new stimulus by introducing the concept of *dasein*, which is the distinctive self-conscious mode of existence experienced by people.

Gottfried Leibniz questioned why anything at all exists.

OBJECTS

When Aristotle addressed the problem, he decided that the existence of objects was a much more promising topic than Being itself, and most subsequent ontologists have agreed. Explaining the nature of objects may at least get closer to the central mystery of existence. Objects show enormous variety.

Objects require:
- unity
- distinctive behavior
- a particular type.

Aristotle explained all three of these facts by assuming that every object has an essence (the "what-it-is-to-be" of that particular thing).

CHAPTER 4

- gives it the necessary unity
- underpins its causal powers

ESSENCE

- dictates what type of thing the object is

OBJECTS ▶ *Have an essence, attributes, and require unity, distinctive behavior, and a particular type.*

Each object has a set of *attributes* (or properties), which only exist as aspects of objects. Some aspects are essential to it, and others *accidental*. These essential natures of objects give rise to the behavior of nature. Aristotelian scientists explain nature by showing the essences of things, rather than giving modern explanations by means of regular laws.

Aristotle argued that we can explain the unity, behavior, and type of an object by identifying its essence.

52

This Aristotelian account of the ingredients of existence had huge influence, and was the standard view until the rise of modern science. For Aristotle, a living creature is the most obvious object, because it is so unified, but inanimate objects have all sorts of problems for the metaphysician:

- A bicycle is an object, but does it cease to be an object if you dismantle it—even if you then put it back together?
- Can one object overlap with another? Are France and Europe objects (since France is part of Europe)?
- Is an army an object if it has a multitude of changing parts?
- Is an electron an object if its location is defined by statistics rather than by boundaries?

One modern approach entirely rejects Aristotle's view, and says any components can make up an object, no matter how scattered, if we choose to think that way. Another approach says any section of space-time can be treated as an object, and when faced with the vague nature of electrons it is tempting to abandon the concept of "object" altogether. The modern word has also been widened in meaning, and abstract entities such as numbers are often treated as objects.

A modern approach to objects states that an object can be made up of various components, even when scattered.

CHAPTER 4

Properties

The conventional concept of a physical object treats it as an underlying entity, with the properties attached which provide its visible and individual character. But modern metaphysicians have found this picture rather muddled.

If all the properties attach to what underlies them (the **substrate** of the object), that implies that the substrate has no properties of its own—so what is it? Objects can't exist without properties. Without a substrate, an object is just a bundle of properties. But what are they properties of, and what binds these properties into a single unified bundle? Neither solution seems satisfactory.

Nevertheless, we all understand that a hot, heavy, red spherical object has some properties, and we can discuss those properties independently from the object, because other objects also have those properties.

> **PLATO'S THEORY OF FORMS** ▶ *Properties (and other larger idealized concepts) have an existence of their own, even when no object embodies them.*

Plato's **Forms** explain why we can discuss redness without mentioning objects. They also explain the order of the universe, because, unlike the physical world, their structure is eternal. Aristotle found the Forms implausible, because it is unclear how abstract "redness" can be embodied in a physical thing, or how we could even know what redness is if it has no causal powers. Modern platonists sometimes defend the independent existence of mathematics, but physical properties seem more down-to-earth.

However, some support for Plato's view is seen in our use of language. What does the word "red" mean? It refers to a familiar color, but not to any one instance of it. We can refer to long vanished objects, or future objects, or possible objects as "red," and even refer to the color on its own. The word needs a consistent meaning, or we can't talk to one another. "Red" is an example of a **universal**—a word that can apply one concept to many instances.

"Red" is a property of the object, and can be discussed independently from the object itself.

> **UNIVERSAL** ▶ *A word that can apply one concept to multiple instances.*

If we reject Plato's claim that redness exists on its own, we need some explanation of how this works. If it is just an idea, are we therefore saying that the property "red" does not exist? Maybe the different instances of red are not the same; and each one is a particular thing which resembles the other red things. Or maybe there is nothing more to it than language, and *properties* are just talk—the predicates in our sentences. In that case, "not red" is as much of a property as "red," and "being ten feet from a red object" might also be a property.

Categories

Because redness is shared by many objects, we can group them together, under the heading "red things." So are such groups or categories a feature of reality? Not always, because we can make up categories, and they could be quite eccentric (such as all the objects in cupboards in Paris). Some categories merely reflect our interests, rather than the structure of the world.

The denial of real categories is common among philosophers who see language as central to philosophy. The obvious categories of living creatures seem like part of nature, because their species are fairly obvious, but the way we categorize clouds (as cumulus, nimbus, and so on) is much less precise, and when we divide up areas of the sea for shipping forecasts that is just for our convenience, and doesn't indicate real boundaries at all. It is just a matter of words. Defenders of natural categories prefer to focus on animal species, and the elements in the periodic table seem a good case of genuinely natural categories, whether we like it or not. We take all gold atoms to be identical, and so their category is undeniable, but critics say that actually each atom's electron shell is in a different state, and we are deliberately ignoring that when we treat gold as perfectly uniform.

> **THERE ARE THREE VIEWS ABOUT THE PERSISTENT CATEGORIES OF REALITY:**
>
> - They don't exist (and we merely find them useful).
> - They are natural, and reflect fairly well the real structure of the world.
> - They reflect the structure of our minds, and we cannot help imposing this structure on things.

CHAPTER 4

Immanuel Kant divided categories into "creations" and "limitations."

These categories can be seen as either creations (constructing the world as we experience it), or as limitations (forcing us into a restricted viewpoint). For example, Kant suggests that the unity of an object comes not from its hidden essence, but from the human need to unify things. Similarly, the presumed causation of lightning producing thunder is not really there but is imposed by our minds. Ontology concerns not only what exists, but also the order and structure within existence, and so categories and relationships are of as much interest as the objects and properties.

CHANGE

Ontology treats objects, properties, and categories as if they were static and timeless, but in practice reality continually changes. The response of Heraclitus to this was that "you can never step into the same river twice," implying that rivers (which we describe as objects) change too much to be real entities. Some ontologists build on this thought, seeing reality as made of "processes" rather than objects. Even a mountain made of solid rock can be seen as an extremely slow process, as it erodes and shifts.

REALITY ▶ *Made up of processes rather than objects.*

An object that changes, such as a ripening fruit, seems straightforward in daily life, but there are some puzzles in the process.

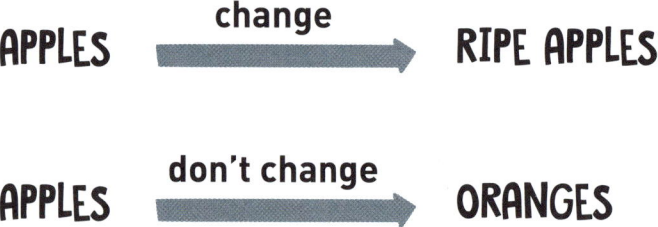

For this to be true, something must remain the same during the change. If we think of an apple as a "substrate" with properties, then the substrate remains while some properties change, but a property-less substrate is a very odd entity. If the apple is just a bundle of properties, then a change makes it a different bundle. Unless we know what made it an apple to begin with, we can't say whether the apple has modified or changed into a non-apple.

A modern view suggests that apples and ships occupy periods of time, as well as volumes of space. This *four-dimensional* approach to apples sees them as unripe at one time and ripe at another, just as they might be bruised on one side and healthy on the other. When I look at a ripe apple, I am seeing only part of the object—a *time slice*. In this account, which is encouraged by the theory of relativity, change is not a feature of an apple once we see it in the correct timeless perspective.

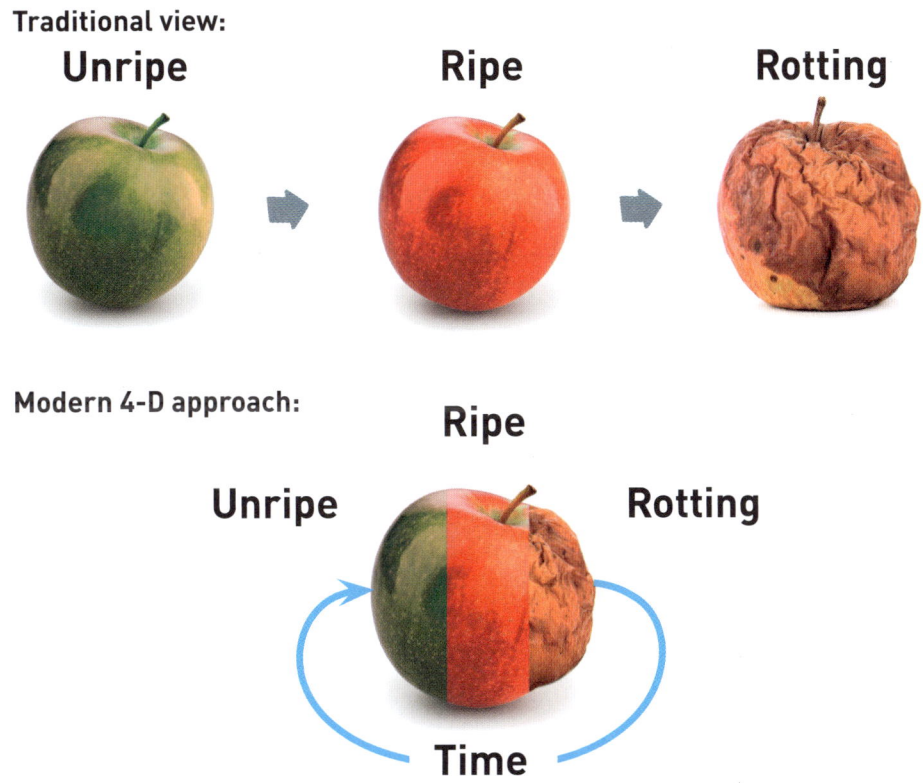

CHAPTER 4

REALISM VS ANTI-REALISM

We can form theories about aspects of fundamental reality, but we also form views about reality as a whole.

ANTI-REALISTS
Skeptical about the real existence of objects, properties, and categories:
- The strong form gives up on attempts to talk about "reality." We should be content with orderliness and practical success in our own thoughts, concepts, experiences, and language, forgetting about what they are supposed to refer to.
- The weaker form permits reference to "reality," but says that the way we "cut nature at the joints" (as Plato put it) only reveals how we think, and tells us nothing about real structures, which are beyond our understanding.

REALISM
Not only is there a reality, but also our attempts to think about it cut somewhere near the true joints. Given that view, more positive assertions can be made about the nature of reality. Most scientists assume that they are describing reality, although quantum physicists may incline towards anti-realism, settling for whatever the mathematics tells us.

ATTITUDES TO REALITY

NATURALISM
Everything that exists is (as far as we know) part of what we call "nature," and there is nothing supernatural. This seems like a flat denial of (for example) ghosts, which are normally taken to be supernatural, but it might be said that ghosts are also part of nature.

PHYSICALISM
Nothing exists except the postulates of physics. This says that absolutely everything is physical, but defers to expert physicists to decide what exactly "physical" means. The strongest opposition to this view is expressed in religions, which are committed to a spiritual realm of reality, but also in the platonist view that there are all sorts of truths—about mathematics, logic, necessities, and even moral values—which stand outside the physical world. The view that the mind is in some way non-physical is also defended, in opposition to physicalism.

Necessity and Possibility

In addition to the ontological facts about reality, there are also modal facts. These concern what has to be true, what might be true, and what couldn't be true about reality. In addition to the substance and properties of an object, we can talk of its *modal profile*, meaning the array of possibilities associated with it. On a larger scale, we can consider the modal aspects of reality as a whole, in the features that have to be either true or false, no matter what.

We say "I must catch the last train," meaning there is a local short-term necessity involved. We might also grandly claim that "all existence is necessarily good," which (if true) applies everywhere and always. We can distinguish types of necessity in two ways:

- by the scope of what they refer to
- by what gives rise to them.

Apart from local necessities, of having to do one thing if you want to achieve another, the main difference in scope is between metaphysical and natural necessity. The biggest claims are *metaphysical*, and the *natural necessities* are those like gravity, which seem to be true "given the laws of nature" (which might be different in some other reality).

Trains cause local necessities, and maybe all possible reality has metaphysical necessities. If P implies Q, and Q implies R, then necessarily P implies R. This is *logical necessity*, because it arises from the nature of implication, which is a central feature of logic. Common sense logic ("four lunch guests will need four chairs") has its own necessity, and so does classical predicate logic. However, there are many systems of logic, and each one has its own distinctive necessities, and a sentence which is necessary in one system may not be necessary in another.

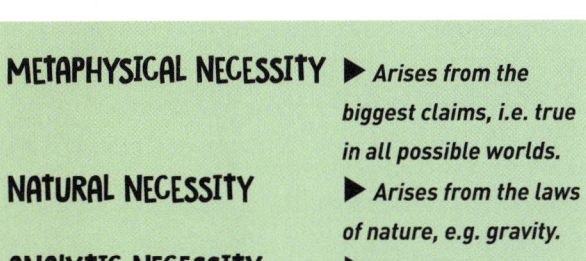

MODAL FACTS	▶ What has to be true.
	▶ What might be true.
	▶ What couldn't be true.
METAPHYSICAL NECESSITY	▶ Arises from the biggest claims, i.e. true in all possible worlds.
NATURAL NECESSITY	▶ Arises from the laws of nature, e.g. gravity.
ANALYTIC NECESSITY	▶ Arises from the meanings of words and concepts.

CHAPTER 4

Analytic Necessity

There is also *analytic necessity*, which arises from the meanings of words and concepts. A pair of boots necessarily has two boots, and an ocean necessarily contains water, because that is what the words mean. But whether a fact is necessary may depend on how it is described. It seems right to say "seven is necessarily less than eight," but not "the number of days in the week is necessarily less than eight." The number of days in the week *happens* to be less than eight, but it doesn't *have* to be less than eight (because we could all switch to ten-day weeks). Willard Quine said necessities *always* depend on how you describe them, so the concept of necessity is dubious. Modern empiricists are inclined to say that the only necessities are the analytic ones, because the logical necessities are analytic necessities in disguise, and natural and metaphysical necessities are beyond our experience. Big metaphysical claims about necessity seem to depend on the insights of pure reason, favored by rationalist philosophers, but are often scorned by empiricists.

Traditionally, trying to understand the types of necessity, and different examples of them, has been the highest ambition of philosophy. In real life, though, it may be the possibilities that are more interesting, while the necessities (being inescapable) are normally ignored.

Willard Quine was skeptical of the concept of necessity, as it always depends on how the necessity is described.

Chapter Five
KNOWLEDGE

Nature of Knowledge—Knowing Reality—A Priori—Perception—Rationalism and Empiricism—Justification—Objectivity—Skepticism

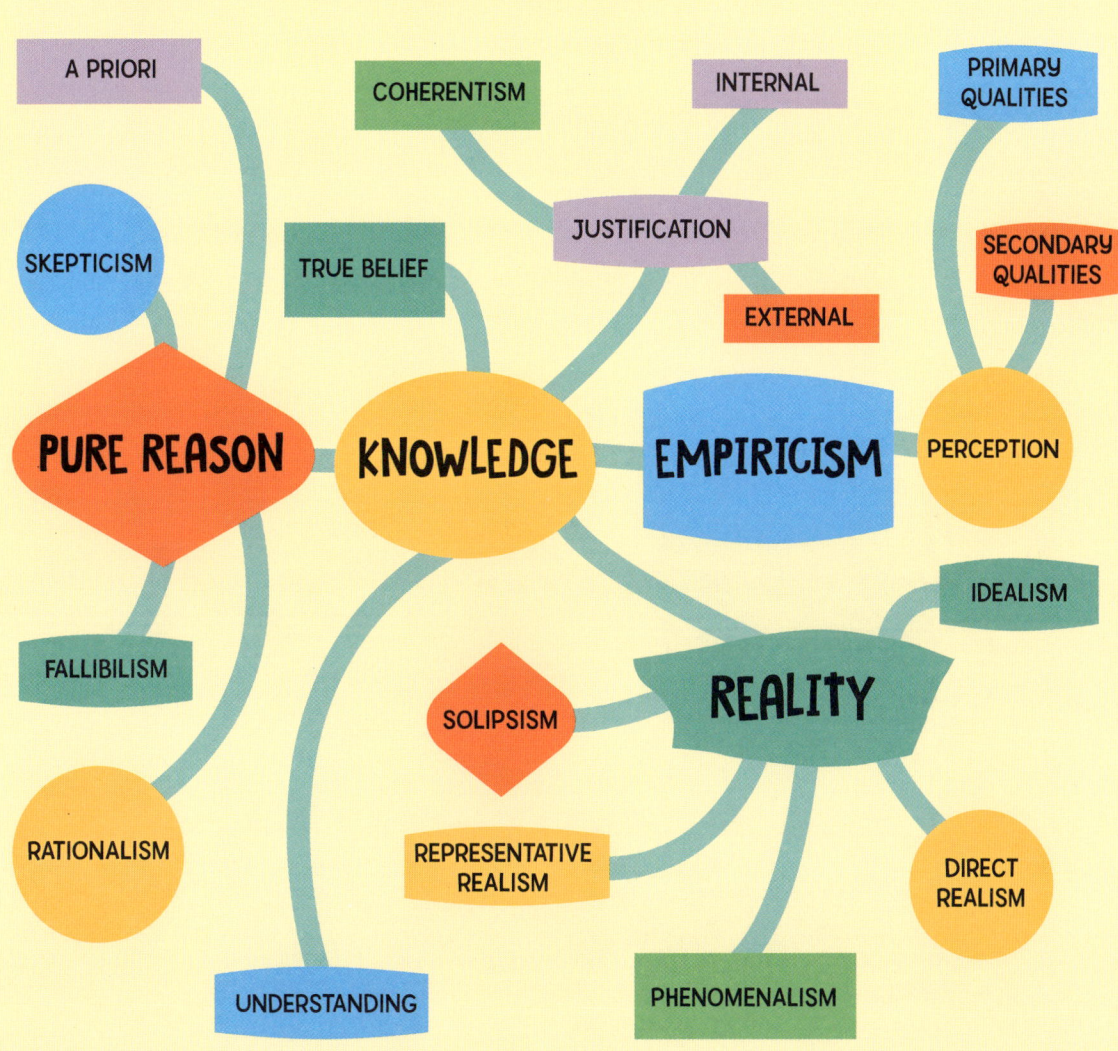

NATURE OF KNOWLEDGE

Philosophers may boldly assert truths and tell us about the nature of existence, but how do they know such things? Our lives depend on what we know, and science has discovered remarkable knowledge. Hence a major topic in philosophy is *epistemology*, which aims to understand the basis and reliability of what we think we know. We usually start with the success or failure of our beliefs. If you believe something but you are wrong, then you do not know. You can't "know" that the Earth is flat if it is not flat. Hence truth is a minimum requirement for knowledge, and most epistemologists assume a fairly robust idea of truth.

EPISTEMOLOGY ▶ *The study of knowledge.*

To say: "I know this, but I don't believe it" sounds like a contradiction, so we normally say that *only a belief can qualify as knowledge.* You might hold accurate information in your head but not believe it, or you might not even understand the information, so we normally say that knowledge must at least be "true belief."

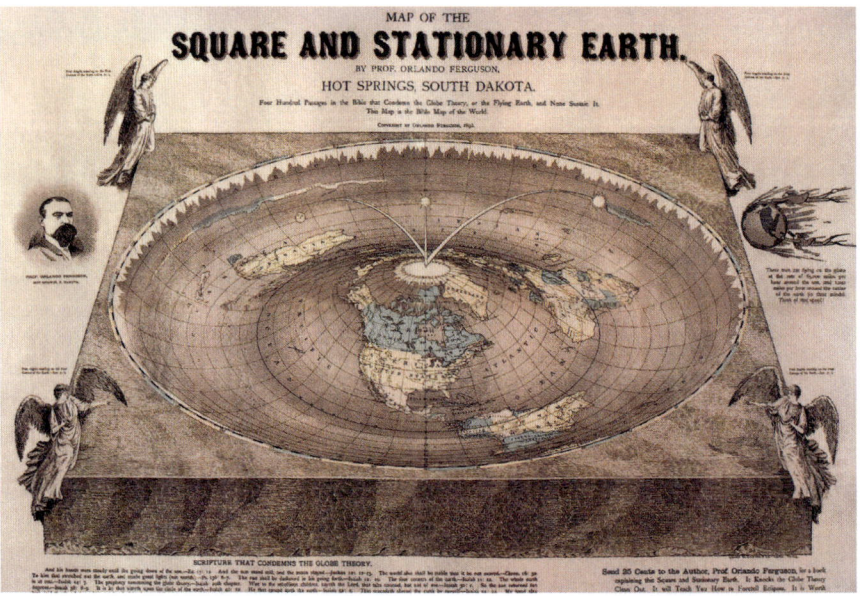

If the Earth is not actually flat, it is impossible to know that it is flat.

KNOWLEDGE

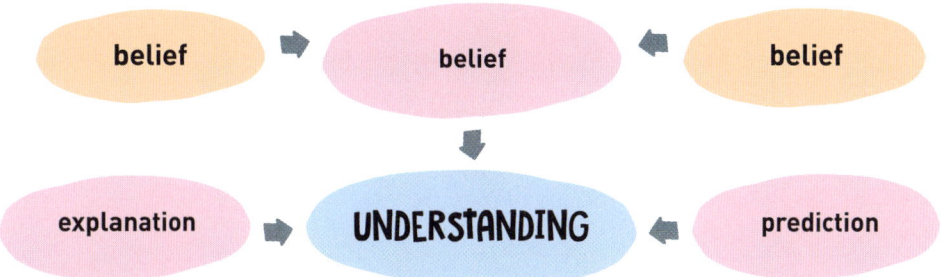

If you unquestioningly believe everything your mother tells you, and most of it is correct but some of it is wrong, then you will have a lot of true beliefs and also some false ones—but you can't tell the difference. She might teach you 50 capital cities, and only 48 of them are correct, but you can't distinguish the two that are wrong. Hence your true beliefs will be a matter of luck, and you don't really know them, so knowledge needs a bit more than just true belief.

Most discussion in epistemology focuses on the nature of this "bit more." Knowledge needs a guarantee, so that we can all agree on it, and accept the authority of experts. You might find a list of capital cities in an encyclopedia, but how did the compilers of the information ensure that the list was accurate? Have they visited all of these countries? Epistemologists are too fussy to just ask an expert, because they want to know what makes someone an expert. Having the status of really knowing something, or being an expert, is hugely important in politics, journalism, the law courts, and science.

Mere success in quiz shows will not qualify you as an expert; we also seek "understanding" of a topic. In addition to having well-supported true beliefs, understanding needs connections between them, and the ability to explain and to predict. However, understanding is impossible without specific knowledge, and epistemology usually focuses on knowledge, which is a clearer concept.

Success in a quiz show does not make an expert—understanding is necessary as well as knowledge.

CHAPTER 5

KNOWING REALITY

Metaphysics and ontology tell us what exists, but how do we know these assertions are right? We can doubt our senses, our reason, the meaning of our language, and the reliability of our concepts. That gives a lot of scope for error. We know, for example, that some people are color-blind, and that insects see colors not experienced by human beings, so facts about colors depend partly on who is looking at them.

SOLIPSISM

The most extreme response to these worries is **solipsism**, which says I am trapped in a private mental world, and don't even know if other minds exist, let alone reality.

IDEALISM

A less extreme view is **idealism**, which may concede that other minds exist, but says that reality can be no more than the sum of our experiences, because we have no evidence beyond that. So-called reality is a feature of minds, not an external objective fact.

REPRESENTATIVE REALISM

Representative realists are impressed by the series of steps from the stimulus of a nerve end, in a fingertip or the eye, to the actual experience in a small locality of the brain. Such a complex chain of events doesn't seem to be a very direct contact with reality. Information must go through stages that represent the incoming information, in a form that can make an impact on conscious thought. These representations (sometimes called **sense-data**) may accurately represent reality, but also raise doubts about realism, because the representations need interpretation, and have to be taken on trust.

The complex chain of steps from the eye through the nervous system to the brain suggests fairly indirect contact with reality.

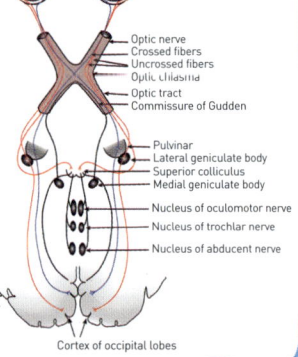

KNOWLEDGE

PHENOMENALISM

The standard views allow that there is some sort of reality out there, but differ over how closely and directly we are in contact with it. If we say, with the idealists, that existence is entirely a matter of human experience, this means we can't assume that the cat exists when it is behind the sofa. It seems more sensible to believe that if you look behind the sofa, you will have a cat-experience. That is, the cat still exists, but as a potential experience. This view, called **phenomenalism**, keeps the intellectual integrity of idealism by not straying beyond experience, but adds the more normal view that the existence of a cat is not intermittent. Phenomenalism is still a form of **anti-realism**, though, because it says that reality is (for us) a wholly mental construct.

When the cat is hiding, it still exists, according to the phenomenalist view, so there must be more than simply human experience.

DIRECT REALISM

There are also more robust views of reality. **Direct realism** takes the optimistic view that experience really does reveal reality. Color-blindness is dealt with by saying color is just an aspect of the way we experience reality. We don't say that someone loses touch with visual reality if their eyesight is blurred, and we similarly ignore other unusual modes of experience. If we close the gap between mind and reality in this way, then philosophy comes much closer to common sense.

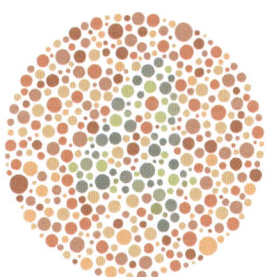

Color-blindness is an unusual mode of experience, but it does not prevent someone from experiencing reality.

CHAPTER 5

A PRIORI

Apart from our experiences, we also know truths of mathematics, of logic, and of what must always be true, by pure thought. This is *a priori* knowledge, meaning either that it can be known without the involvement of experience, or that its truth could never be affected by experience. To know that 7 + 5 = 12, we just need to think about those numbers, and any experience which seemed to contradict it would be dismissed as a misunderstanding. If knowledge is a true belief with further support, then knowledge from experience can offer evidence, but what grounds can be cited for a priori knowledge? We can say that it is "clear and distinct" or "self-evident," and we can cite "the natural light of reason" or "intuition."

> **A PRIORI** ▶ **Knowledge which cannot be affected by experience.**

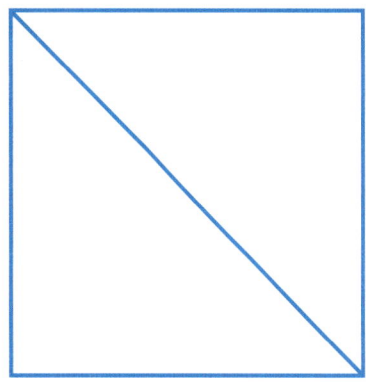

Certain forms of geometry provide a priori truths.

Contradictory Propositions

Nothing is more obvious to pure reason than that contradictions are unacceptable. If two propositions contradict one another, they can't both be right. Hence we know that something must be true if its falsehood implies a contradiction, which gives a strong basis for some a priori knowledge. Other a priori truths can be seen from the concepts involved. From the symmetry of a square, we see that its diagonal produces two triangles equal in area. Other a priori truths are undeniable generalities about experience—that actions in the past can no longer be changed, or that longer distances take a longer time to traverse.

Innate Ideas

Some ideas seem to be *innate*, meaning that they arise naturally within the mind, and are not put there by experience. Thus it is claimed that simple concepts of arithmetic and geometry, and even larger ideas, such as the concept of goodness, or of a supreme being, are innate. If that is so, then we can have a priori insights into these concepts, and may be able to infer important theoretical or religious or moral truths without reference to any evidence.

Empiricists are doubtful about innate ideas (because all knowledge is experiential), and say that the mind just connects experiences together, and "abstracts" such ideas from experience. For them, the mind is close to being a *tabula rasa* (a blank page), which only becomes knowledgeable when experience writes on it.

If a priori knowledge could never be contradicted by any experience, this implies that it could not fail to be true, and is necessary. On the one hand, something known a priori may have to be necessary (because it is a truth of pure ideas); on the other hand, something necessary may only be knowable a priori (because no mere evidence could ever prove a necessity). This would mean that necessary truths and a priori modes of knowing are closely linked together. Rationalists, who have great hopes for rational insight, favor this view.

Fallibilism

Modern discussion has doubted the simplicity of this two-way link. It is suggested that some necessities, such as the atomic numbers of elements, are discovered by scientists, and are thus *a posteriori*, rather than a priori.

A POSTERIORI ▶ *Knowledge which derives from experience.*

The more cautious, modern *fallibilist* view says that insights of pure reason may nevertheless be wrong, and are not a basis for knowing necessities. An even more skeptical view sees a priori knowledge as entirely a matter of how human-made concepts and language fit together. If so, then knowing about the areas of squares, relationships of numbers, and even general truths about religion and morality, are merely descriptions of concepts invented for human convenience.

The atomic number of an element is an a posteriori truth.

CHAPTER 5

PERCEPTION

The most direct awareness of reality comes through experience, which relies on perception. Sight is particularly important and vivid, but the sense of taste varies more between individuals, and the sense of touch seems closer to reality. The two main issues concerning perception are:
- whether it puts us in very close contact with reality
- the extent to which pure information from outside is modified by the processing and concepts of the mind.

If perception offers reliable information about external facts, that offers a secure foundation—but if the information cannot avoid heavy interpretation, that needs a different approach.

The simplest perception is glimpses of movement or color in peripheral vision. But if we have not even begun to identify the object, this is normally referred to as a *sensation*, rather than "perception," and doesn't involve knowledge. Beliefs begin with relationships between things, especially when we add concepts and categories. But in normal perception we are not aware of adding concepts to them. If I see a bird, I see it directly as a bird, which is experienced as unified and instantaneous. The concept "bird" is ingrained in us, but presumably it was built up in our language, from perceptions of many birds. In an adult human, the concepts are so closely embedded in the perceptions that they are barely noticed.

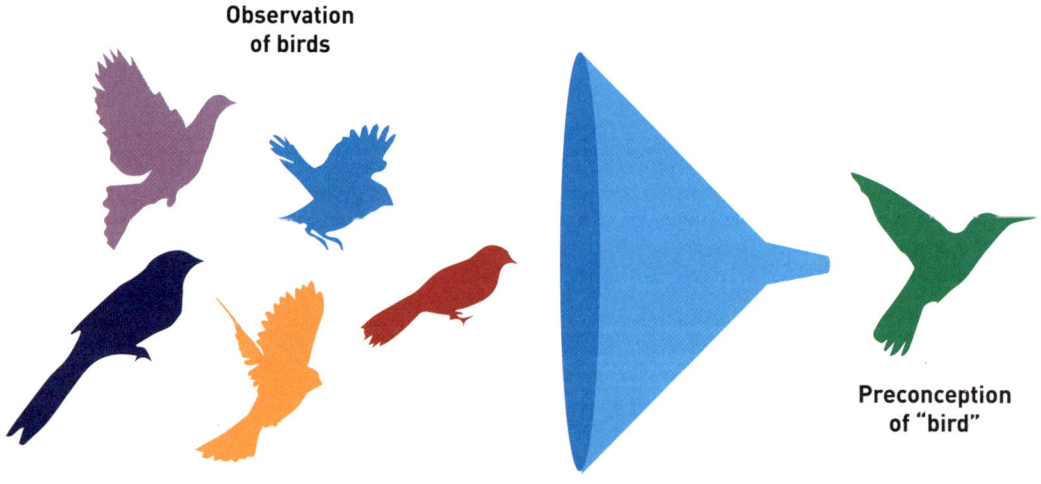

Spiders can invoke fear for some people—not everyone has the same experience.

For most people, seeing a spider is like seeing a bird, but people with a phobia about spiders have a different experience. Our concepts are molded by loves, fears, and prejudices, and they are also molded by past experiences, our culture, and the language we speak.

Primary and Secondary Qualities

When you see a square object, it also feels square, and a dropped brick looks, feels, and sounds quite heavy. But when you taste honey, or see violet, no other perception can confirm it. The first type of encounter is said to be with *primary qualities*, and the second type with *secondary qualities*.

Primary Qualities

The primary qualities look more promising for objective knowledge. Not only can my other senses confirm the perception, but other people are likely to agree on it, whereas other people may be color-blind or differ in their sense of taste. Science focuses on the primary qualities, which offer a consensus among observers, and can also be treated mathematically.

Secondary Qualities

The secondary qualities (such as color, taste, and smell) offer real information, but are more subjective. The distinction is important—although critics, especially anti-realists, reject it, claiming that primary qualities are constructed from secondary ones.

CHAPTER 5

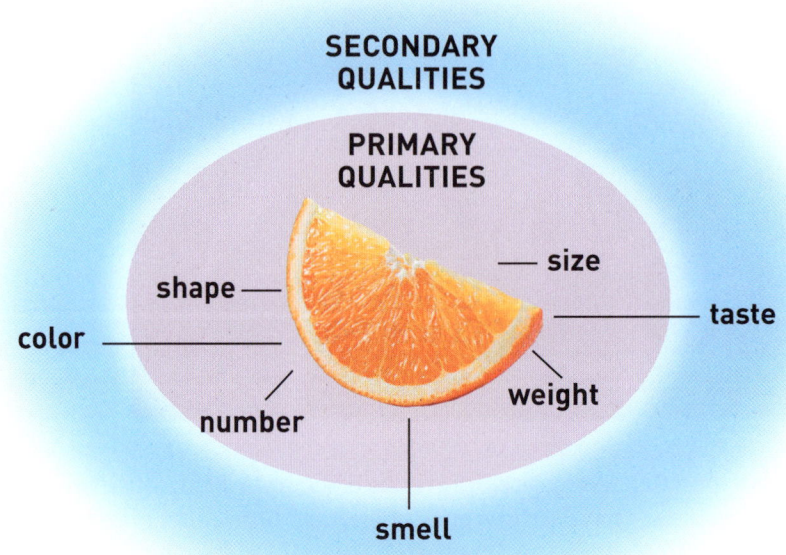

RATIONALISM AND EMPIRICISM

Two major views are in conflict over the basis of knowledge: rationalism and empiricism. *Rationalists* say what turns our tangle of beliefs, concepts, and raw experiences into knowledge is a judgment.

> **RATIONALISTS** ▶ *What turns our tangle of beliefs, concepts, and raw experiences into knowledge is a judgment.*

Descartes illustrated this view with a lump of candle wax. We feel it, tap it, look at it, and taste it, and conclude that it is wax. If we then melt it into a puddle, the experiences change dramatically, but we still say it is wax. Since the judgment overrides the changed experiences, the knowledge must have come from a judgment.

> **EMPIRICIST** ▶ *Everything relies on perceptions, and a judgment is just a comparison of experiences.*

Empiricists say that everything relies on perceptions, and a judgment is just a comparison of experiences. David Hume offers the example of a golden mountain (a fantasized solid gold mountain). No one has experienced such a thing, but we know of gold and of mountains, so we put the two together for the fairy tale. All concepts, says Hume, are like that, and the mind sifts patterns out of multiple experiences. Knowledge is rooted in our perceptions, not in reason (which is probably overrated by rationalists).

This debate was at its height in Enlightenment Europe, when the great empiricists (John Locke and David Hume) rivaled the great rationalists (René Descartes, Baruch Spinoza, and Gottfried Leibniz). Once Immanuel Kant claimed that experiences were deeply entangled with the rational and conceptual aspects of the mind, the debate became more complicated. However, many philosophers still incline to one or other of the two positions, so the discussion is far from over. Even if all sensations involve thinking and all thinking is rooted in the senses, most philosophers believe knowledge is based primarily either on our experience or on our understanding.

David Hume was a leading empiricist in the philosophical debates that raged through the Enlightenment.

CHAPTER 5

JUSTIFICATION

Most epistemology focuses on that "bit extra" which turns a lucky true belief into knowledge. You believe a truth, but how do you justify believing it? Big problems were spotted in ancient discussions. If you pick some piece of information to justify your belief, then presumably you must know that information. But then the information must also be justified—and so on.

We face an *infinite regress* of justifications. If the various justifications support one another, that sounds circular. Or we might say that the knowledge eventually rests on something which needs no justification—but how do we know it if it isn't justified? This three-way puzzle (***Agrippa's Trilemma***), seems to make pursuit of the foundation—or criterion—for knowledge hopeless.

The point of the Trilemma is to show that knowledge is impossible, because it can only be justified in one of three ways, and none of them work. The justification is either founded, unending, or circular. If the series of justifications ends in a foundation, that obviously has no further justification, so it can't be knowledge. If the series goes on forever, you can't be sure of any of them. If the series is circular, that may be a group of lies that endorse one another.

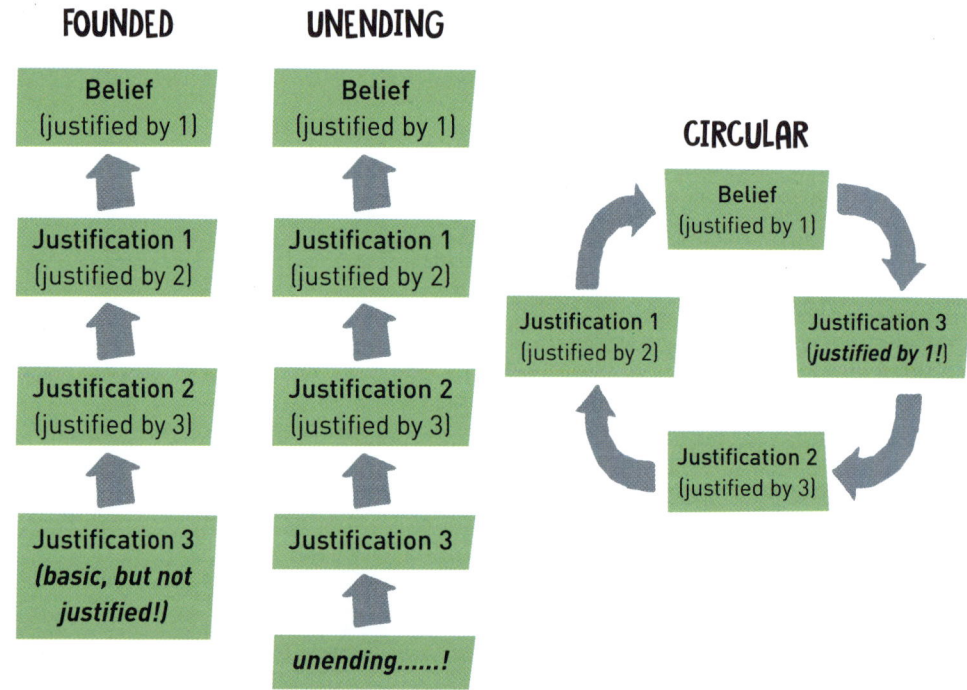

Solutions to the Trilemma suggest either rationalist or empiricist foundations. Rationalists say the basis of knowledge is a direct insight or intuition that something is obviously true. If we have a priori insights that are certain, we can securely deduce other knowledge from them. Descartes claimed that whenever he was thinking, it was certain that he must exist, in order to think. This famous argument (*cogito ergo sum*—"I think, therefore I am") highlights some sort of certainty, though it is questionable whether he has proved that he is a continuous and unchanging person.

> **EMPIRICISM** ▶ *All knowledge comes from experience.*

Empiricism

Empiricists seek their foundations in experience. G. E. Moore, for example, claimed that he was more certain that he was holding up his own hands than he could ever be about skeptical arguments that denied it. Facial recognition is offered as foundational knowledge, because even tiny infants immediately know their own mother. Both versions of *foundationalism* divide our beliefs into two groups, with the "basic" ones (whether rational or experiential) needing no further justification.

The philosopher G. E. Moore, like all empiricists, looked to experience for his foundational knowledge.

Coherentism

Skeptics say experiences might be mere dreams and reasoning can be misguided, and critics of foundations say they are either too elementary to count as knowledge, or too complex to be known without further justification. Hence a rival view, *coherentism*, offers a different approach.

> **COHERENTISM** ▶ *Our experiences and reason must fit together coherently to count as knowledge.*

Although a set of justifications supporting one another sounds circular, in real life we believe something if many pieces of evidence point toward it, and if they all fit together like a jigsaw (as in a successful prosecution in court), then that is as good as justification can get. The coherent picture can include both rational and experiential ingredients. The main difficulty with coherentism is that a collection of evidence can be highly coherent but still not true, as in a carefully plotted novel.

> **RELIABILISM** ▶ *Beliefs must depend on reliable connections to the facts.*

Both basic beliefs and coherence focus on the mind of the knower. A recent challenge says that this *internalist* view is wrong, because good justifications are *external*, since we need good connections to the facts, rather than private states of mind. The preferred version of externalism is *reliabilism*, which says that the best connection with the facts is through means which have proved reliable, such as good eyesight, intellectual ability, or efficient scientific instruments. Internalists say that we must act on what we know, so final decisions must be internal, but the robust realism of externalism is attractive, and it fits well with modern views of objectivity in science.

> **INTERNALISM** ▶ *Final decisions must be internal.*

OBJECTIVITY

Extreme relativism says there can be no knowledge, because there is no "truth" and there are no "facts." Hence there are merely individual private beliefs, or perhaps shared viewpoints within a culture. But knowledge also needs beliefs to be justified, and we can still try to distinguish between good and bad justifications.

GOOD JUSTIFICATION	BAD JUSTIFICATION
"I believe this happened because ten of us saw it happen"	"I believe this happened because I hope it happened"

Therefore we can try to make our beliefs more objective, and edge closer to the truth or facts, even if that can never be fully achieved.

Relativism relies on doubts about perception, about reason, and about language. We each perceive from a different location, and employ different concepts in the experience. It is often said that reason, once seen as universal, is strongly influenced by cultural prejudices and private emotions. And it is said that each language changes over time, has unique inbuilt assumptions, and can never be accurately translated.

Greater objectivity seems possible through agreement, either of different senses, or from different observers. Assuming we trust memories (and it seems crazy not to), we can perceive an object and remember an earlier identical perception of it (implying objective stability in the object). We also find two different senses offering the same information about an object (one of its primary qualities) and we can trust other people to report their perceptions, and possibly support our own. A motto for scientists is "if you don't believe it, go and look for yourself."

Prejudices

Reasoning can be subject to prejudices, and we produce "rationalizations" for things we are determined to believe anyway. Mathematics, formal logic, and computer languages try to eliminate such influences, and produce results that are beyond dispute. It is more difficult to be objective about evidence, because it needs interpretation, but modern law courts offer forensic analysis, recordings, and photographs, aiming for a consensus on something close to the facts.

It is claimed that it is impossible to fully translate between two languages, because a sentence is only really understood as part of a whole language, and each language embodies a unique worldview. This implies that no two languages can report identical facts, and full objectivity is impossible. The best defense of objectivity dismisses this as too pessimistic. Poetry may be hard to translate, but science papers and instruction manuals should be fine. Specialist languages can be made more precise. Science favors mathematical language, and avoids emotive terminology.

Contextualism

An influential modern idea is that whether someone qualifies as knowing may be relative to a context. Someone may be accepted as an expert in a relaxed context, but not in a demanding one, and I may think I know a topic very well until I encounter people who know more. Could it be that the word "know" changes its meaning in different situations? Or do we either know or not know, but sometimes demand weak justifications (in casual conversation) and sometimes strong ones (in a law court)? If the contextualists are right, then objectivity is only found in the most demanding contexts—but that is a common assumption in modern societies.

The context can determine who is an expert. In a court of law, the standard for an expert is very demanding.

SKEPTICISM

Relativists doubt facts and truth, but skeptics merely doubt our ability to know such things, even if they are available. *Global skepticism* is the wide claim that all knowledge is impossible (and presumably, we can't even be sure of that claim).

> **GLOBAL SKEPTICISM** ▶ *All knowledge is impossible.*

Presumably we can't even be sure of that claim. More local skepticisms in philosophy include doubts about:

- religion
- moral values
- other minds
- the self
- necessities
- meaning
- rationality
- induction
- causation.

We are free to doubt anything, but philosophers offer reasons for skepticism. The Greeks said that any falsehood can appear to be true, and for every reason to believe something, there is another reason to deny it. Descartes said it was hard to deny that life may be a vivid dream, given that we usually believe what we dream. If you don't accept that, it may still be that some outside force is deluding us. We might think of the evil scientist feeding lifelike data into a **brain in a vat**; or the simulated reality created by the machines in the film *The Matrix*. The question is not whether these scenarios are likely, but whether they are possible. If either of them is possible, then our knowledge is insecure.

All of epistemology can be seen as attempts to address such doubts. If there are certainties that are foundational, or beliefs stronger than any skepticism, then knowledge may be reliable. Pragmatists say that successful action is a good guarantee for knowledge. Even if global skepticism seems undeniable, we can still decide to dismiss it as an academic exercise, since even people in a state of ignorance must get on with their apparent lives, with all their frightening dangers.

CHAPTER 5

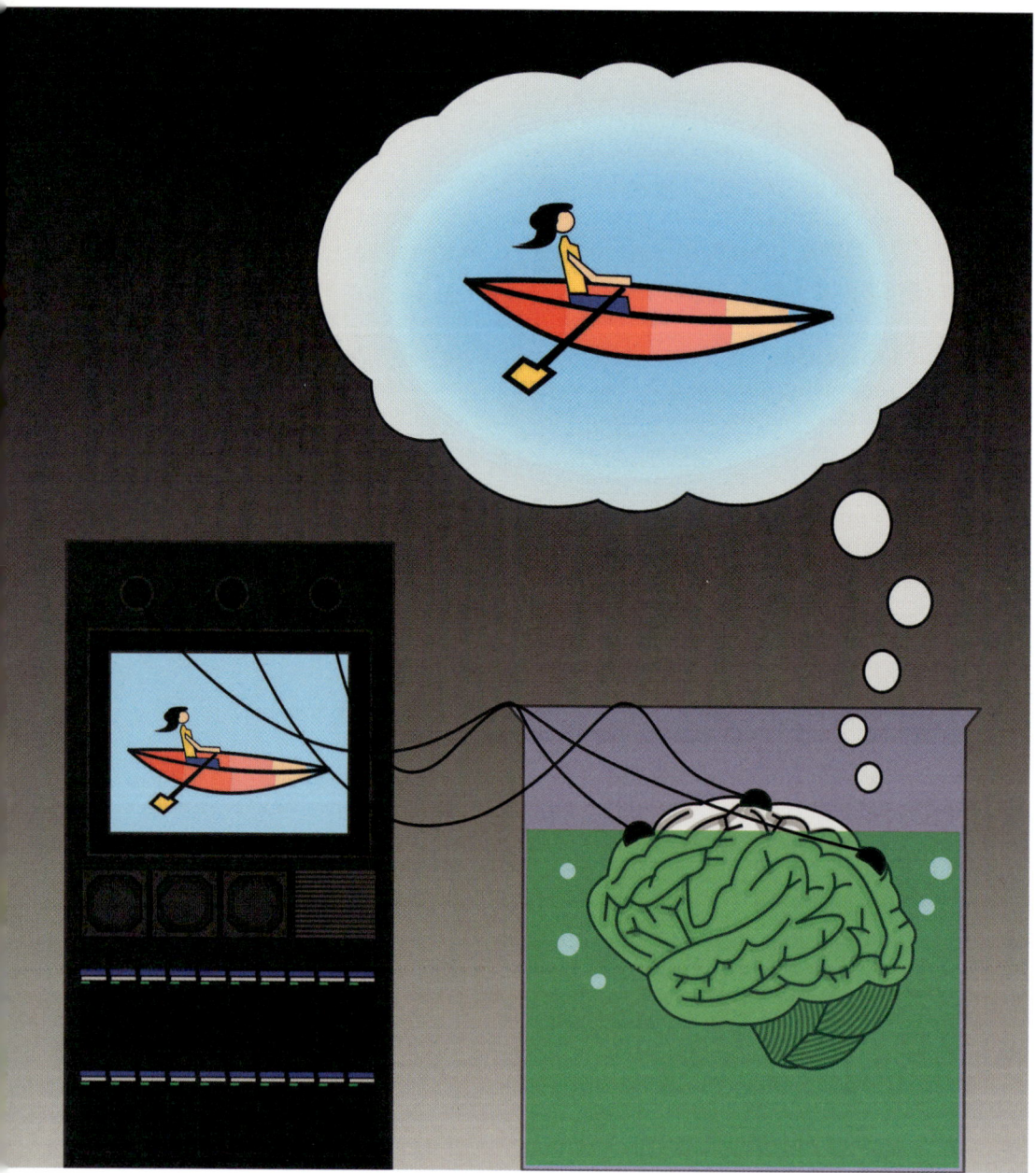

The thought experiment of the "brain in a vat" asks whether we can trust our own experiences.

Chapter Six
MIND

Nature of Mind—Consciousness—Mind and Body—Dualism—Behaviorism and Functionalism—Property Dualism—Physical Mind

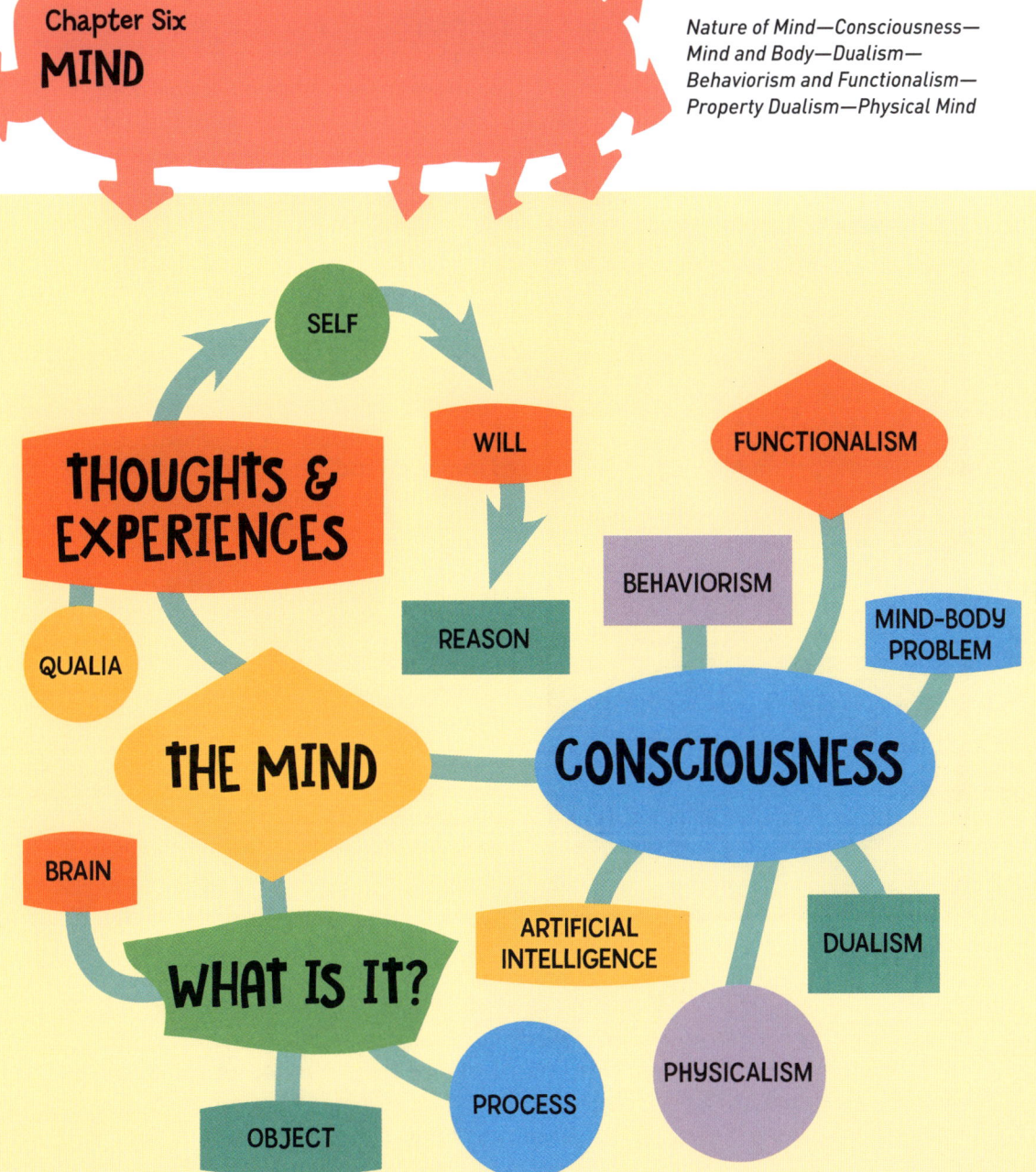

CHAPTER 6

NATURE OF MIND

For philosophers, the mind is interesting because of its essential role in knowledge and understanding, its active role in choices and morality, and the relationship between human minds and the language they employ. We need an account of the mind's functions and capacities, and an understanding of the relationship between mind and brain, in a way that fits with broader theories about the world.

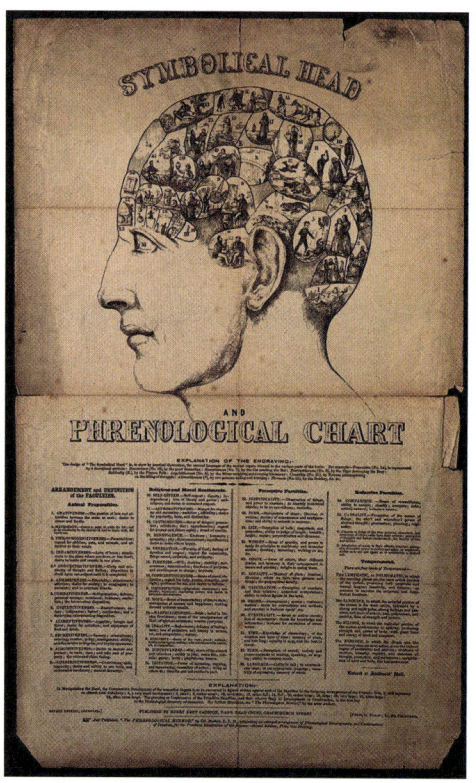

Can we really understand what is going on in our own minds?

What is a mind?
- Is it a distinct entity or a process?
- Is it the same as consciousness, or is it much more extensive?
- Is it entirely separate from the body, even though involved in it?
- Does it extend out into the world, in the information we store on phones, for example?
- Is it just a collection of tiny physical activities?
- Does it control the body, or simply respond to it?
- Are we experts on our own minds, or are we too involved to see what is really going on?

Some major questions about the status of human beings loom behind these puzzles. If we are no different in principle from any other mammals, then our account of the human mind will not differ much from our account of the mind of a laboratory rat. If, however, we have a more elevated view of ourselves, as having immortal souls, or as agents with much more freedom of choice than rats, or as reasoners who can grasp truth, logic, mathematics, and the secrets of nature, then our account of the human mind must make such things possible.

We can try asking what a mind is *for*. Minds need brains, which are only found in organisms that navigate in their environments, so that is a good starting point. If a larger moving creature cannot navigate, it won't last long in a dangerous world. Multi-tasking is required, at high speed.

If you are heading to the store to buy bread, you have to juggle the target and its location, the reasons for the target, your own body movements, incoming sense experiences, awareness of dangers, and what to do when you have bought the bread.

All of these activities have a striking unity to them, and the mind somehow produces this seamless whole. Animals clearly have minds, in varying degrees, but we are not sure how aware or thoughtful they are. The only way we can understand animal minds is by seeking the best explanations of their behavior, and the complexities of animal life seen in wildlife films seems impossible without planning, comparisons, and mental maps of the locality. Consciousness may not be essential for linking together such activities as nesting, chasing, and setting cunning traps, but it probably helps a lot.

CHAPTER 6

Thoughts and Experiences

If that summarizes the basic role of a mind, what do minds need for the task? Philosophers have focused on two aspects. We need to experience the world, in order to respond to it. You quickly remove your foot if you tread on something sharp. The feeling of pain does this job, without any need for reasoning or beliefs. The word *qualia* (qualities) is used for these immediate sense experiences, and refers to the hurtful quality of a pain (or the redness of a color)—that precedes any thoughts about what to do. On the other hand, your mind may have many general beliefs that involve no particular experience at all. They are mental states which are "about" something, and the word *intentionality* is used for this capacity to think about things. Beliefs are about things, in a way that the Sun cannot refer to or be about the Moon.

> **QUALIA** ▶ *Immediate sense experience.*
> **INTENTIONALITY** ▶ *Mental states about things.*

We have thoughts about the Sun and Moon, but they have no thoughts about us, because they lack minds.

Minds have raw experiences (qualia) and thoughts with content (intentionality), and both activities imply that the mind represents the external world.

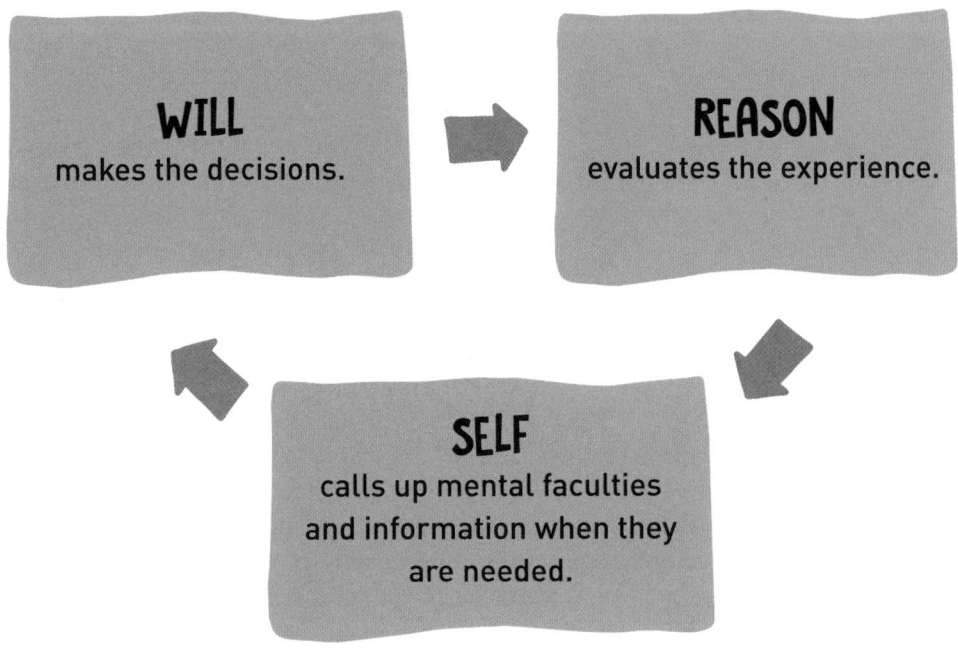

In humans we also find the phenomenon of second-level thought—thoughts about thoughts, such as "do I really want this bread?" or "have I taken a wrong turning?"

Our perspective on other people's minds is different, and we can even wonder whether other people have minds. We normally take this for granted, but what grounds have we for being so sure? Maybe you are the only conscious one, and the rest of us are non-conscious (known to philosophers as "zombies"). You could reply that your behavior is explained by your mind, and other people have similar behavior, so the explanation of them must be the same. It also seems important that they probably have a brain like yours.

CHAPTER 6

Might some people experience this as blue?

Because a mind is so private, this problem of proving *other minds* remains a puzzle. Even if we accept the existence of other minds, a further question is whether their experiences are like ours—the puzzle of *inverted qualia*. If you and I experience quite different qualia when looking at tomatoes or tasting sugar, we might never discover the fact, as long as we used the word "red" or "sweet" in the normal way. I may see tomatoes as blue, and taste sugar as sour, but never realize that your experiences are different. We certainly shouldn't assume that we all have identical experiences of a given object.

CONSCIOUSNESS

The early Greek approach focused on the word *psuché*, which refers not just to your mind but also to the feeling of your body being alive. Hence psuché is also found in plants. For a long time the Greeks were unaware that thinking occurs in the brain (although head injuries eventually confirmed this). Once the crucial importance of the brain became clear, the discussion narrowed down to the conscious mind. The next step was a slow realization that there are non-conscious aspects to the mind, seen in the influence of perceptions, memories, desires, anxieties, and motives of which we are unaware.

> **PSUCHĒ** ▶ *The feeling of being alive.*

Conscious vs Unconscious Activity

Modern research has greatly extended our knowledge of unconscious mental activity, such as decisions that are detected in the brain before we even realize we have made them. Patients with *blindsight* have suffered brain damage and report that they are blind, but tests reveal that they can still pick up visual information without realizing they are doing it. This non-conscious flow of visual information must occur in all of us, so straightforward vision is much less conscious than we thought.

MIND

Robots are able to perform many tasks without possessing consciousness, which makes it difficult to define what "thinking" is.

CHAPTER 6

Consciousness remains the most vivid part of the mind, and it still retains central importance, because what is conscious can be spoken of, assessed, compared, and subjected to reasoning. Since robots can perform many simple tasks without consciousness, and we describe such machines as "thinking," the explanation of human consciousness has been labeled the ***hard problem***, for both philosophers and scientists. In particular, if we ask "what's it like to be a robot?", the answer is probably "nothing," so the biggest puzzle is to explain why we experience mental activity, rather than just perform it. This suggests that explaining qualia is much tougher than explaining intentionality: a robot can be programmed to build a car or vacuum the stairs, but a robot is unlikely to have a favorite perfume.

MIND AND BODY

If we only want to understand thought, the way in which the mind and the brain are related is a minor problem. However, when wider philosophical issues are discussed, this mind-brain relationship has major importance. The debate moves between two extreme views—that mind and brain are entirely different, or that they are exactly the same.

The first view implies that mind has a quite different mode of existence: it may be non-physical, and have quite different constraints from ordinary physical matter. This might allow it freedom from causal control (making free will possible), allow it to exercise pure reason (untainted by biology or social influence), and make possible bodiless existence (and perhaps immortality). In general, it would imply the independent existence of a world of thought (containing mathematics, perhaps), and make a spiritual realm more likely.

The second view, that the mind just is some aspect of the brain, is encouraged by modern physics and neuroscience. It faces great difficulty, though, in giving decent explanations of our experiences of thought, emotions, choices, and reason.

Are the mind and body two separate entities?

> **PHYSICALISM** ▶ *Nothing non-physical exists, and so the mind must be entirely physical.*

Physicalism can come in *reductive* and *eliminative* forms.

REDUCTIVISTS	ELIMINATIVISTS
The mind is real.	The mind does not exist.
The mind arises entirely from physical events in the brain.	Minds are simply physical activity—like "the weather," they drop out of the catalog of what exists, once we have identified the winds, temperatures, pressures etc.

DUALISM

Democritus held that only atoms and their movements exist, so he rejected the separateness of mind and body. But dualism gradually became orthodoxy.

> **THE DUALIST VIEW** ▶ *The belief that the mind is non-physical.*

There were good reasons to support dualism. The mind was associated with the brain, but that was just featureless stuff, which showed no signs of thought going on—no microscope had yet revealed the brain's neurons. When Descartes considered the mind, he identified a number of features that cannot be physical:

- The mind is wholly unified, while the brain can be sliced up.
- We can doubt whether we have bodies (since we may be dreaming them), but we can't doubt that we have minds, as we need minds for the very process of doubting.
- The mind (unlike the brain) seems to be intangible, having no measurable volume or shape or weight. Hence it seems that the mind is not physical.

CHAPTER 6

An obvious problem had to be dealt with. If the brain and the mind are entirely different types of substance (physical and non-physical), and have nothing in common, how do they influence one another? The mind feels pain, and the body obeys decisions, but what is the communication link? One approach says there has to be a link (perhaps at one locality in the brain), but we cannot explain it. Alternative views say there is no link, and the harmony of mind and brain must be explained in some supernatural way.

> **OVER-DETERMINED** ▶ *When the mental cause is surplus to requirements.*

Critics of Dualism

Critics say this *interaction problem* is too serious, and *substance dualism* must go. In particular, our standard causal account of one physical event leading to another seems to break down if there is this sharp mind-body boundary, and the mind is not physical. We are faced with chains of physical causes abruptly coming to an end (when the pain moves from the physical brain to the non-physical mind), and then abruptly reappearing (when the decision to move the foot moves from the non-physical mind to the physical brain). The movement may even be *over-determined*, if all the causation needed to move the foot can be seen in the physical events, and the extra mental cause is surplus to requirements.

In addition, dramatic advances in biology and neuroscience (such as watching the brain gobble up glucose when it is thinking hard) have made the physical account of the mind much more plausible. If our general view of humanity is that we have resulted from natural selection, then we see ourselves as more closely related to small animals, whose behavior can be explained without reference to a separate mind. The dualist view of mind has consequently become unfashionable nowadays, and subtler accounts of the mind have been developed.

BEHAVIORISM AND FUNCTIONALISM

> **BEHAVIORISM** ▶ *The mind can be understood by observable public behavior.*

One approach is to rethink what the mind is. If the mind is not a thing or a substance, but an activity or a process, then there are not two different entities. The brain is a physical thing and the mind is an abstract aspect of the brain, such as a pattern of behavior. The doctrine of **Behaviorism** emerged in psychology, to make that subject focus on observable public behavior, rather than on unscientific introspection of private minds. Philosophical behaviorism said that the mind simply is such patterns of behavior, thus dissolving the problem. The popularity of behaviorism was short-lived, because external behavior doesn't fully explain the mind. An actor can exhibit pain behavior when they don't feel it, and tough people can show no behavior when actually feeling horrible pain. There are also lots of mental states, such as doing mental arithmetic or knowing an historical date, which normally produce no behavior at all.

Functionalism

An improved theory was *Functionalism*, which kept the idea that the mind is a system of behavior, but placed this behavior inside the brain itself, instead of in what is externally observable.

> **FUNCTIONALISM** ▶ *The mind is a system of behavior, based in the brain itself.*

The mind is like computer software, running on the brain's hardware, and it can be visualized as a flow diagram. Various versions of the theory propose that computation is involved, or that each function is seen in terms of its causal role, or that the purpose of each function must be mentioned. There

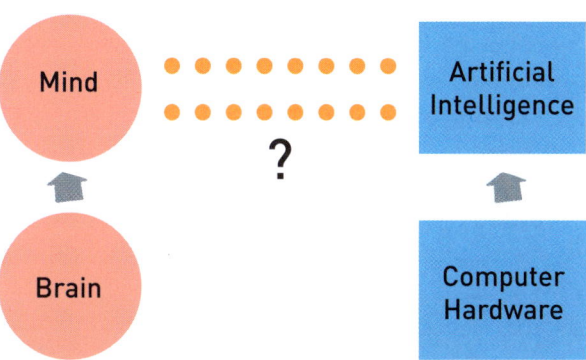

CHAPTER 6

is no mysterious substance involved, and the mind is an abstract description of the pattern of brain processes. This could be supported by a non-physical substance, but it is more likely to just be ordinary biology.

One objection to this is that you could set up a mechanical system that had all the functions of a good language translator, but without the understanding that minds bring to translation. There is more to a conscious mind than its functions. If someone had *inverted qualia* (privately experiencing red as a blue experience), their functions and behavior might remain unchanged when they talked about red things, so functionalists can't explain the difference in their inner experience. The theory cannot answer the hard problem: why do we experience things in a certain way? If all you need is the functions, maybe we don't need our experiences? Functionalism explains everything in the mind by its relation to something else, so it can't say anything about its intrinsic properties.

PROPERTY DUALISM

If you think the mind is special, but not that it is a non-physical substance, then *property dualism* offers a compromise.

> **THE VIEW OF PROPERTY DUALISM** ▶ *The mind emerges from the physical substance of the brain.*

For Donald Davidson, one particular feature of mind that prompted this proposal is our ability to act according to reasons. Our reasons determine what we do, but they are nothing like physical causes, and certainly don't obey strict laws, the way physical matter does. Hence the mind is an "anomaly," a misfit, in nature, and yet it is obviously an aspect of a physical system, the brain. The mind is said to be a new kind of property, rather than a different substance. The property is *emergent*, meaning it is not contained in the physical stuff of the brain, but is produced by the brain. The important feature that results is *downward causation*—that the mind which emerges has causal powers (our reasons for doing things) which are not caused by the brain, but which can affect the brain and body. The mind is said to track brain events (and never wanders off on its own), while retaining its independent powers.

This theory captures the idea that the mind is very special, without diverging too far from modern scientific views. Skeptics about the theory tend to view it as traditional dualism in a modern disguise. Because the mind has emergent independent causal powers, they can never be predicted from observations of the brain, which makes them a permanent mystery (for physical science). So the theory seems to abandon attempts to fully understand the mind. Some philosophers—the *mysterians*—accept this situation, and say the mind is an insoluble puzzle. Minds have no direct awareness of brains, and brains show no visible sign of containing minds, so there is no evidence on which to build a theory.

> **THE MYSTERIAN VIEW** ▶ *The mind is an insoluble puzzle.*

PHYSICAL MIND

At the other extreme is the *physicalist view* of the mind, which either denies the existence of the mind or reduces it to purely physical events.

> **THE PHYSICALIST VIEW** ▶ *All mental events are physical events.*

Modern science encourages physicalism, because more and more is explained in physical terms. Life, for example, which formerly seemed like magic, is increasingly well understood in terms of chemistry. But many philosophers resist physicalism, because it threatens the status of the most precious things in life—such as reason, values, art, and love. In a purely physical world, values seem to be leveled out, and no one thinks complex molecules are superior to simple electrons.

The main support for physicalism is seen in the objections to substance dualism:
- The physical world has a continuous flow of cause and effect, all of it observable, but a non-physical mind makes a large and baffling breach in the flow.
- The familiar laws of science are taken to be universal, but dualism suggests that they are not, because they don't apply inside human beings.

CHAPTER 6

The key question is whether all of our mental life can be explained in physical terms. Given modern research into the brain, physical explanations are becoming more and more thorough, but some features of the mind (such as qualia and pure reason) seem hard to explain in this way. We can physically acquire information from the surface of a tomato, but how can we physically produce the experience of its redness?

Death

If a brain stops working (with death), physicalists assume that the mind ceases too, so the best way to understand the physical mind is as an active process. Its mode of existence is like that of a waterfall, which is a distinct and dramatic entity, but is just made up of the behavior of ordinary water. Our common dualist talk is explained by the concepts we use, not by the physical reality. Because humanity failed to grasp the unity of mind and brain, two entirely different ways of talking about them have developed, and now are deeply entrenched in our languages. At this point the critics of physicalism point to consciousness, because that is a very startling thing to emerge from a mere collection of whirling physical activity, no matter how complex. They remind us that the mind is exceptionally unified by its consciousness, in a way that no mere collection of molecules could ever be.

Artificial Intelligence

Another support offered for physicalism is the development of artificial intelligence, which replicates skills such as great chess-playing, which we previously thought were only achieved by minds of genius. The more inroads AI makes into human intellectual activity, the more likely it becomes that minds are just as physical as computers. Critics reply that this progress is deceptive, because AI has limits: no one ever expects a computer to write a good novel or invent wonderful jokes—but who knows what the future holds?

The mind is like a waterfall—a dramatic and impressive entity which is made up by the behavior of something very simple.

Chapter Seven
PERSONS

Humans and Persons—The Self—Continuity of Persons—Free Will

CHAPTER 7

HUMANS AND PERSONS

A human being comes into existence before they are born, and remains a human being even after death. The idea of a *person* emerged because the law needs it, to refer to the phase of a human being when they can be held legally responsible for their actions. To be guilty of a crime or be committed to a contract, a person must remain the same person over time. What matters are mental characteristics, such as being conscious and sensible, rather than having a human body. To be a person, according to the legal definition, it is not even essential to be a human being—a person can be a corporation or even a city. Three key questions arise:

- What counts as a "person?"
- When does someone remain the "same" person?
- What is the status of a human who is not a person?

What characteristics are needed for personal responsibility? If a person has no excuse for an action, they must have been in full control. John Locke suggested that a person needs to be conscious, rational and reasonably intelligent, self-aware, and continuous—and as long as the person is capable of choice, that view remains generally accepted.

John Locke's Person
Conscious	Rational
Intelligent	Self-Aware
Continuous	Capable of Choice

John Locke argued that a person must be conscious, rational, self-aware, and continuous.

How a person remains the same is trickier. We think of a new-born human being and their possibly senile variants as being the same human being (keeping the same DNA). But remaining the same person (in Locke's sense) is harder because mental states change so much, and a person in infancy or in extreme old age has almost nothing in common with the person in their prime. The easiest solution would be if you had a *Self*, which forms in infancy, and remains exactly the same as long as your brain is undamaged. Then we could say that while your thoughts, moods, and experiences change, your Self remains fixed, as the subject of those activities. The majority of discussion about persons therefore focuses on the Self or Ego.

THE SELF

We can ask whether you have a Self at a given instant, and save for later the question of whether your Self persists over time. Early Buddhists entirely denied the existence of the Self, but there are good reasons in favor of it. Our thoughts and experiences don't drift randomly—they belong to a subject. This subject remembers the past and plans for the future, and compares and reacts to what happens to it. If a chain of reasoning occurs, such as a mathematical proof, the thinker needs to remain the same throughout, to hold the whole thing together. At a given moment you are not a mass of shifting fragments, because all of your mental events can be focused on a single aim (such as running to catch a train). Some mental events are transient and trivial, but others are of great importance to you, such as your memories, relationships, and major beliefs.

Does a plant or a ladybug have a Self? A united organism has unified interests, but we probably don't think a plant has a Self because it is not conscious. So is consciousness essential for having a Self? The part that unifies mathematical proofs and focuses on the train seems to need consciousness, but your unconscious mind is also part of you, so the Self may not be very precise, and having a Self may not be all-or-nothing. Even if a ladybug is somewhat conscious, it seems to lack the other criteria for selfhood. It probably has very brief trains of thought, few plans, and minimal beliefs (though you never know…). The more complex the mental life, the more an enduring focal point seems to be needed. Language, for example, needs a single speaker to unify a long speech.

Immanuel Kant admits that we cannot detect an inner Self, but there is an obvious need for such a thing, which can be known a priori. We do not know it from observation, but infer it as a precondition of experience and of reasoning. It is an undetectable presence, which is essential if we are to make any sense of mental life.

However, maybe these arguments focus too much on mental states, and ignore the role of the body. Internally you may think you have a Self, but other people identify you by your face and physique. The mind is nowadays seen as closely integrated into the body, and thought has a strong bodily dimension. So maybe your sense of self is much more like your image of your own body—which means that losing a leg really is losing part of your Self, and if you change gender you become a different person.

Kant believed the Self was a precondition for experience and reasoning.

CHAPTER 7

Self-Awareness

Most of the arguments in favor of a Self are based on introspection—looking into our own minds. This may help us to understand ourselves, and also give a reliable foundation for knowledge. Rationalists say that there are self-evident truths available to introspection (after a little thought), from which many further truths can be inferred, when they are combined with experience.

There is, though, an obvious problem with trying to see your Self by ***introspection***, which is like a cat chasing its tail, because there are no mirrors for a self to see itself. Introspection has all sorts of limitations such as distinguishing your own emotions, or knowing whether you understand something. When you are angry or urgently doing something, introspection becomes impossible, so those states cannot be studied directly. Modern psychological research has also shown that people's reports of their motives and moral principles are very unreliable, because what they actually do so frequently contradicts what they say they are aiming to do. Reports of recently witnessed events can also be amazingly inaccurate. Hence introspection has obvious limitations, so it should be treated with great caution.

Trying to observe your Self by introspection is like a cat chasing its own tail.

However, dismissing introspection as a source of knowledge is too drastic. Your awareness of your mental life may be uncertain, but it is better than anyone else's assessment of it. Brain scanning and psychological experiments could get nowhere without the introspective reports of subjects about the thinking involved. The conviction that your childhood experiences, especially the vivid ones, happened to you is too strong to be dismissed by occasional reports of mental unreliability. This may not mean we know the Self, but it offers a lot of understanding of our own nature and continuity.

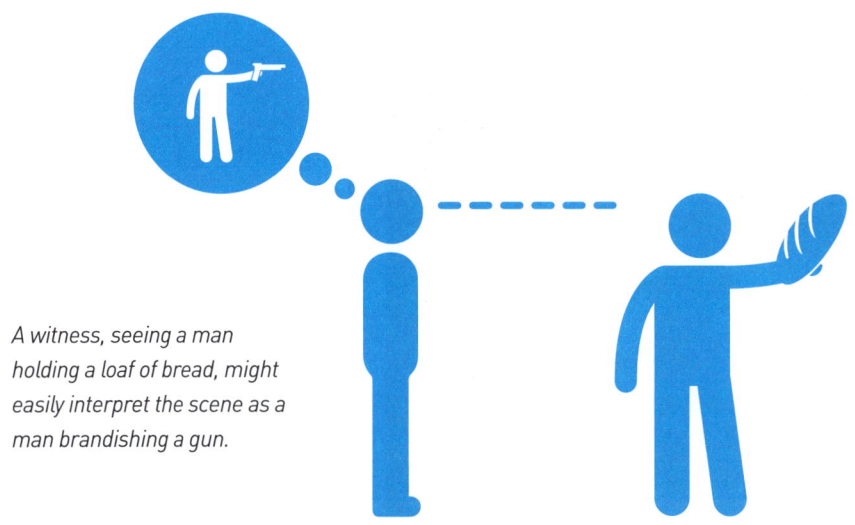

A witness, seeing a man holding a loaf of bread, might easily interpret the scene as a man brandishing a gun.

Rejecting the Self

DOUBTING THE SELF				
Buddhists	**Immanuel Kant**	**David Hume**	**Friedrich Nietzsche**	**Modern Neuroscience**
There is no Self.	We cannot detect it, but infer it due to our experience and reasoning.	There is no Self, only a "bundle" of mental events.	We are driven by unconscious desires, and there is no fixed entity that constitutes "me" throughout life.	There is no brain structure to play the "Self" role, but second-level thoughts may give it a basis.

CHAPTER 7

A more drastic challenge to selfhood came from the empiricist David Hume, who reported that he could see no sign of a Self when he examined his own mind. He just found an unstructured tangle of mental events, which he referred to as a "bundle." We can imagine a Self, but there is no evidence for its existence. Neuroscience offers some support for this view, since no known brain structure plays the necessary Self-role—although thought would clearly be impossible without some co-ordination. The presence of "second-level" thoughts (thoughts about thoughts) might give some basis for a Self—as the part of you that decides what to focus on (concentrating on this book, for example), or judges your own behavior.

Skeptics say we must concede that the idea of some fixed unchanging entity which constitutes you throughout your life is simply false. Nietzsche was even more pessimistic than Hume about our prospects for knowing ourselves by introspection. Hume at least had direct acquaintance with the contents of his "bundle" of experiences, but even these are misleading if they entirely depend on how we interpret them, and they may even be swamped by unconscious mental "drives" we don't understand. Nietzsche felt himself to be swept along by powers buried deep within the mind.

David Hume could only discover within his mind a "bundle" of mental events rather than a coherent Self.

The Changing Self

More influential has been Hegel's claim that introspection won't reveal the Self, but we do come to understand our essential nature when in relation to other minds. This view has been developed by sociologists into a rich account of the Self as a "social construct." If there is a fixed Self, where does it come from? It seems to be fixed by our parentage and DNA ("nature"), and perhaps by training in childhood ("nurture"). In adult life we experience influences on our emotions, opinions, and choices, but the traditional view says we remain the same while doing this. But if the Self is a social construct, all of that is wrong.

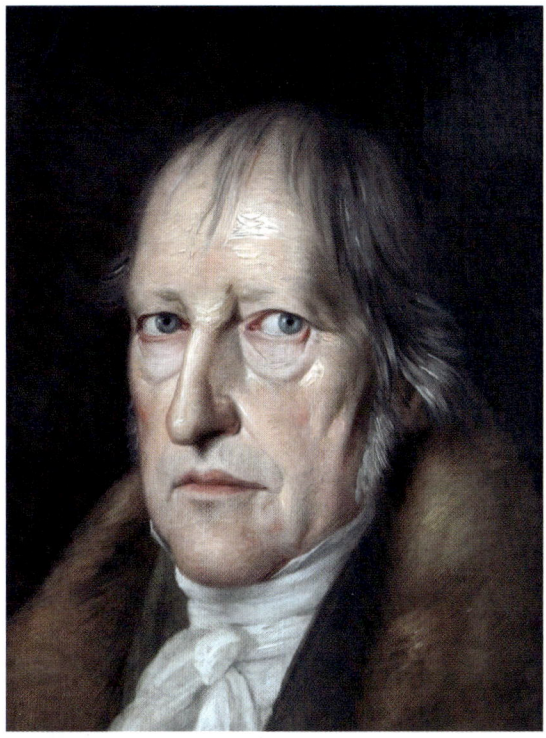

Hegel claimed that we could understand the Self through its relation to other minds.

MOLDING THE SELF			
Georg Friedrich Hegel	**Karl Marx**	**Existentialism**	**Postmodern Philosophy**
We can only know the Self through our experience with others. Self is a *social construct*.	Our minds are molded by the economic and political situation.	We can remake our Self according to our own ideals.	The Self is the main character in the ongoing narrative of our lives.

CHAPTER 7

According to Karl Marx, our consciousness is molded by the economic and political situation.

An early version of this social view came from Karl Marx, who said that the essential nature of our consciousness is molded by the economic and political situation in which we find ourselves. Our minds are molded by whoever controls society, and most of us become whatever suits our social position.

A more individualistic approach is existentialism, which says that the Self can indeed be molded in unlimited ways, but urges us to take control of the process, instead of being passively influenced by society. Because we have second-level thought, we can make and re-make our Self according to our own ideals. A modern approach to the Self relates it to our deep love of storytelling, and treats the Self as an ongoing narrative, an image of ourselves which develops (almost without thinking about it) as we progress through life. We have a "narrative self," which is the main character in an unfolding drama. In the narrative view our lives have unity and purpose, and other people develop their own stories alongside our own. We are fixed as the main character, but changed by events.

CONTINUITY OF PERSONS

Lawyers need us to remain the same person, and we all think of ourselves as essentially the same from infancy to old age, but how can that be, if the Self is constantly changing and is largely molded by social influences? Can we hang onto something about the self, despite such variation? An obvious solution is to focus on the body, which at least follows an unbroken trajectory through space and time. If you are not the same as the infant you, at what moment did the change happen? Your DNA remains identical, and your photographs are recognizably of the same person. We place a high value on someone's bodily existence, even before or after they have the qualities that make them a "person." However, we have very little in common with our infant selves, and we wouldn't expect someone aged 30 to keep a promise they made when they were five.

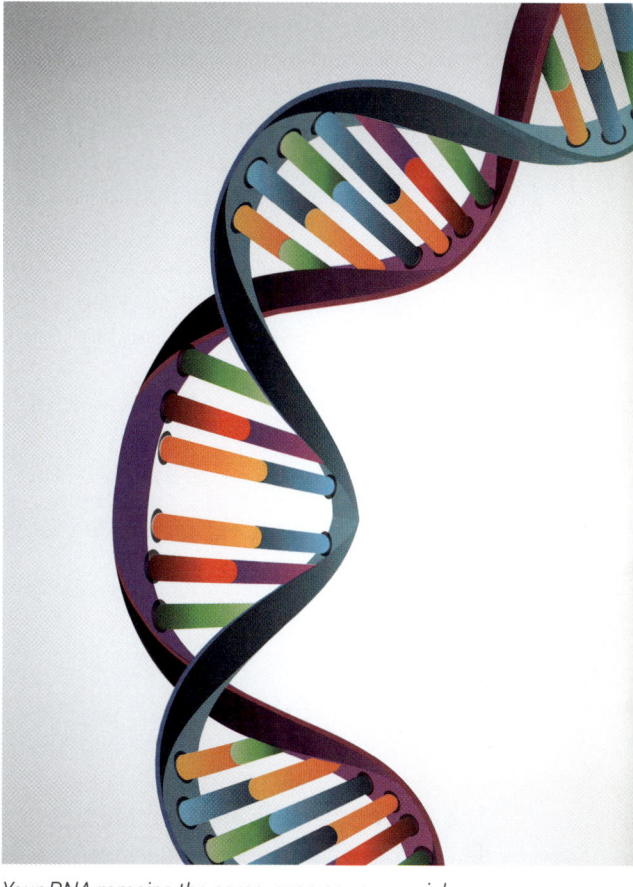

Your DNA remains the same, even as your social situation changes.

Memories

Locke suggested that what matters is not that you believe you are the same as five-year-old you, but that you *remember* being five. Our days and years are held together by long **chains of memories**. We may see them as part of a *narrative*, but we also treasure trivial private memories, which are valued for their own sake. Locke boldly suggested that you remain the same person only insofar as you can remember the events, and if you have entirely forgotten them, they cease to be part of you. He also added that your body is part of your person if you are conscious of it, so that your little finger is part of you but your hair may not be. So you are your consciousness, and you remain identical as long as you are part of this awareness extended over time.

Thomas Reid soon saw problems with this theory. According to Locke, if you have childhood memories when you are 30, then you are the same person as that child, and if an old person has memories of being 30, they are the same person as that 30-year-old. But what if that old person can remember being 30, but not remember being a child? Then the old person both is not the same as the child (because they've forgotten), and is the same as the child (because they are identical to a 30-year-old who is identical to the child). Contradiction. It also seems that you cease to be guilty of your crimes if you no longer remember doing them—which makes amnesia a great advantage for criminals.

If Locke's theory is correct, when you remember yourself as a child, you are that child.

WHERE IS THE SELF LOCATED?			
Where?	The Body	Our Memories	Our Brain
Criticism	Our bodies change over time.	Things can be forgotten—so a criminal with amnesia must be innocent.	When a brain is cut in two, the result appears to be two people living in a single body.

The Evidence from Modern Medicine

These criticisms are serious, but the theory has seen a modern revival because of interesting new evidence. As long as the body functions properly, it is possible for a human being to survive with only half a brain, and when surgeons have (as part of a medical procedure) cut the connections between the two brain hemispheres, the result is behavior which suggests that there are two people inside the same skull. Hence we can imagine (*fairly* realistically) one half of your brain being transplanted into another body. In such an event, which one is you? If you mainly want to track where your consciousness continued, you will have a real interest in both halves of your brain, which suggests that you want to track where your consciousness goes, and the two lives that go with them.

The original criticisms still stand, though, and maybe there can't be memories or a unified consciousness if there isn't some enduring central controller which not only co-ordinates current thought but also makes future plans, remembers events, and even shapes them into a narrative.

PERSONS

We do not blame a fox for its behavior, because we believe it has no choice.

FREE WILL

Is the will of a person "free?" That is, has it full control over its actions, in a way that the weather does not? Many thinkers believe that moral responsibility is impossible without *free will*. We don't usually blame foxes for their behavior, because they cannot choose otherwise, but we praise and blame mature people because they can have total control over what they do. First, though, we must ask what exactly free will is, and whether it is possible for anything to have such a power.

The strongest claim about free will is associated with a supreme being. To be "supreme," such a being must dominate nature, and not be subject to its laws (and indeed may be the creator of those laws). This needs a power of choosing which is not subject to any outside influence. If causation forms chains of cause-and-effect, a fully free being must generate causes which are not the effects of any previous event but which are initiated out of nothing. It is hard to imagine a purely physical being having such a power if they are entangled in the normal causations of nature. Some aspect of the mind must break free of physical nature, either as a separate substance or as unique property.

> **COMPATIBILISM ▶ Physical beings cannot have total freedom, but still have agent causation.**

A weaker claim (called *compatibilism*) is that although physical beings cannot have total freedom, they still have a distinct type of natural causation (**agent causation**) which enables more controlled actions than those caused in weather systems. Such agent causation arises either because the being has a conscious mind, or because it is capable of reasoning, or because it has second-level thinking.

In favor of free will, it is sometimes said that there is nothing more obvious. When faced with a choice, we contemplate the options, take our time, and then initiate an action when we judge it to be best. We are conscious of the whole procedure, and we can see that we have full control.

> **Facing Temptation**
> We are able to choose even when faced with the strongest temptations:
> - Drug addicts are able to break their habit
> - Prisoners resist torture

There is never a point where we *must* succumb to temptation. Our reasoning processes also seem to offer good support for free will. The whole notion of reason requires a calm detachment which rises above causal pressures, so lack of free will implies we are in no way rational beings (which seems false). Whenever we find a reason to act, we can find an alternative reason not to, and in such situations only the will can break the tie, so it must rise above all pressures. If second-level thought is important, then even thinking about freedom may prove we are free.

Opponents believe that such optimism is a delusion. Spinoza said that when you think you are choosing freely, that is only because you can't discover the hidden causes of your behavior. Nowadays the subconscious mind gives a location for secret motives, and even secret reasons, and it is impossible to prove that real powers of choice are not hidden from us. If we will something with apparent freedom, we don't actually know where that final decision came from; decisions may simply come to us, just as all our other thoughts arrive in consciousness uninvited. Neuroscientists have even demonstrated that the brain initiates the final action before it reaches consciousness.

Spinoza argued that you never chose freely—you just didn't know the hidden causes behind your choice.

CHAPTER 7

> **DETERMINISM** ▶ *Every event, including human actions, has a prior cause necessitating it.*

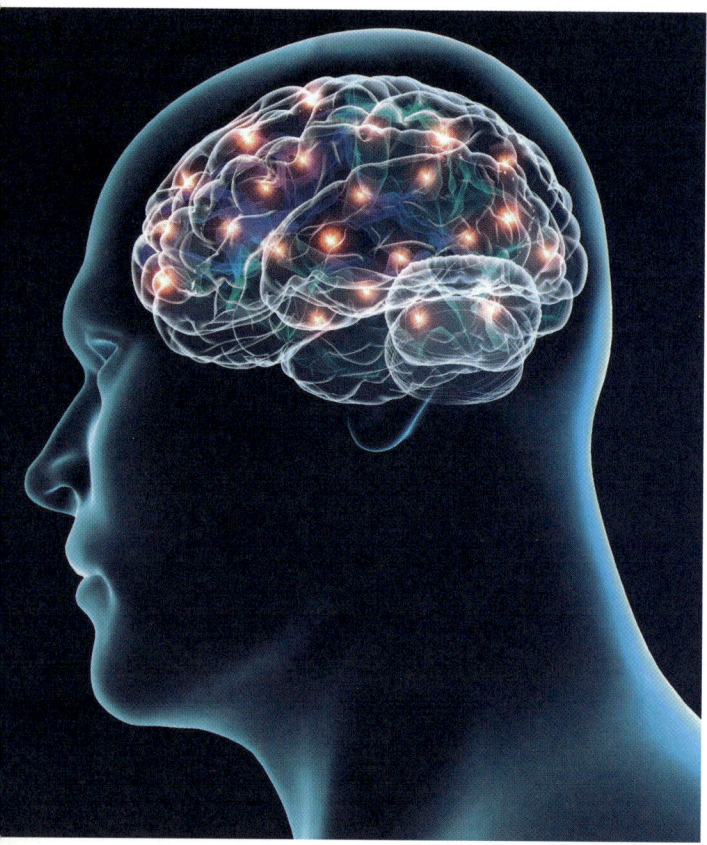

Modern neuroscience has shown that decisions begin in the brain before they reach consciousness.

> **FATALISM** ▶ *The future is already determined.*

If free will is rejected, then the alternative seems to be *determinism*, which says that every event, including human actions, has a prior cause which necessitates it. Rain has to fall when the conditions are right, and human thoughts and decisions are no different. In principle, it was thought that if the present moment was completely known, the entire future could be predicted—although quantum mechanics (which deals in probabilities rather than certainties) has undermined such confidence. Some thinkers even embrace *fatalism*, the belief that our decisions are pointless, because the future is already decided.

Most philosophers laugh at such a claim, because our choices are part of what has been determined, so we may as well carry on choosing.

Chapter Eight
THOUGHT

Modes of Thought—Mechanics of Thought—Content—Concepts—Understanding Action—Intention to Act—Willed Action

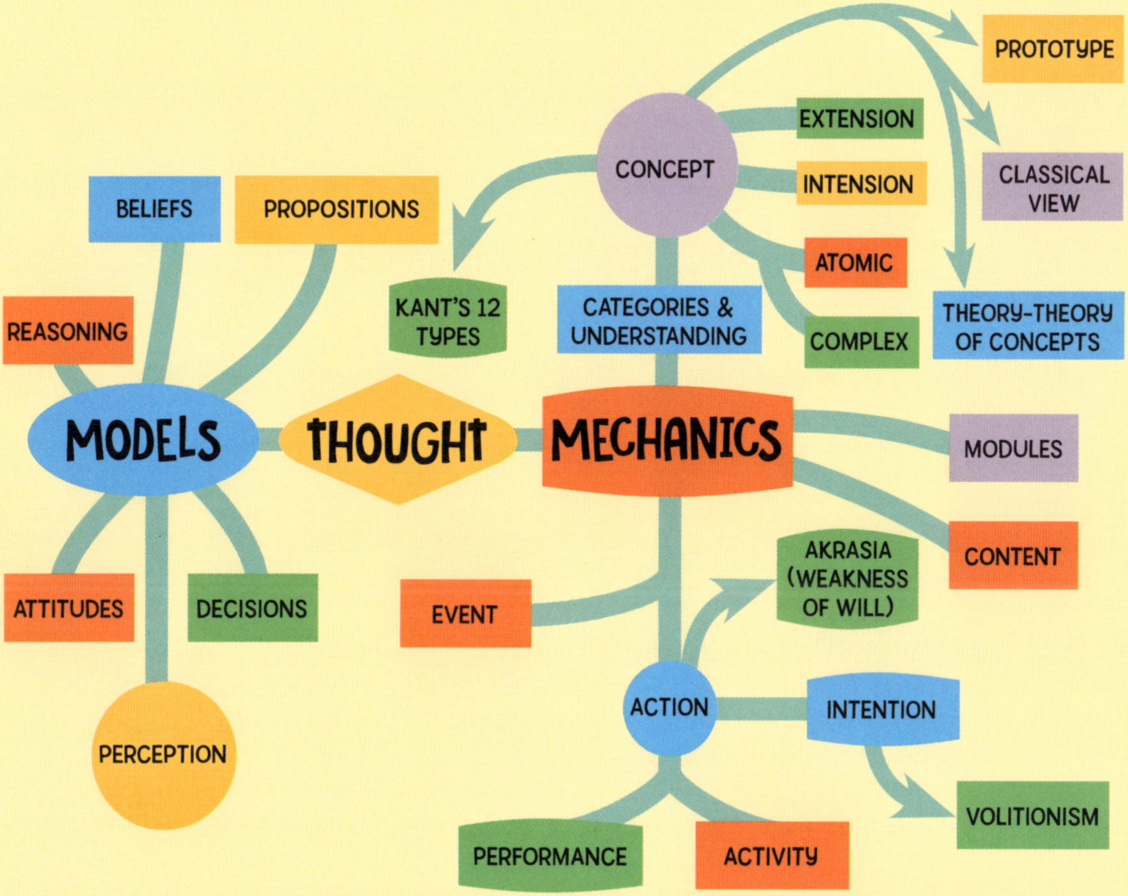

CHAPTER 8

MODES OF THOUGHT

Apart from the questions of what the mind is, how it relates to the body, and whether it is controlled by a Self, we can also try to understand the nature of thought, without worrying about where it comes from. Philosophers study thought in relation to the truth, knowledge, actions, and values which are their wider concern.

"Thought" is a vague term covering everything that occurs in consciousness (and possibly some unconscious mental events), so sorting them into types is a useful start.

THOUGHTS	MENTAL CAPACITIES
Emotions	Focusing
Propositions	Following rules
Attitudes	Abstracting aspects of things
Judgments	Generalizing
Beliefs	Treating topics as objects (such as the economy)
Perception	Seeing resemblances (such as assuming a stretched string is "straight")
Imagination	Idealizing things
Memories	
Reason	
Motives	
Decisions	

Some emotions are about something (such as fear of rats), and some (such as melancholy) are simply moods. Desires, which are part of our motivation, involve an emotional aspect, and neuroscience tells us that every thought, even mental arithmetic, is in some way emotional.

PROPOSITIONS ▶ *Thoughts that can be true or false.*

Propositions are thoughts which can be true or false; if I can express the thought that the train is late in English or in Spanish, then the unexpressed thought is the proposition. *Propositional attitudes* are the responses we have to propositions, such as wondering whether, or fearing that, or hoping that, or resenting that the train is late. A particularly important attitude is a judgment that the proposition is true, or "believing" that the train is late.

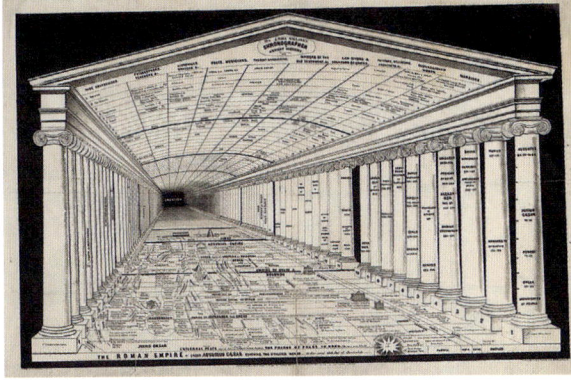
Memories fill our mind, but they are not always clear or accurate.

Perceptions produce mental events, which may either be instant raw thoughts, or may be shaped by our scheme of concepts. Our mind is also filled with memories. We may think memory is what we can recall, but we remember far more than this, because we recognize places and faces when we encounter them again, despite not being able to recall them beforehand. Our struggles to remember things give an infuriating glimpse of how little control we sometimes have over our minds. We also have a remarkable ability to imagine things that we have never experienced. These images are not assembled but arrive complete, as when you imagine a face you have never encountered.

Reasoning is a major mode of thought for philosophers, and comes in theoretical and practical forms, aiming at either true beliefs or appropriate actions. The status of reason ranges from the highest value placed on pure reason, to serious skepticism about various versions of rationality which emerge from different cultures. Studying its role in thinking may help to arbitrate in this debate.

MECHANICS OF THOUGHT

Philosophers work back from the larger features of thought to suggest what sorts of structure must underlie them. An important suggestion from Kant was that the mind has "categories of the understanding." He wondered what was essential to enable a mind to have experiences like ours, and proposed 12 categories of concept, grouped under the four headings quantity, quality, relation, and modality. Rival thinkers, such as Aristotle and Hegel, offer alternative category systems, so there is no consensus here, but we may well unthinkingly impose structures on our mental life.

CHAPTER 8

A modern development started with thought about how we acquire language. Children quickly learn to speak very accurately, with virtually no lessons, which suggests that the mind has an inbuilt module that contains the necessary skills of grammar and concepts, which are then triggered by experience. But if we have one module for language, why not other modules, for mental capacities dealing with psychology, biology, physics, and geometry?

We all have an inner personal assistant, reminding us where our phone is and when it is time to go out. Each module might represent a step forward in human evolution. Jerry Fodor, who proposed that the mind is *modular*, also surmised that the brain needs an inner language (the *language of thought*, resembling machine code in computers), in order to represent the images and concepts we manipulate when thinking.

THE MODULAR MIND

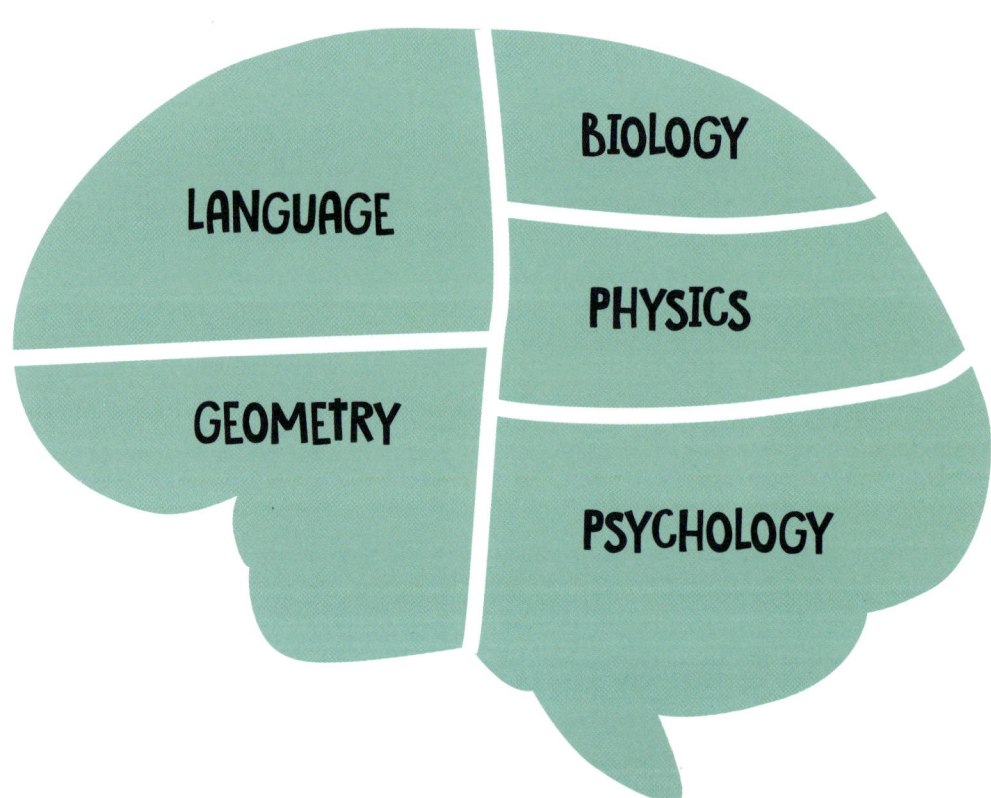

If someone says to you a single word, such as "zebras," this triggers a whole area of your knowledge.

The word *Zebra* triggers:

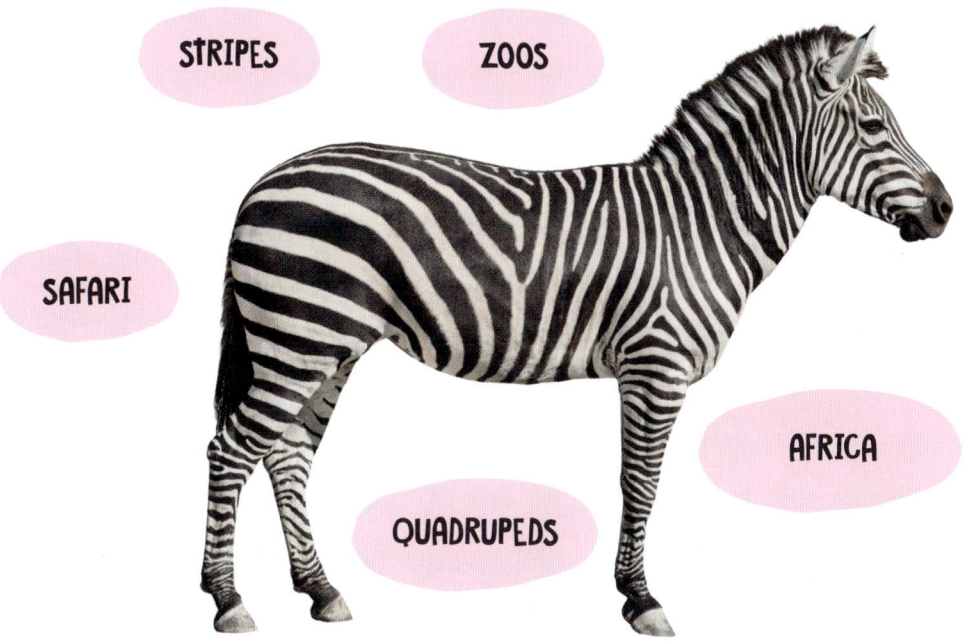

Our mind can be thought of as an elaborate filing system.

This is exactly like opening a file in an organized data system, and so the idea of **mental files** offers a helpful account of thinking. "Zebra" is the label of this particular file. Occasionally one file may have two labels (such as "Mumbai" and "Bombay"), or two files may have the same label (such as two towns called "Plymouth").

CHAPTER 8

The Frame Problem

A different approach to the mechanics of thought is trying to build a machine that thinks. Artificial intelligence has so far been very successful with precise, rule-based thinking, such as chess, but is not much good at tasks which need a lot of background—the so-called ***frame problem***, such as speaking appropriately at a funeral. At what point a machine counts as "thinking" is not clear, although the ability to hold a sustained conversation has become one ideal for AI researchers to target.

Artificial intelligence has proven very effective at rule-based thinking, for example in the game of chess, but it is not clear at what point this becomes true thought.

THOUGHT

CONTENT

If a detective and a criminal are thinking about "crime," they are thinking about the same thing, but their thoughts are likely to have different *content*. The content is what the thought is about, and if the thought is expressed in words, then the content is their "meaning" (which is what the listener must grasp to understand the words). A single thought might change its content (such as "Venice is beautiful" before and after a visit). When we first encountered horses, did the presence of horses generate a concept in human minds, or was the concept invented like a tool, to help us think about them? The relationship can't be simple, because other concepts about animals (such as feeding and running) are also involved in the concept of "horse."

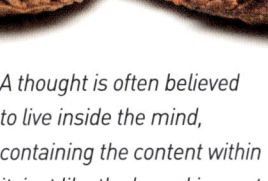

A thought is often believed to live inside the mind, containing the content within it, just like the kernel in a nut.

We visualize a thought as something inside the mind, with its content contained like a kernel in a nut. However, there has been an important challenge to this: Hilary Putnam observes that many of us cannot identify an elm tree by sight, yet when we talk about "elm trees" we all mean the same things—namely, the actual elm trees. We can only do this if knowledgeable people decide which trees are elms, and the rest of us go along with them. This implies that the content of "elm" is not internal to the mind, but is part of the social nature of language. This view is known as *externalism* about content (or *broad content*). It implies that our minds and thoughts spill out into the world, with implications about individuality and society.

CONCEPTS

The notion of a *concept* is central to our understanding of thought. We can only explain the behavior of animals if they are thinking, and a bird could not focus on a nest without a concept of it. Even if we reject that view, humans have concepts that are prior to language, since small infants can categorize things and adults can formulate a new concept before they think of a word for it. Once language is involved, two words (such as "pavement" and "sidewalk") can express the same concept, and ambiguous words like "bank" can express two concepts.

A bird needs a concept of a "nest" to focus on it.

CHAPTER 8

The extension of "cloud" refers to all the clouds in the world, both actual and possible.

A concept has an ***extension*** and an ***intension*** (note the "s"). The extension of "cloud" is all the actual and possible clouds in the real world, and its intension is the criteria which decide whether something belongs in the extension. Most discussions of concepts focus on intensions, but logicians like extensions because they are the objects we reason about, which are more clearly understood. The simplest concepts are said to be "atomic," and the others "complex"—though it is not easy to say when a concept qualifies as "simple." We may have a few innate concepts (such as "object"), and it is possible that they are very numerous. There seems no way to settle the question of where concepts come from, so the main focus has been on their essential nature.

The classical view says that the essence of a concept is given by an accurate definition, which gives the necessary and sufficient conditions for applying the concept. So a "cloud" must necessarily be in the atmosphere, made of vaporized liquid, be visible, be unified, and be not large enough to cover the sky. Something with all of these may be sufficient to be a cloud. (Notice that philosophers' definitions are usually more thorough than those found in dictionaries).

THE PROTOTYPE	THE EXEMPLARS	THE CLUSTER OF KNOWLEDGE
The perfect cloud	A variety of cloud specimens	Standard information about clouds

If you introspect your concept of "leopard," you probably visualize a very average leopard—a prototype against which other candidates can be assessed, by comparing features. This is efficient for thinking, and centers on what is obvious about the concept. However, it leaves open the question of which features are important—spots or whiskers?—and in many cases it is not clear what the prototype should be. What is typical "furniture" or "transport," for example?

The Theory-Theory of Concepts
The idea that concepts are small collections of knowledge (the so-called **Theory-Theory of Concepts**) gets away from visualized examples, and emphasizes that a lot of information may be involved in grasping a concept: that horses are mammals, which must eat, drink, and sleep, and which can be ridden. The theory-theory is also rather subjective, suggesting we never share the same concepts because we each have different knowledge about them.

If you have only seen boats, and no other means of transport, you will have a very particular concept of what transport is.

The range of a concept is better explained by many exemplars—such as different modes of transport. However, if you've only seen boats, and I've only seen horses, our concepts of "transport" would be entirely different. The correct account of concepts may be some combination of these theories.

UNDERSTANDING ACTION

We all (even philosophers) spend more time thinking about practice than about theory, so the mental activity that surrounds actions is of great interest, especially when morality is involved. We plan, choose, and judge actions, and we need a clear picture of their stages and ingredients, particularly when we are assessing responsibility.

The first step is to distinguish between an "action" and an "event." An earthquake is an event but not an action, because no one "does" an earthquake. Someone's leg twitching in their sleep is an event rather than an action, because actions concern "agents" who make decisions, usually with intentions, reasons, and motives. It is not clear whether a robot could be an agent, but action theory mainly studies conscious and deliberate human actions.

Activity and Performance

If I drive to work, is that one action, or a combination of several actions, or a sequence of tiny actions too numerous to count? What counts as an action, and how long can it last? This only matters if we want to classify actions, or show their relationships, or predict outcomes. For example, walking is an "activity," so you can say "I have walked today" when you are in the middle of doing it, but washing up is a "performance," so you need to finish it before you can say "I have washed up." The important question concerns causal relationships between actions. We normally say one distinct event causes another, such as an earthquake causing a tsunami. But my frying some eggs didn't cause me to cook breakfast. If we picture reality as continual chains of causation, we need to separate all the actions, but they overlap, and partly depend on how we describe them. Throwing a ball has a clear ending, so performances are more clear-cut. But does an action begin with an intention, or an act of will, or a movement? If actions are movements, then we can observe and measure them, but once desires, motives, intentions, and decisions are involved, it becomes hard to describe them accurately.

WHERE IS THE BEGINNING?

INTENTION

ACT OF WILL

MOVEMENT

INTENTION TO ACT

In law, if someone drops a brick on your foot the action is a crime only if they intended to do it, but what does this mean?

- Is an intention an emotion or a judgment?
- Must people know their own intentions and be able to explain them?
- Are intentions a distinct category of thought, or are they composed of other mental capacities? Is there more than one type of intention?
- Can a group of people have a shared intention?

A motive is not the same as an intention, since your reasons and desires may push you toward an action, but you may never actually form an intention to do it. The motive, rather than the intention, is the main explanation of an action, because it tells us why this intention was formed and then enacted. Hence motives seem to involve reasons, which can be expressed in words. Some philosophers say desires are the main reasons for acting, but a strong desire could be a reason for *not* acting (if it was seen as wicked). The idea that reasons predominate is strengthened if reasons are seen as having causal powers, so that the reasons can actually trigger the action. It is hard to discuss actions and responsibility sensibly if we don't think reasons are motivating them.

A brick that falls on you is not a crime in itself—it requires someone's intention to drop it on you.

CHAPTER 8

Prior and Sustained Intentions

If you examine your own intention to do something, you don't find a raw emotion like anxiety, because intentions largely focus on what has to be done. We can often see an animal's intentions, by seeing what it does. But intentions have internal as well as external aspects, because they can be either determined or half-hearted. There are also prior intentions and sustained intentions; you intend to press a button and then do it, but you keep intending to travel to Venice while you are doing it. Maybe an intention is like a private promise to yourself.

You can keep intending to travel to Venice over a long period of time.

Judgments and Desires

The main disagreement is between those who see intentions as judgments, and those who reduce them to a desire and a belief. If someone intended to drop the brick, then they can (if they are honest) give their reasons for doing it, which implies that the reasons guided the decision. The rival view (associated with David Hume) says that they just have an emotional desire, combined with beliefs about the behavior of bricks, and nothing further (such as a judgment) is needed. Critics of that say we may not form an actual intention even when we have the appropriate desires and beliefs, but it can always be replied that what restrains us (such as laziness or conscience) can be reduced to further desires.

Before we can eliminate intentions from our theory of action, we must recognize their own distinctive characteristics. For example, you can't simultaneously intend to turn left and to turn right, you can't usually intend to turn left when your destination is to the right, and you can't intend to fly to the Moon on a swan, so intentions must be consistent with one another, coherent with the desired end, and appear to be possible. This suggests that intentions are more rational than mere desires.

One individual cannot intend to lift a bus off a trapped person, but a group of people can, so can a group have an intention? Each person can focus on the shared goal, but they must also intend that the other people share their intention, so there is a communal aspect to intentions. The team goal may be reducible to individual states of mind, but those are more complex than simply wanting to do something.

You can't intend to turn left and to turn right at the same time.

CHAPTER 8

WILLED ACTION

Traditional accounts of actions usually say that they originate in the will. The simplest version of this is *volitionism*, which says that there is nothing more to an action than the act of will involved, but this seems wrong because it leaves out bodily movements.

> **VOLITIONISM** ▶ Action = the act of will

Willing to walk is not the same as walking. It is even suggested that the will has its own causal powers ("agent causation"), which have a unique independence of action. The biggest challenges to this say either that there is no such thing as the will (because introspection reveals nothing like it), or that we are mistaking the intellect or the last desire before action (whichever one does the job) for a distinct mental entity. That is not the end of the discussion, though, because modern neuroscience gives some support for a central controller of thought and action, for which "the will" is the best name. When all the intentions, reasons, and desires have been lined up, there still needs to be a starting gun to get the action going; actually doing it needs an initiator.

Weakness of will

An ancient puzzle concerns the phenomenon of *weakness of will* (Greek *akrasia*, lack of control). What is in charge of your actions—your judgment or your desires? If you firmly judge that you must give up chocolate, but then succumb to temptation and eat some, this suggests that desires have taken charge, and that your mind has conflicting sources of action. Socrates, however, believed only judgments lead to actions, so his explanation was that you didn't really believe your own judgment to not eat chocolate. You must have a hidden belief that it is good to eat chocolate, or that any harm it does won't apply to you. Our attitude to moral responsibility is influenced by our view of how we act, and it is important to remember that we also have second-level thought—we can desire not to desire something, and judge that our reasons are bad reasons.

The will to walk is not the same as actually walking.

Chapter Nine
LANGUAGE

Nature of Meaning—Reference—Semantics—Propositions—Analyticity—Communication

SEMANTICS
- SYNTAX
- COMPOSITION
- INDEXICAL WORDS
- POSSIBLE WORDS

MEANING
- TRUTH CONDITIONS
- INTENTIONS
- USAGE
- VERIFICATION

LANGUAGE
- REFERENCE
- PROPOSITIONS
- ANALYTICITY

COMMUNICATION
- CONVERSATIONAL IMPLICATURE
- PRIVATE LANGUAGE ARGUMENT
- CHARITY

NATURE OF MEANING

Modern philosophy has focused more on how the mind relates to the world than on the world itself. Language was once treated as "transparent"—leading directly from thought to knowledge—but we now see that it is not so simple. The key concept is "meaning"—what distinguishes language from the hubbub of noise that surrounds it. The earliest approach said that words simply attach to "ideas," but Gottlob Frege found different components in meaning. If I say "the password is 'swordfish,'" that has a literal meaning and its meaning as a password. If I say "James is ill," the predicate "is ill" gives information, but "James" just points to someone. So Frege said meaning can involve *sense* (the contents of the words) and *reference* (which picks out items for discussion). There are other aspects to meaning as well—seen in metaphors, emphasis, sarcasm, and so on. The first task is to understand the literal meaning or sense of words and sentences.

The science of Linguistics explores meaning through analysis of the way people acutally speak. This often results in complex theories in which many aspects of speech (such as intention, tone, context, and body language) combine. Philosophers focus more on logic and truth, and tend to study the "strict and literal meaning" of sentences. So the first task is to understand how straightforward statements connect to the world.

Frege claimed meaning required both sense and reference.

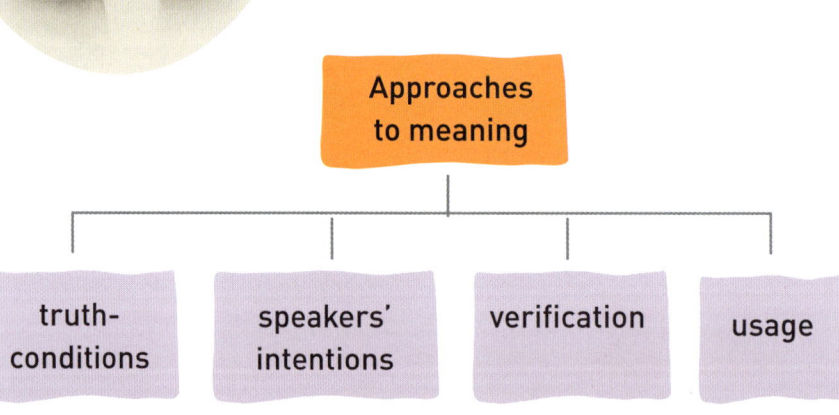

Truth-conditions

The truth-conditions of a sentence are how the world would be if the sentence were true. So the meaning of "pigeons fly" is the situation where they do fly, and the meaning of "pigs fly" is how the world would be if they really did fly. This theory has the advantage of directly connecting meaning with reality (reducing the opportunity for skepticism), but it is not clear how physical objects can count as "meanings."

We could say instead that the truth-conditions are in our representations of the pigeons (rather than in the real thing). These can be thought of as pictures, but that makes it too specific (how many pigeons are in the picture?), and puts meanings back among our ideas, which loses the main attraction of the theory. We might even learn the truth-conditions of a sentence in German, without knowing what it actually means.

The truth-conditions theory is attractive because it makes speaking the truth a basic human activity (with lies and falsehoods as an afterthought), and its emphasis on truth (rather than metaphors and expressions of feeling) seems to offer the required account of strict and literal meaning. The biggest objection is the observation that we need to know the meaning of a sentence *before* we can assess its truth-conditions (though this is an objection to many attempts to explain meaning).

The meaning of the sentence "Pigs fly" refers to how the world would be if pigs really did fly.

CHAPTER 9

Speakers' Intentions

Speakers' intentions come into it if language is seen primarily as communication. In a conversation, one thinker tries to pass what they are thinking about to a listener, so meaning can be seen in terms of the intention to make a listener understand what the speaker is thinking about. This theory is usually seen as capturing the important psychological dimension of meaning, without pinning down what is being transmitted.

Verification

Strong versions of empiricism require that all mental life is directly or indirectly tied to actual experiences, and meaning should not be an exception. The logical positivist movement defined the meaning of a sentence as the method by which it is (or could be) verified. Definitions might be an exception, but the theory implied that if a sentence can't be verified, then it is meaningless. The lofty claims of metaphysics and religion were said to lack meaning, since evidence for or against them is irrelevant. The theory made the important point that impressive words can actually be empty of meaning, but *verificationism* soon ran into difficulties.

> **VERIFICATIONISM** ▶ *Meaning is defined by the method by which it can be verified.*

Words are like chess pieces. You have to know how to use them.

The basic problem is that some unverifiable sentences are obviously meaningful. We can speculate whether "Socrates once had a headache," which we understand even without hope of verifying it. Even simpler objections are that in order to verify a sentence you must already know what it means, and that the theory itself doesn't seem to be verifiable. Modifications have been attempted (perhaps by requiring verification "in principle"—if, say, you had been a friend of Socrates), but verification seems to be too demanding.

Usage

Philosophers who find so-called "meanings" highly dubious often favor approaching meaning through *usage*. Wittgenstein said the meaning of a word is like the meaning of a chess piece, which is just knowing how to use it (which only requires the ability to follow a rule). This greatly simplifies the question of meaning, but there are inevitable problem cases (such as being able to use "Amen" correctly without knowing that it means "so be it"). Understanding language seems to go beyond knowing how to use it—as we might suspect if we encountered an impressive talking robot.

REFERENCE

The reference of a word is the entity to which it refers. If words have reference as well as meaning, this explains how language can plug into the world, helping to show how a sentence can be true. If scientific terms don't connect to anything, then it is impossible to compare theories and say which theories are best. So is this direct link to reality possible? At one extreme, if a sentence mentions Napoleon, we can just include the man himself in the meaning of the sentence. At the other extreme, we only understand the reference because of our descriptions of him, which means reference is all in the mind, rather than linking directly to the world.

The debate about reference is a key one in modern philosophy, because the extent to which our language can express truths about the world depends on it. A descriptive theory of reference pushes us toward the anti-realist view that thought cannot connect with reality, while a direct theory of reference is more realist.

At one extreme of the debate, in a sentence mentioning Napoleon we can understand the reference only because of our descriptions of the man.

CHAPTER 9

Compositional and Whole Sentences

If reference connects language to the world, it is assumed that sentences are *compositional*, meaning they are assembled in the mind piece by piece. If you read: "Napoleon had a hard time returning from Moscow," the compositional view says you put the words together like Lego bricks to make a complete structure.

A rival view says we grasp ideas and sentences as complete wholes, rather than a bit at a time, and we only understand the words by their role in the whole sentence. If that is right, then the references of words are less important, and we must explain how complete thoughts connect to reality.

> Two theories of reference correspond to the two compositional and whole-sentence views of meaning:
>
> - **The *direct* view** ▶ The meaning of "Napoleon" can't just be the man, but the word "Napoleon" has some direct historical connection to him.
> - **The *descriptive*** ▶ The reference to Napoleon involves knowledge of facts and descriptions, which uniquely specify him.

The direct view relies on the realist assumption that there was an actual specific person to whom we connect by using the name. The descriptive view only relies on a few ideas about Napoleon (which may not even be true), which enable us to agree who we are talking about.

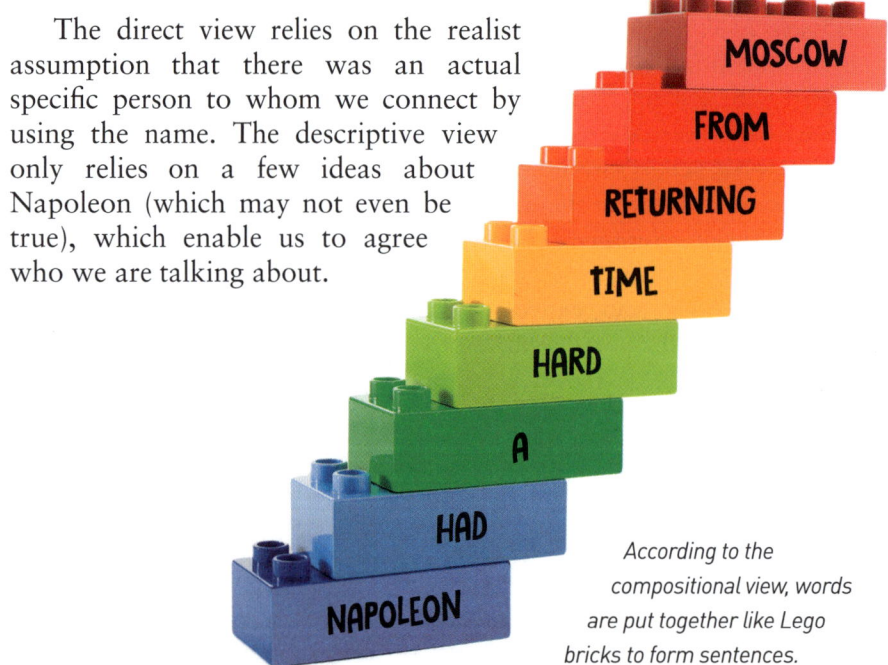

According to the compositional view, words are put together like Lego bricks to form sentences.

Napoleon was the victor at Austerlitz, but the reference cannot depend on that description if it might be contradicted by a historian.

Causal Chains

The strongest direct link would be a causal chain leading back to the moment when that baby was given the name "Napoleon." Problems arose with this *causal theory*, however. You can have a causal link running back to the baby Napoleon, but not to the concept of a "hypotenuse" (which has no causal powers, because it is abstract), so the theory doesn't work well for mathematics, and talk of "Bigfoot" seems to refer to something which does not exist, so there can be no causal link. A better theory merely says that reference starts with the term's original use, and then is sustained by a language community.

The descriptive theory has received strong criticism from Saul Kripke. If Napoleon is actually specified as "the victor of Austerlitz," then a historian's claim that "actually Napoleon didn't win at Austerlitz" would be a contradiction (equivalent to "the victor at Austerlitz did not win at Austerlitz"). All the descriptions we use to fix the reference of "Napoleon" would be undeniable, because they would be essential to who he is. The fact is that we can successfully refer to "that man holding a martini" even if the description is wrong (because he is holding a glass of water), so the reference can't depend on the truth of the descriptions.

Both the direct and descriptive theories claim that language itself has referential properties (of inherited links, or descriptive success), but an alternative view says it is people (not words) who refer to things. "Napoleon" could refer to a man or a pig, depending on what the speaker intended. Reference can be achieved by a meaningful look, or by the phrase "you know who I mean," as well as by standard methods.

CHAPTER 9

SEMANTICS

A distinction can be made between the "syntax" (the structure) and the "semantics" (the meanings) of a sentence. The syntactic structure of a sentence is distinct from its meaning: "he likes grapes" and "she likes strawberries" have the same *syntax*. The distinction is not always clear, since "he is easy to please" and "she is eager to please" seem to have the same structure, but the meaning shows that this is not so. The standard picture, though, is that syntax is fairly mechanical, and leaps into life when it acquires semantics.

Subject-Predicate Form

Should the semantics have the same structure as the syntax? Most languages have a subject-predicate form, where a standard sentence picks out a subject, and then attributes a predicate (some feature) to it, as in "the willow tree is dropping its leaves early this year." For this we can have a semantics of objects and features, assigning them to components of the syntax. But there are many problems:

- The subject of "no leaves are blocking the drain this year" is "no leaves," but that doesn't refer to anything.
- Remembering the distinction between narrow and broad content for thoughts, how do I assign "an elm tree grows in the wood" if I can't recognize an elm tree?
- What object do I assign to "Pegasus is a winged horse" if Pegasus doesn't physically exist?

Logicians such as Bertrand Russell introduced the idea of the *logical form* of a sentence, which may be quite different from the superficial syntactic form. Once the logical form is clear (about which objects are claimed to exist, for example) the assignment of meanings becomes easier. Formal logic can help to state the logical form unambiguously.

In the compositional view of meaning (where sentences are built up), the semantics has to be detailed and complete, but it may be easier if the whole thought comes first. Then we can start with what the sentence is about, rather than what the subject refers to. The sentence "our walk will be after sunset" refers to the sun, but it is probably about the darkness or the timing of the walk. We may be able to specify the truth-conditions of the sentence without bothering about reference, or we may focus on situations (without mentioning truth).

Bertrand Russell came up with the idea of the "logical form" of a sentence.

CHAPTER 9

When describing a sunset walk, we may be referring to the darkness or time of the walk rather than to the sun.

Concepts in Sentences

A further problem concerns the "extension" of a concept—the entities which it picks out. The word "cordate," when applied to an animal, means that it has a heart, and "renate" means that it has kidneys. It is a fact that in live animals the two always come together. That is, the extension of "cordate" (the animals with hearts) is identical to the extension of "renate" (the animals with kidneys). So the words have the same extensions, but different meanings. Hence you cannot give the semantics of a word merely by specifying the entities to which it refers. This has led to "possible worlds semantics," which shows the difference between "cordate" and "renate" as possible worlds where an animal could have a heart but no kidney, or vice versa. That is, meanings are given by what they *could* refer to, rather than just what they actually refer to.

LANGUAGE

cordate

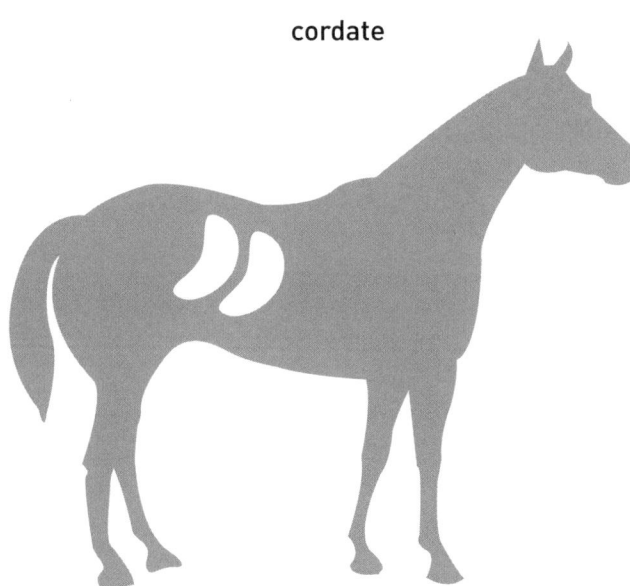

renate

The extension of "cordate" is the same as the extension of "renate," so words can have the same extensions but different meanings.

Indexical words

A second problem concerns *indexical* words, such as "here" and "now," and "we," which depend for their meaning on the place, time, and speaker of the utterance. The word "now" has a fixed meaning—the present moment—but *which* present moment?

The meaning has two components, the universal meaning, and the meaning on a given occasion, and the semantics of indexicals must specify both:

- If you ask "what does the word *now* mean?", the answer might be "the moment at which the word is uttered."

- If you ask someone "what do you mean by *do it now?*", the answer could be "do it this morning."

Both parts must be specified to explain the usage of the word "now."

This has led to a general system called "two-dimensional semantics," which tries to capture the complex aspects of meaning throughout language.

CHAPTER 9

PROPOSITIONS

If we compare the three sentences, "Snow is white," "Schnee ist weiss," and "La neige est blanche," they seem to say exactly the same thing, in three different languages. If there is a "thing" of which these are three expressions, it is called a "proposition"—a complete meaningful thought which can be expressed in a language, and which can be either true or false.

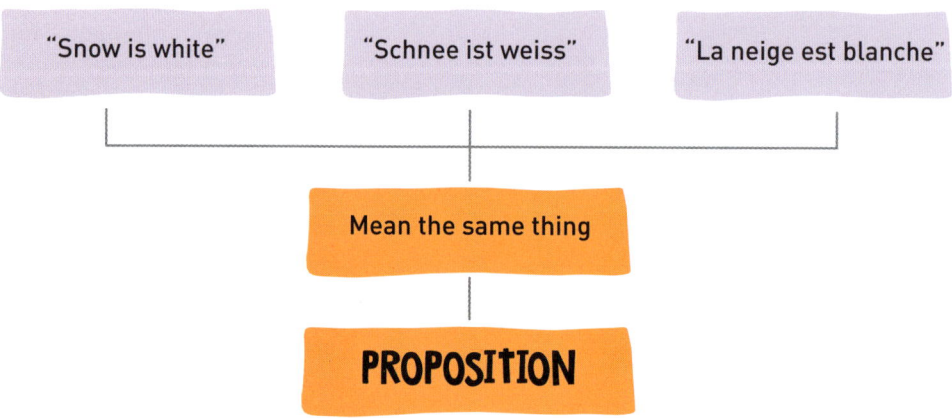

Critics say that the three sentences about snow are just three "equivalent" responses to a simple fact about the world. Why add "propositions," if we can explain everything without them? Defenders of propositions say we need them for logic, for the psychology of thinking and talking, and to make sense of translation. Whether some truth is proved by logic shouldn't depend on which language it is expressed in. If we find the logical form of a sentence, which is an accurate account of the underlying proposition, then speakers of all languages should agree on it. Each language may have untranslatable nuances, but the proposition is meant to be the core of meaning, on which we can all agree. We understand the remarks, "what I meant to say is . . ." or "what he is trying to say is . . . ," which implies that we formulate thoughts in our minds before we find the words for them. The very process of translation requires that we grasp what a sentence says, and then express that idea in another language.

There are four main theories about propositions. They can be seen as:
- specific aspects of reality
- events in the mind
- simple abstract entities
- selections of possible worlds.

Bertrand Russell said a sentence about Mont Blanc contained the actual mountain, so a proposition about it is a set of features (height, danger, etc) arranged in a certain order. This has the virtue that in conversation we are all talking about the same thing, but it is hard to explain talk of imaginary mountains, and generalization and abstractions don't fit easily into this account. It also left a puzzle about why these ingredients are unified into a single proposition.

Propositions may be mental events, formulated before we put them into words, but we aren't actually aware of propositions in our minds, since we focus on what the proposition is about, rather than the thing itself. If Russell's view is too concrete, an alternative says they are abstractions, consisting of all the thoughts it is possible to have. That is a lot of propositions, but no worse in quantity than the infinite numbers, which we seem to accept. A proposition can also be treated as the set of possible worlds in which it is true, which is all its possible truth conditions. This presents a proposition as some situations, but says nothing about the structure of the proposition.

A sentence about Mont Blanc included the actual mountain, according to Bertrand Russell.

CHAPTER 9

ANALYTICITY

If you can assess the truth of a sentence just by analyzing its wording, it is said to be *analytic*. The truth of "a kitten is a young cat" is known simply from the meanings of the words. It is tempting to divide our language into two groups: *analytic* ideas about concepts (our "dictionary"), and *synthetic* ideas about the world (our "encyclopaedia"). It has been suggested by empiricists that the only necessary truths are the analytic ones (because they are true by definition), and none of the synthetic truths are necessary, because their necessity can never be revealed by experience (since every case, both actual and possible, would have to be observed). The issues concern the nature of an analytic truth, and whether the sharp analytic/synthetic distinction is a genuine one.

Analytic Ideas	Synthetic Ideas
Truth can be determined by the wording of a sentence.	Truth can be determined by a sentence's relation to the world.
About concepts	About the world
Example: Dictionary	Example: Encyclopaedia

Kant said an analytic truth has its predicate "contained in" its subject, so the word "kitten" is said to contain the concept "young cat." Hence to check its truth, you unpack the ingredients of the subject, and denying the sentence (such as "this kitten is an old cat") is a contradiction. However, this only works if there is a subject to unpack, and a sentence like "either P or Q, and not P, so Q" is true for any content, so it is analytic but without a subject. Also "this kitten is an old cat" could be seen as a redefinition of "kitten," rather than as a contradiction. Later discussions suggest that being analytic means you can substitute "young cat" for "kitten" in any context.

Willard Quine denied the analytic/synthetic distinction. Using substitution as a test for analyticity is rejected, because it relies on "young cat" meaning exactly the same as "kitten" (being a "synonym" for it), but different terms can't be exactly alike, because the words involved have different relationships in the wider language. Also, meanings are always tangled up with facts (e.g. about cat lifespans), and stating the facts needs meanings, so analytic and synthetic truths are linked within one big scheme of understanding, and can't be distinct. If Quine is right, then even mathematics and logic are dependent on the real world (because they are not analytic), and could be changed if necessary.

LANGUAGE

COMMUNICATION

The main use of language is for transmitting thoughts. The early Greeks argued over the value of rhetoric (the skills of public speaking) because it had a major role in their society. Is the main aim of a speech to get people to agree with you, or to speak the truth? Socrates defended the second view, but in modern law courts and elections we know the aim is still to persuade the audience, rather than to get it right. Modern "pragmatics" focuses on language in practice, and how having a context and listeners can shift meanings, references, and even truth.

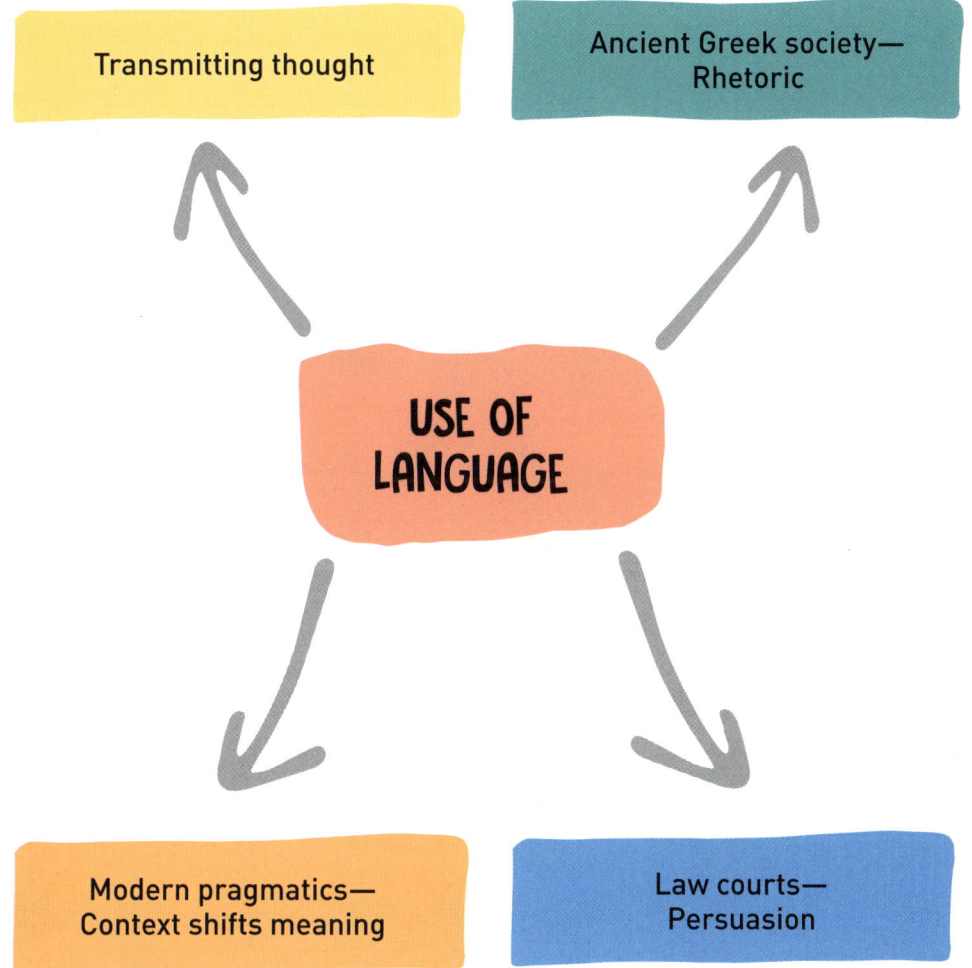

CHAPTER 9

Rhetoric played a major role in Ancient Greece.

Private Language Argument

Wittgenstein claimed that a language which cannot communicate is an incoherent idea. His famous *private language argument* says that language is essentially rule-following, which is impossible without external checks on conformity to the rules (just as tennis needs a ruling body). A private language is particularly hopeless when reporting hidden states of mind, because the meaning of "blue" must be public, even though the sensation of blue is not. The argument is controversial, but important because it implies that we are much less individualistic than is normally assumed.

Meaning and understanding greatly depend on the context. Justification, for example, will be demanding when doing university exams, but relaxed when preferring one restaurant to another. Indexicals like "here" and "now" only have full meaning in a context, and "they will be trouble, so we must pull together" only makes sense in a context. Some argue that this goes much further, and innumerable words and statements have subtle differences of meaning dictated by the situation. If so, clear communication is much harder than we thought, but it would explain a lot of human misunderstandings.

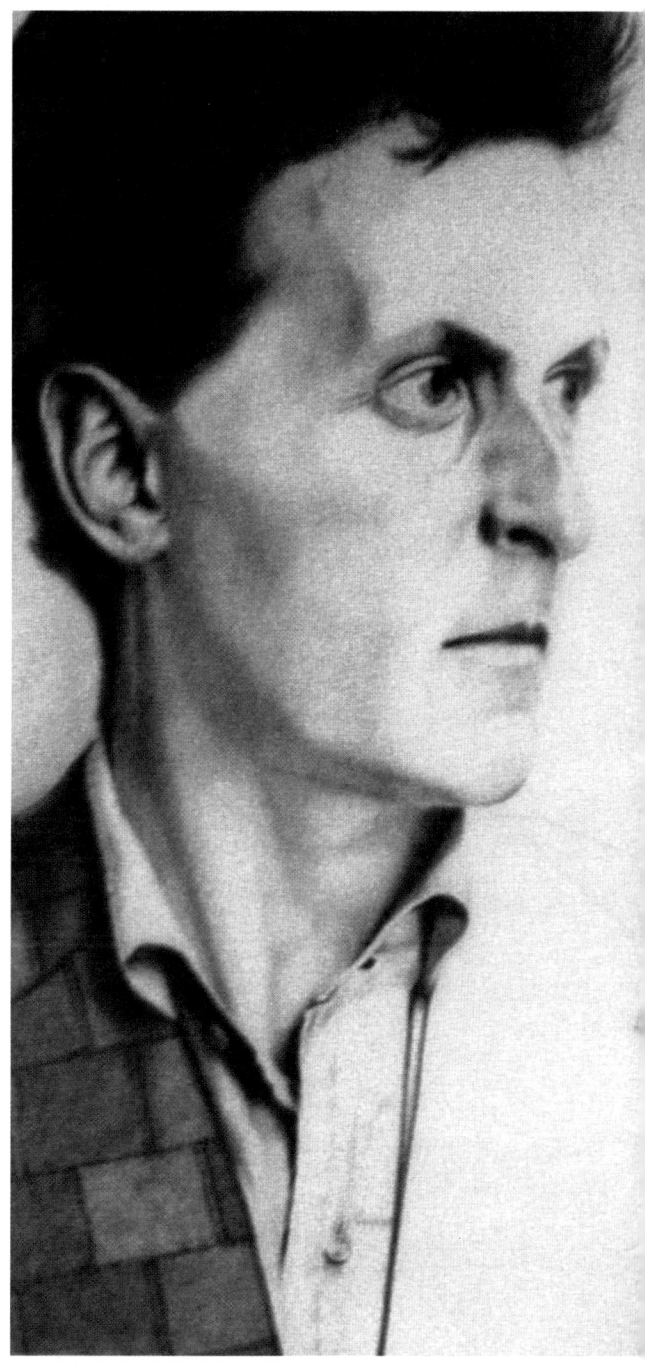

Wittgenstein devised the private language argument.

CHAPTER 9

Conversational Implicature

Paul Grice identified a set of unspoken rules (called *conversational implicature*) by which we interpret conversations.

> **CONVERSATIONAL IMPLICATURE** ▶ *A set of unspoken rules for interpreting conversation.*

We all agree that what we say should contain the appropriate quantity of information, assert only what we believe, be kept brief, and avoid obvious triviality. These rules are broken all the time, but people are criticized for doing so. Conversations also rest on unspoken presuppositions, most notably what the conversation is about, and unnoticed shifts of topic occur in many conversations. In philosophy, distinguishing presuppositions is vital, so that their truth can be checked.

Translation between languages puts our concepts of meaning and propositions to the test. Quine raises doubts about whether perfect translation is ever possible, because a whole network of beliefs and language is involved in our understanding of each word. If he is right, this also makes the comparison of scientific theories difficult. A possible response is the *principle of charity*, which says we have to assume that the speakers of an unknown language are human like us, and their logic is like ours.

> **CHARITY** ▶ *We must assume speakers of other languages share our humanity and logic.*

Translation can then be largely successful, even if there are important differences between the cultures. Terrible misunderstandings can arise from translation errors, but scientific theories are successfully compared, and (with serious effort) remote cultures can be fairly well understood.

Chapter Ten
VALUES

Aesthetics—Art—Moral Value—Basic Values

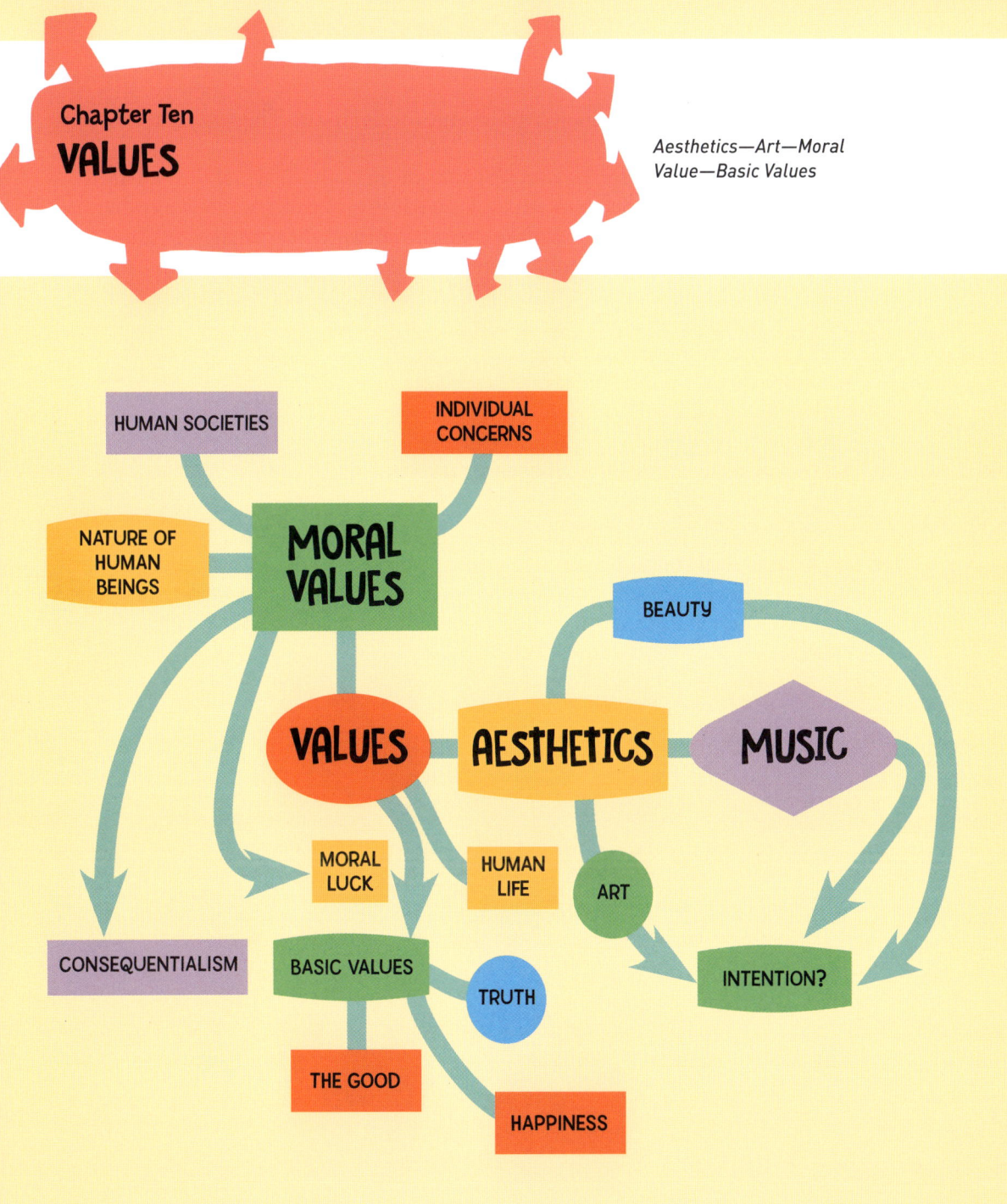

CHAPTER 10

AESTHETICS

Values are general concepts which attract and motivate us. They are a focus for what we consider important, and we hope to share them with the people around us. The key values for us are personal moral values, which are more basic in our ethical system than the principles we follow. Principles such as "do your duty" have no appeal for us if they are not motivated by what we value. There are also "civic" values, which are considered important in a society, and "aesthetic values," concerning what we find attractive. Values thus have great importance, but are puzzling in their nature.

- Do they express eternal truth?
- Do they sum up sensible strategies for living?
- Are they irrational?
- Can we give reasons to support our preferred values?
- Can we only assert them, like emotions?

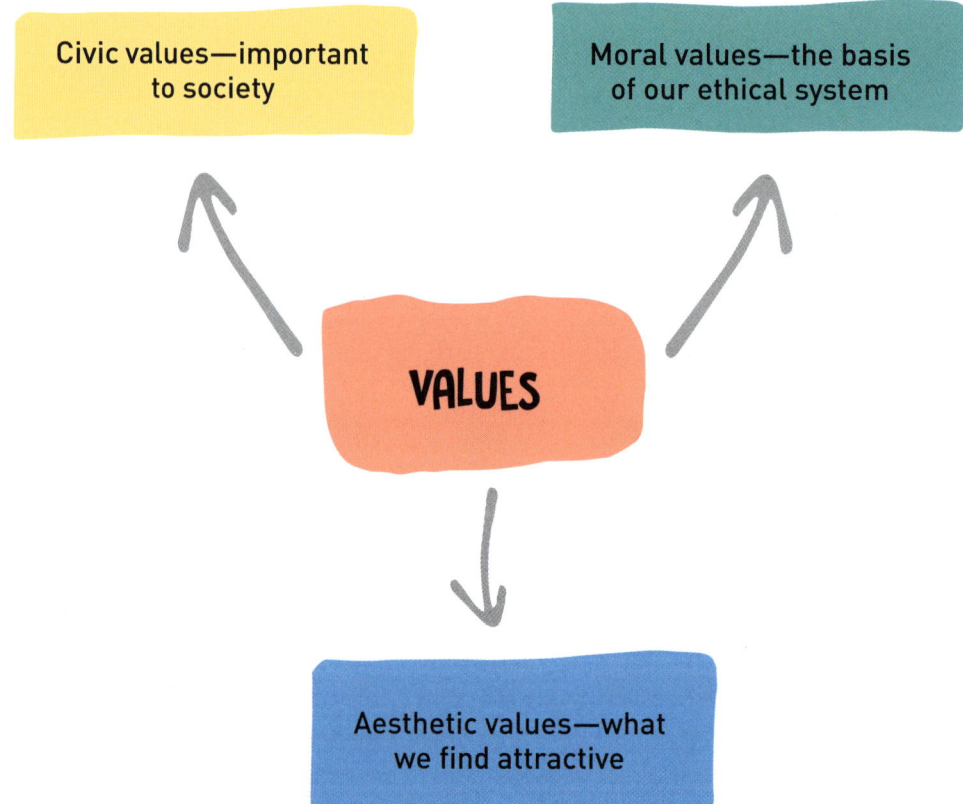

VALUES

Beauty

Some people have little interest in what is said to be "beautiful," but we all admire clever, skilful, or challenging achievements. For the ancient Greeks, these concepts were virtually the same, but in modern times aesthetic appreciation is seen as a distinctive reaction, which may require sensitivity or taste. Most people are sensitive to natural beauty (of a face, or a landscape), even if they don't like the arts. Aesthetics concerns a distinctive and significant experience we have of nature and the arts. It may embody reason, truth, and wisdom, as well as pleasure and other emotions, and it plays an important role in all modern societies.

"Beautiful" is a broad term, applied to sponge cakes and carpentry, as well as to sunsets and paintings. For Plato, beauty was hugely important. It was an indicator of moral worth, and its appreciation was the first step on the road to wisdom. At the other extreme, the popularity of the saying "beauty is in the

Beauty is an incredibly broad term, referring to people, artwork, nature, and more—most people can appreciate some form of beauty.

eye of the beholder" expresses the relativist view that being beautiful is never a fact but just the private responses of each observer. Those who doubt such relativism distinguish between aesthetic *preferences* and aesthetic *judgments*. On the one hand, "I know what I like," but on the other hand, music critics or curators of art shows try to predict what we will *all* like, and even to suggest what we *should* like.

AESTHETIC PREFERENCES	AESTHETIC JUDGMENTS
Individual	Critics
What I like	What we all like/what we should like

If there are objective and tasteful judgments to be made about what is beautiful, then these are best made by experienced observers with a good track record for spotting what the rest of us agree is good. If a long-dead artist is said to be unappreciated, this implies that their work has fine aesthetic qualities, even if no one is currently experiencing them.

It is a pleasure to experience beauty, but it is hard to define what gives the pleasure. Romantic philosophers distinguished the *sublime* as a special sort of beauty: found in starry skies or dramatic landscapes, which induces an exceptional state of awe, humility, and insight. More normal beauty is found in things which are harmonious (like elegant furniture), or perfectly attuned to a purpose (like a running leopard), or show exceptional imagination (like a Shakespeare play). A familiar puzzle is why we can find literature or art beautiful even when it depicts horrible events, which reveals that being beautiful is very different from being merely "pleasant." Beauties can be compared for their qualities, as well as for their intensities, so it is not just a matter of feeling.

Art can be beautiful even when it depicts a horrible event.

ART

Most modern aesthetic discussion focuses on works of art, and the close resemblance between experiencing music, painting, literature, dance, and other arts invites us to give a unified account of their nature. In what way do artworks exist? Which aspects are essential to them? What is their purpose and value? What distinguishes the best works from the rest?

Paintings and buildings have an obvious mode of existence, as physical objects, but what sort of thing is a Beethoven symphony? It behaves like an object, because it has a name and various features, and an audience can focus on it, but it is spread over time, so it never all exists at once. The written score is silent so that can't be the symphony, and each performance is slightly different, so no one performance counts as the real thing. It may have multiple existences or it may be an abstraction, but it remains a problem for students of ontology.

What is a symphony? It is not the written score, which is silent, and each performance is slightly different.

CHAPTER 10

The Ingredients of Art

The ingredients that make up art are:
- the ideas, feelings, intention, and imagination of the artist
- the form and content of the work
- the focus, feelings, and ideas of the audience
- art's social role.

Debates center on the relative importance or unimportance of each of these. Modern discussion began with the suggestion that an *artist's intention*s are irrelevant, because only the work itself can be judged. The idea that art expresses the creator's feelings also looks doubtful, because exuberant artworks can take months to create, which is a long time to feel exuberant. However, once we see how important a title can be for a painting, it becomes obvious that the aim of the work is important. It is hard to enjoy any work without sensing some communication with its creator. Hence many thinkers have urged us to attend to the historical context if we want a good understanding of an artwork.

Clearly, good art must engage its audience. Romantic art is highly emotional, and can evoke tears, but other art is elegant, surprising, dazzling, or intellectually satisfying. The best artists strike us as wise people, with an admirable gift for capturing their insights in a unified work. Some thinkers have focused entirely on the form of the work, seeing the best art as being organically unified, with its structure in harmony with the subject matter. Modern visual art has undermined these theories, by defining art as nothing more than whatever established artists say it is—such as an object found on a beach but displayed in an art gallery.

Marcel Duchamp's Fontaine *is the classic example of conceptual art, as modern art is often defined by whatever established artists say it is.*

Philosophers who accept this claim see art as a social institution, rather than any specific type of creation. Nowadays, we can accept a large building wrapped in fabric as an artwork, which would have been unthinkable a century earlier.

The "Wrapped Reichstag," by Christo and Jeanne-Claude, is today considered a striking piece of artwork, which would have been unthinkable a century ago.

Just as attempts to define the nature of art have led to artistic rebellions, so have theoretical assertions of its purpose. A traditional view that art is a branch of moral education led younger artists to entirely reject any moral purpose in art. But despite these rebellions, the older views won't go away. As long as art is beautiful, or involved in moral and political issues, it will be important to us, and we will always revere the unified structures of the best traditional art. Whimsical triviality may entertain us for a while, but most audiences want to be gripped and inspired, rather than just amused.

MORAL VALUE

Artistic ideals like beauty can inspire us, and moral values such as "good," "right," "duty," and "virtue" play a similar role. The best approach to values is to ask about their source. If a large rock smashes a small rock a trillion miles from here, that has no moral interest if no minds are involved. If a random meteor hits a town on Earth, that is a very bad thing, but it also fails to be moral if no one intended it. If someone drops a bomb on a town, the intention and the suffering make it a moral issue. There may be other moral beings in the universe, but our moral values arise out of human affairs.

> **There are three main sources of values within human affairs:**
> - the nature of human beings in general
> - the customs of human societies
> - individual concerns

If there were no **human values**, we would all have disappeared long ago, because we need security, warmth, nourishment, health, upbringing, and so on. This group of values is sometimes neglected (especially in wartime), but is almost impossible to deny. The customs of a **society** produce many important values, such as loyalty, legality, and obedience, even though other societies may do things differently. The values of individuals may be overruled in many situations, such as slavery or the army, but modern liberal societies encourage individuals to develop values of their own, based on what matters to them. These are not, of course, the only sources of value. We recognize the importance of the environment and of other animals, and specialist areas such as mathematics and gardening have their own values, concerning precision or planning—so environmentalists need to take a long-term view when studying deforestation, mathematicians value precision and consistency, and gardeners must respect seasonal changes.

The Truth of Values

But do these values contain truth and authority, or are they just attitudes, arising mainly from emotions, which could easily have been quite different? David Hume famously said that no reason could ever be found which proved the correctness of values or duties from the plain facts. This strict distinction between facts and values is associated with the scientific view of reality, and with the demand of empiricists for evidence. We may like human kindness, but could we prove that it is valuable?

If there are many objectively correct values, then we would expect most people to agree on them. There may be a consensus on human values, but much less so on cultural and individual values. Critics say that the *fact-value distinction* is not a sharp one. If we describe someone as "inconsiderate" or "treacherous," or say that someone "owes" you something or "needs" something, these look like facts with values built into them. It is even argued that we are incapable of ever seeing things in a value-free way (as cold facts), even when we are doing science.

SITUATION	Good	Pet in town
	Bad	Dangerous animal in town
ACTION	Right	Shooting dangerous animal
	Wrong	Shooting pet

CONSEQUENTIALISM ▶ *The ends justify the means.*

Consequentialists defend the view that all that matters in moral actions is that the consequences are good. What we want are good situations (where people are happy, healthy, and so on), and if we have to perform unpleasant actions to achieve good ends, this may be a worthwhile trade-off. The rival view says we must always do what is right (even if we don't like the consequences, as when you admit guilt over some bad action) because morality concerns our actions, not the resulting good or bad situations. Thus, we should hardly ever tell lies, and casually lying whenever it is convenient strikes us as wicked. The puzzle of *moral luck* is often cited against this view. For example, if you casually lob a brick over a wall, we judge you more harshly if you kill someone than if it falls harmlessly. Intentions seem to matter most, and you will quickly lose friends if you lob bricks over walls, even if it does no harm.

Optimists see values as containing universal truths, so that all societies have very similar underlying values, despite appearing to be very different. Their source may be in pure ideals, or in our love and care for other people, particularly our children. But skeptics see this as wishful thinking. Empiricists, who see no tangible evidence for the existence of real values, often accept the *expressivist* view, that assertions about morality are nothing more than feelings of approval or disapproval.

CHAPTER 10

> **EXPRESSIVISM** ▶ *Morality is nothing more than approval or disapproval.*

Modern political thinkers see values as arising from social structures, especially those concerned with power. Values such as obedience, duty, discretion, and punctuality are needed in a reliable employee, so the powerful elites promote them, and the rest of us must accept them. But there are also revolutionary values, arising from weaker social groups, which see arrogance and displays of wealth as shameful, and may approve of whistle-blowers who reveal corruption.

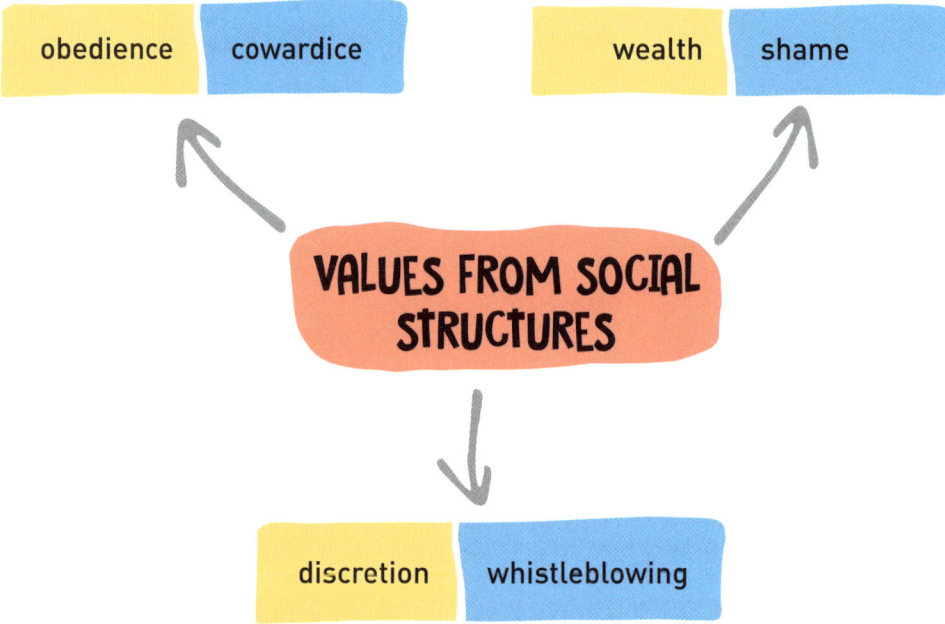

Modern discussion of values is strongly influenced by evolutionary theory, which sees them as biological rather than rational in origin. Thus, the basic drives of any creature are for survival and breeding, and values are part of the strategies to achieve this. For all larger creatures, friendly and co-operative values are successful methods of achieving selfish ends, and the main reason why you should be nice to people is so that they will return the kindness and help you live successfully.

BASIC VALUES

Values retain the highest importance, whether they arise out of emotions, good sense, biology, or political power. So is it possible to identify some values around which all of humanity might build their moral lives? The strongest commitment to values is found in Plato, who places beauty, goodness, and truth on a pedestal, with the Form of the Good (the eternal, unchanging, non-physical source of all values) as supreme. Plato and the Greeks also acknowledged other basic values, such as reason, knowledge, harmony, human flourishing, and pleasure. Religions introduce further values, such as faith, love, and humility, and modern democratic values have elevated attitudes such as respect. There are, of course, less elevated values which are given some priority, such as longevity, wealth, or being "a winner."

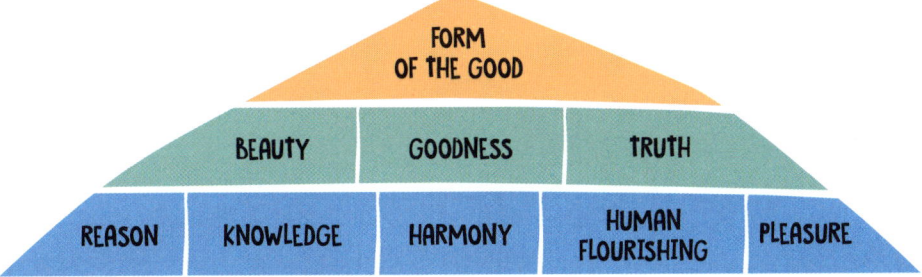

The idea of a supreme value—*The Good*—has been criticized for its vagueness and the uncertainty of its existence, but it is defended on the grounds that the word "good" can never be defined in terms of something else. For example, if someone says pleasures are intrinsically good, you can ask whether they are talking about good or bad pleasures. Nowadays it is rare for beauty to be offered as a supreme value, although for many people life would be empty without it. Truth has taken a battering in modern times, and the relativist denial of its existence has become a commonplace. Nevertheless, social life is in trouble if we continually lie, science makes no sense if it doesn't pursue the correct answers, and historians want to know what *really* happened.

Enlightenment philosophers were attracted to the rational life, but Romantics rebelled against this, and different cultures can disagree over what counts as rational. Lovers of rationality point to mathematics, logic, and the precise sciences as role models, but even there it is questioned whether there can be absolute standards. Pure knowledge and wisdom have lost status in modern times. The frontiers of physics generate excitement and awe, but it may only be *new* knowledge which has high value.

CHAPTER 10

> **EUDAIMONIA** ▶ *The activities that promote happiness.*

The Greeks valued the harmony of the universe, and we see the value of harmony in society, as in our admiration for "peace and reconciliation." Aristotle built his account of ethics round the ideal of *eudaimonia* ("flourishing"). This Greek word is often translated as "happiness," but *eudaimonia* is not just a nice feeling. It means life is going well, and is best translated as "flourishing." The concept is more concerned with what you do. A person's life was *eudaimon* if it was successful and admirable. A depressed person can still have a successful life, despite frequently feeling unhappy.

> **HEDONISM** ▶ *Pleasure is the supreme value.*

Hedonism is the doctrine that pleasure is the supreme value, and modern secular cultures have become highly hedonistic.

Most philosophers have their doubts about pleasure. Even Epicureans, who are noted for valuing pleasure, also placed a high value on restraint. Constant indulgence in food and drink leads to obesity and hangovers, and the supreme epicurean good is friendship. The idea that pleasure is the only good should certainly be treated cautiously. If, for example, thinking hard about philosophy makes you unhappy, would you submit to brain surgery which increased your pleasure but made you think less?

Of all the values derived from our basic humanity, the simple value of a human life is the most obvious. Killing someone for no reason is universally condemned, and we would all want to save people from drowning or a fire. There are, however, problem cases. Can a human life completely lose its value to an extent that justifies suicide, or euthanasia, or capital punishment? Are some people more valuable than others, because of their great talents (which is put to the test if there is only one seat left in a lifeboat)?

A good way to discover our highest values is to ask what we consider unthinkable (or even what we would "sooner die" than do). If wicked friends tempt you to misbehave, at what point do you say, "no, we can't do that!"? Even thieves are unlikely to deliberately steal a child's favorite toy, and defrauding a hospital is particularly despicable. The ethics of warfare highlight what is unthinkable on an even more significant scale.

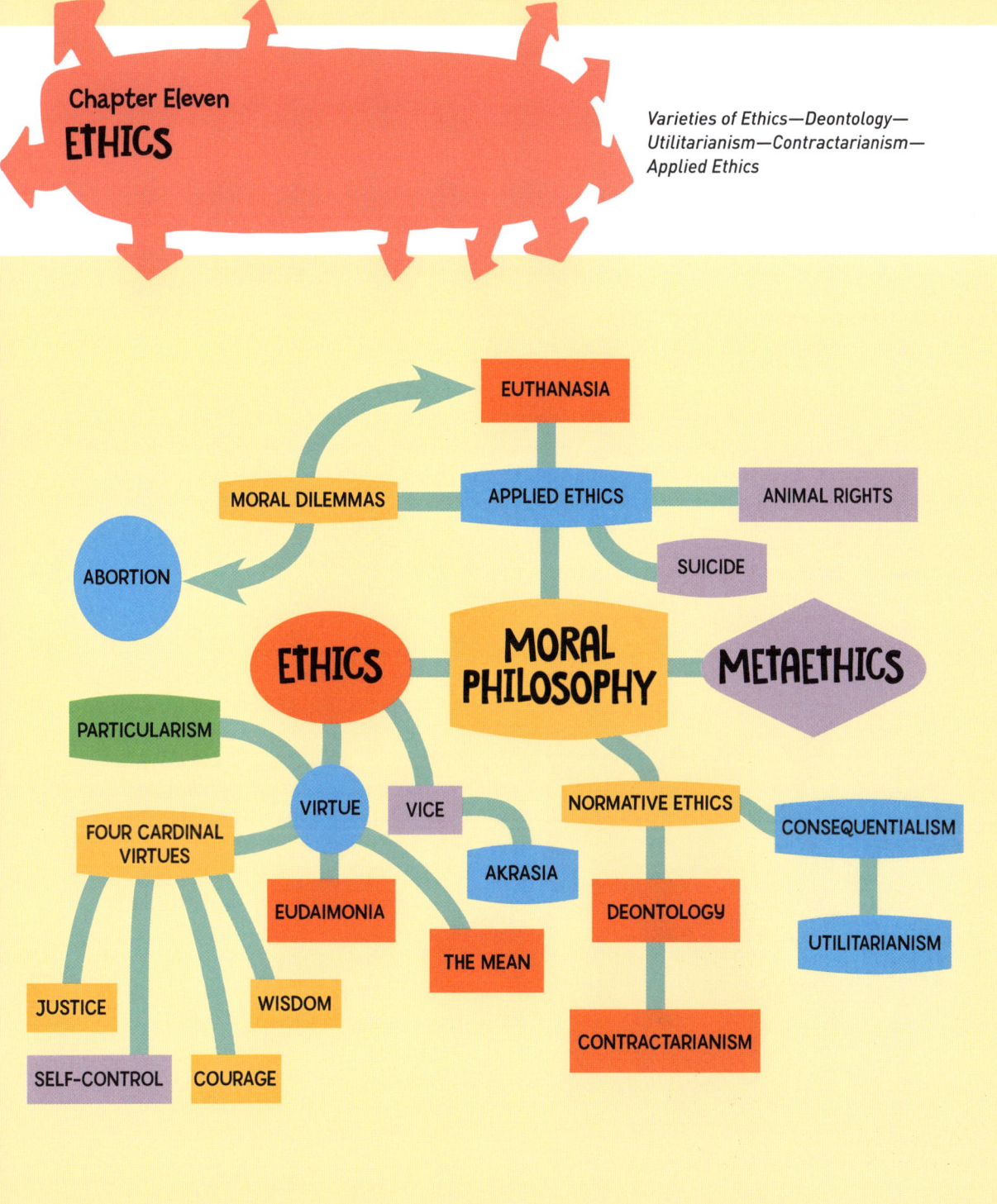

Chapter Eleven
ETHICS

Varieties of Ethics—Deontology—Utilitarianism—Contractarianism—Applied Ethics

CHAPTER 11

VARIETIES OF ETHICS

Moral philosophy involves *Metaethics, Normative Ethics,* and *Applied Ethics*. Metaethics (higher level ethics) concerns the core values and principles of moral thought, and their source and authority. Normative ethics concerns "norms" or standards and rules of moral behavior, and applied ethics looks at moral dilemmas in ordinary life.

METAETHICS	NORMATIVE ETHICS	APPLIED ETHICS
The principles of moral thought	The rules of moral behavior	The moral dilemmas of ordinary life

Greek ethics focused on the nature of a good human being, and the virtues which make a good character. Good actions were understood as the typical behavior of a person with good character. This interest in virtues dominated until the Renaissance, when lawyers saw that in a courtroom right and wrong actions are more important than character, since a good person can be guilty of a particular crime and a bad person can be innocent. Hence the quest was launched for principles of right and wrong action.

Two views came to dominate: that right actions are either those which involve agreed universal duties (*deontology*), or those improving welfare and happiness (*utilitarianism*). The view that morality only concerns mutually beneficial contracts between people also had supporters, though it was often dismissed as cynical. Recent dissatisfaction with these three theories has also led to a revival of virtue theory.

From the Renaissance on, lawyers determined that what mattered was right and wrong actions, rather than character.

Virtue Ethics

A piano is valued if it performs its function well. Virtue theory rests on the idea that a human being is valued for the same reason. If human beings have a function, then a good human succeeds in those functions. Aristotle identified two human functions: reasoning (since that distinguishes us from other animals), and living in society (which we have in common with ants and bees).

This assumption can be challenged, if we are free to decide our function, but virtue theorists favor the idea that there is a universal "human nature," which everyone of our species shares (despite local differences).

On this basis, there are said to be "intellectual" virtues—of good reasoning—and "moral" virtues—of good citizenship. The aim of the moral virtues is *eudaimonia* (see page 150).

Just like a piano, human beings are valued for performing their function well.

The aim of the moral virtues is *eudaimonia*, or flourishing—a fulfilled and successful life.

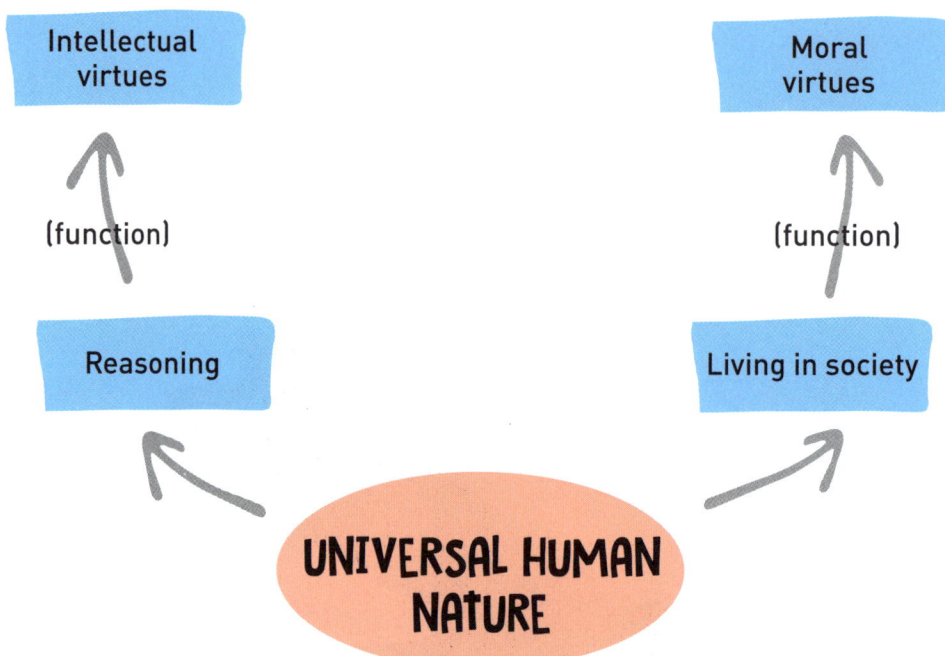

Virtues are motivations for appropriate behavior, such as bravery in battle or self-control when faced with free alcohol. There are five levels of behavior on the path to virtue. Mere "brutishness" is when humans behave like ignorant wild animals. Vice is knowing what is evil but doing it anyway. Weakness of will (*akrasia—lack of control*) is wanting to do what is right but submitting to temptation.

Aiming for the good and having the control to do it is much better, but this is still not virtue, because that requires not only assessing that an action is correct, but also having feelings in tune with reason, so that a virtuous person behaves well and also loves behaving well. Doing your duty may be impeccable behavior, but duty is not virtuous if it is done reluctantly.

Socrates wondered whether virtue can be taught.

The Scale of Virtue

Each virtue occurs on a scale which has extremes, and the virtue is the mean between them. Thus, courage lies between recklessness and cowardice, and self-control lies between incapacity for pleasure and overindulgence. The mean is not an average, but doing what is appropriate to the situation. Thus, it is often right to be angry—*the mean* between being permanently placid and having endless tantrums—but the anger should fit what provokes it.

Socrates on virtue
Socrates saw two big issues about virtue:
- Can it be taught?
- Is there one supreme virtue that produces all the others?

He thought that virtue can be taught—if only we could find a teacher—and that right reason makes us fully virtuous.

Aristotle and Virtue Theory

Aristotle said virtue must be taught in childhood, starting with good habits and learning to have appropriate feelings (such as not laughing at the sufferings of others); as reason develops in the child, this will lead to the pleasure of true virtue. Emphasis on the upbringing of children is a distinctive feature of virtue theory, and good role models are an important part of moral development.

According to Aristotle, it is not virtue which needs wealth, health, and friends. It is the good life, of eudaimonia, *which needs wealth, health, friends, and virtues.*

CHAPTER 11

The unifying virtue, according to Aristotle, is not intellectual power but common sense (*phronesis—practical reason*). People we describe as "thoroughly sensible" will exhibit most of the social virtues. Aristotle thought that the flourishing life must be virtuous, but it also needs the "external goods" of reasonable wealth, good health, and friends. The Stoics disagreed, saying pure virtue is sufficient.

Greek society named four ***cardinal virtues***:
- wisdom
- courage
- self-control
- justice

Since then, other major virtues have been added to the list, such as compassion, respect, honesty, and loyalty. Being very compassionate is now a great virtue, but it was formerly seen as a weakness, and hence a vice. This

highlights an obvious problem with virtue theory, that character traits are rated differently in different societies. We may value people who are witty, but in other societies they can be scorned as disrespectful. This implies relativism about the virtues, if they depend on social approval, and a successful murderer might be admired by other members of a criminal gang. Some relativism is inevitable because times change, and modern courage may be needed for interviews rather than sword fighting, but the social virtues must take a wider view than a criminal gang because such gang members are very bad citizens (and people who start wars may be good citizens of one country, but very bad citizens of the world).

Modern values are a little different, but we still admire the four cardinal virtues of the Greeks.

ETHICS

Values can be dependent on context. A gang member may be admired for murder.

The other main criticism of virtue theory says it is a poor guide to action, and having a good character does not show us what to do. The traditional view sees right actions as the sort of behavior expected of virtuous people. One modern variant of virtue theory is a rejection of moral rules, in favor of *particularism*. In real life, no two situations are ever the same, so simple rules distort our actions. A magistrate who rigidly enforces the letter of the law is much less likely to be just than one who is sensitive to the details of each case.

> **PARTICULARISM** ▶ *There are no moral rules.*

DEONTOLOGY

> **DEONTOLOGY** ▶ *The study of moral duty.*

Deontology is the study of moral duty, of which the best-known advocate is Immanuel Kant. He aims to derive moral principles from pure reason, by focusing on rational consistency. Justice should be impartial, with the cool rationality seen in mathematics. To be morally consistent, we specify a *maxim* for each action, which is the rule being followed. Thus I might return a train ticket to someone who has dropped it, on the maxim, "This could be a disaster, so I should help."

If each action has a maxim, we can compare them and try to make them consistent, by finding the maxim all rational people would agree on (called *universalizing the maxim*). In the train ticket case, the universal maxim is "We should all help people who have had minor disasters." We can all accept that. Kant's *Categorical Imperative* states that you work out what the universal law is for each situation, and then your duty is to follow that law. If an action is wrong, its maxim will conflict with our other universal maxims. A simple slogan for Kant's theory is to ask "what if everybody did that?" Failing to pay for a train journey may look like a minor crime—but what if nobody ever paid?

KANT'S CATEGORICAL IMPERATIVE ▶ *So act that the maxim of your action can be willed as a universal law.*

Other versions of deontology rely on intuition or conscience to reveal your moral duty, but these don't have the appealing precision of Kant's account, and there is no way to resolve a dispute between two people with differing intuitions. Deontology focuses on intentions rather than consequences, but you can't form rational intentions without assessing consequences. Kant himself may have over-emphasized being dutiful when he said you should never, ever lie, because we admire people who lie to protect the innocent. That seems to us to exhibit a good will, but Kant says the duty of a person of good will is not to feel compassion but to follow the universal law, which must never undermine telling the truth. This illustrates the difficulty of achieving perfect rational consistency among your maxims.

The theory is criticized for its unemotional character. It is only motivated by a love of reason, which is not universally appealing, and recommends cold duty more than warmth toward people. It may also be difficult to agree on the maxim of an action (if you are described as a traitor when you thought you were fighting for justice). The biggest problem for the theory is that it presupposes certain values (such as the undesirability of losing a train ticket), and critics say you could universalize all sorts of weird or nasty maxims as long as you were consistent. Stealing seems to be fine, as long as we *all* become thieves!

Defenders of Kant's theory particularly admire its universality. It encourages the idea that very different (and even hostile) cultures might reach moral agreement, by coolly focusing on what is rational and consistent.

Immanuel Kant (1724–1804) said you should never lie.

CHAPTER 11

UTILITARIANISM

Utilitarianism says that all moral actions aim to achieve the best possible *utility*, meaning all the sorts of things that people usually want. The aim is the best possible outcome—and the intentions and character of the agent (though interesting) are irrelevant. Its modern form was developed by empiricists, who wanted a theory that fitted actual experience, which is primarily the desirability of pleasure and the undesirability of pain. So the simplest "hedonistic" utilitarianism says "maximize pleasure and minimize pain." Modern versions are not so explicit, and seek to maximize welfare or preferences.

> **UTILITARIANISM** ▶ *Morality is the achievement of the greatest possible utility (happiness).*

The presuppositions of utilitarianism are fairly democratic, because "everybody counts as one," meaning that the happiness of a head of state is no more important than that of a slave. It also assumes that the costs and benefits of most actions can be assessed fairly accurately, and so if we are all treated as equals and the various outcomes are usually obvious, we can roughly calculate what should be done. Utilitarians are mocked for assigning numerical values to outcomes (for example, they may suggest we go to the restaurant, which is given the value of 78, rather than to the cinema, which assigned the value of 67), but we must make comparisons when deciding what to do. If surgeons are assessing future operations, their assessments of outcomes must be as accurate as possible—so perhaps the utilitarian's numerical approach is not as strange as it first seems.

Jeremy Bentham (1748–1832) was one of the leading proponents of utilitarianism.

Practical Utilitarianism

Utilitarians claim that their system is far more practical than other theories of ethics. For example, a hospital on a tight budget must prioritize its treatments, and assessing the benefits against the costs is the only way a just decision can be reached. A further strength is that animals are included within moral decisions, because they have obvious welfare and can experience pain. Modern animal rights organizations grew out of the utilitarian philosophy.

If we seek to maximize pleasure, then torture is a great evil. But it is possible to imagine a situation where thousands of people might be saved by one successful application of torture. We can also picture a burning building in which you maximize happiness by saving ten people while knowingly allowing your own mother to die. These extreme cases have led to **rule utilitarianism** (rather than the "act utilitarianism" so far described), which maximizes welfare via rules such as "never torture" or "protect your family." These rules are said to be better in the long run, and should never be broken, even when the wrong outcome very occasionally results. Critics say that rule utilitarianism sounds more like deontology (which pursues duties), if it ignores a calculation that offers greater benefits.

The animal rights movement grew out of utilitarian philosophy.

The Dangers of Utilitarianism

Because it is so practical, utilitarianism is plagued with problem cases. You can only judge an action by its consequence—but they seem never-ending. What if a hideous murder produces a wonderful result a hundred years later (by motivating the victim's grandchild to achieve some great public benefit)? If only the consequences matter, then who cares how they are achieved? Instead of performing kind actions for your friends, why not buy a robot which performs them much better? If maximizing welfare is the aim, who cares about fairness? Why not deliberately punish an innocent person, if we are sure it will deter people in future from committing that crime? If all that matters is pleasure, let's invent a cheap and harmless recreational drug and put it in the water supply.

Another line of criticism concerns its commitment to *everybody's* welfare. Not only does this diminish the relative importance of your own mother, but it gives equal importance to billions of people you will never meet. The moral demands are unending. Why are you reading this book when you could be improving the happiness of people in a distant foreign country? The problem is that utilitarianism usually focuses on one moral value, and neglects all the others.

Utilitarian philosophers spend a lot of time fine-tuning their theory to meet these many problems, but it seems worth the effort because anyone who says "never mind the consequences" is a public menace. Utilitarianism remains an important theory.

CONTRACTARIANISM

Even without morality, human life goes better if we co-operate. This is the basis of the *Contractarian* morality, which says that we always perform good deeds out of self-interest, because then other people will then help us in return. You might just pretend to be friendly to achieve this, but people are good at spotting insincerity, so your best chance is to be genuinely kind and loving. Your parents brought you up to be helpful and sincere, because your life will go better that way. Even if a specific kind deed is never returned, your reputation for kindness will bring its reward.

> **CONTRACTARIANISM** ▶ *Good deeds are performed out of self-interest.*

If you agree to exchange helpful deeds with someone, such as taking turns to pay for coffee, the person who acts first is vulnerable because the helpful deed may not be returned. Some preliminary trust is thus required for the theory, though Thomas Hobbes said that making it work needs a political power which enforces broken contracts. The strength of the theory, which is missing from some of the others, is its built-in motivation because we all pursue self-interest, and it describes well the particular immorality we see in broken promises and treachery.

The theory has had a poor reputation in the past. Many people see selfishness as the exact opposite of morality (which is usually *altruistic*, or concern for other people), so to accept self-interest as its foundation seems contradictory. To describe the love of a mother for her child as self-interested seems very cynical, and we mistrust anyone who actually admits to being entirely self-interested. A particular example of this problem is the *free rider*, who only pretends to co-operate with other people while exploiting their good will. The theory implies that it is good to be self-interested, which means that the highest standards of morality are achieved by successful tax evaders and people who avoid their share of a restaurant bill. The theory also favors powerful people, who can offer many favors, and severely disabled people get left out of morality if they can't return the favors done for them.

CHAPTER 11

Thomas Hobbes claimed a political power was needed to enforce contracts.

Modern Developments

Contractarianism has been revived because of two modern developments. These suggest that successful living really does need the generous standards of morality that have always been admired, even if it is based on barely conscious self-interest.

Biology
We now know that many animals are highly co-operative, and exhibit far more altruistic behavior than we had previously realized. Helpful attitudes are built into their DNA, and this is even more true of human beings, who live in complex communities. Hence we cannot help exhibiting behavior that seems to be moral, such as instant sympathy with a stranger who is in pain.

Game Theory
Game Theory studies the rules of co-operation. It confirms that one-off contracts between people are precarious and may need enforcing, but that repeated long-term co-operation is much more successful if the participants exhibit traditional high moral standards, of helpfulness and trust, and even "go the extra mile" for the sake of others.

APPLIED ETHICS

Real moral dilemmas frequently involve life and death issues, where the stakes are high, and Applied Ethics tries to clarify such situations. Moral theories concern individual decisions, and focus on either intentions or consequences. Practical dilemmas involve many people, both intentions and consequences are important, and we must both decide what to do and judge it afterward. Other people's right of self-determination (their "autonomy") also has to be respected in moral disagreements.

THEORY	PRACTICE
Individual Decisions	Involve many people
Intentions *or* Consequences	Intentions *and* Consequences

Several people may share responsibility for an action, or be encouraged, ordered, or forced to do something, and failure to act can sometimes be worse than a bad action. The phenomenon of **double effect** is when a good action has unintended bad side effects. It is easier to judge such things by their obvious consequences than by their hidden intentions. However, the wickedness of bad side effects partly depends on whether they were unpredictable, or could have been predicted, or were actually predicted.

Abortion

Abortion presents the typical dilemmas of applied ethics. Some entity is killed by an abortion, but what was its status? An unborn child changes from a tiny cluster of cells to a "viable" living being in nine months. Do we call it "life," "a life," a "human being," a "child," or a "person?" Or do we lack the necessary vocabulary (other than "zygote" and "foetus")? There is no clear distinction between a fully mature foetus and a new-born child.

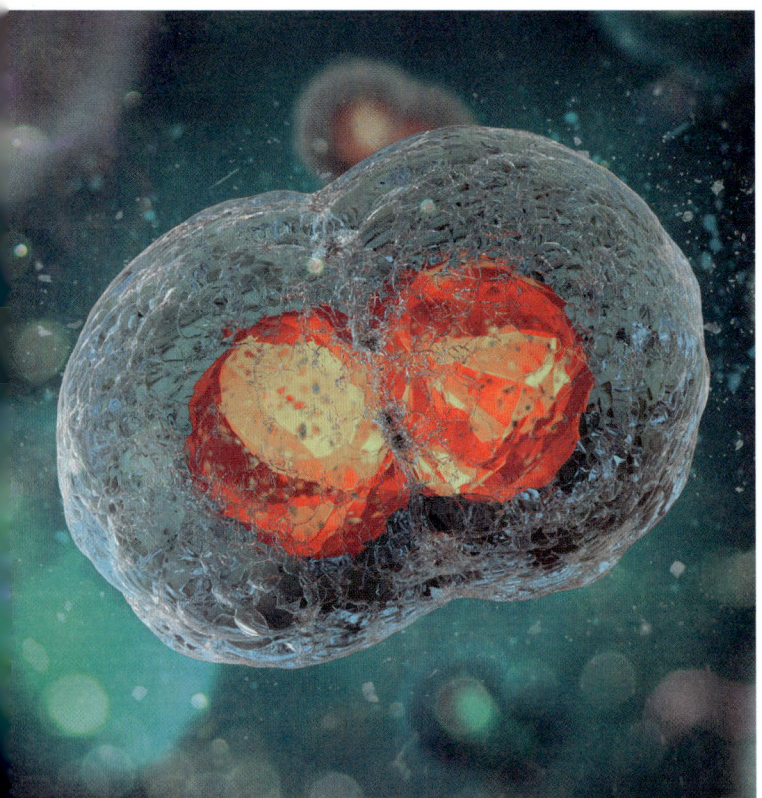

Debate also focuses on the mother. Should we emphasize the intentions or the consequences? Although motives for abortion can vary from trivial inconvenience to the horror of rape, the birth of a child has long-term consequences for a woman's life. We try to balance the rights of the unborn and the mother, but also of the father, and other people involved.

At what point is a child a person? Is it as a zygote, a foetus, or as a newborn baby?

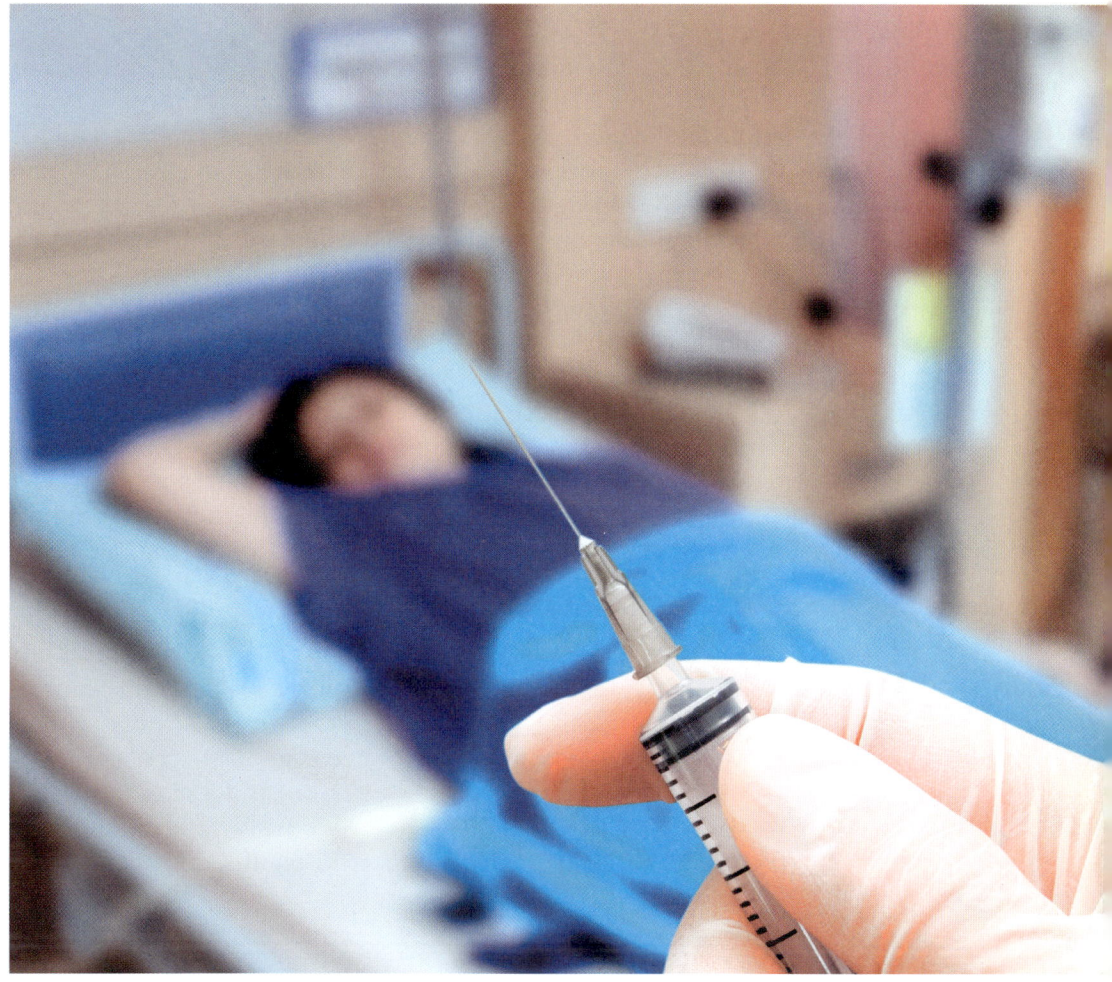
Is euthanasia murder, or simply the withdrawal of treatment?

Euthanasia
Euthanasia (merciful killing) produces similar dilemmas. At one extreme are obvious murders, and at the other are inevitable withdrawals of treatment in hopeless cases. Freedom of choice is crucial, and discussions concern cases which are "voluntary" (allowing patient choice), and "involuntary" (patient overruled) and "non-voluntary" (where the patient cannot express a view). A great concern is pressure on patients (or felt by them) when other people may benefit from their death. The vocabulary used is again important (since a case might equally be "prolonging life" or "prolonging the process of dying").

Animal Rights

In the past, humanity has shown little concern for animals (though mistreating them was a vice of character). They became morally important for utilitarians if they suffer pain, and modern understanding of animals such as jellyfish reveals them to be much more sophisticated than we thought—and thus commanding respect. The strongest champions of animal rights refuse to eat them, try never to kill any living thing, and may value a healthy chimpanzee above a seriously damaged human. At the other extreme, animals are subjected to medical research, act as "slave" labor for us, and are used as entertainment. By comparing animals with the concept of a "person," we can place them on a scale that commands increasing rights. Hygienic human living kills trillions of microbes, to our great benefit. But pets are considered as named family members, and bonobos participate in simple sign-language conversations. There are also great concerns about extinctions (even of lowly species), and most meat-eating humans are concerned about ruthless types of animal exploitation.

Other debates in applied ethics focus on suicide, punishment, sexual morality, children's rights, and attitudes to the very old. Most of them need a clear concept of a person, and a sense of what it is we truly value when faced with painful dilemmas.

Pain has often been inflicted on animals for the purpose of entertainment—but for utilitarians this is a significant moral issue, as both the animals' and the humans' well-being must be considered.

Chapter Twelve
SOCIETY

Legitimacy—Power—Freedom—Equality—Justice

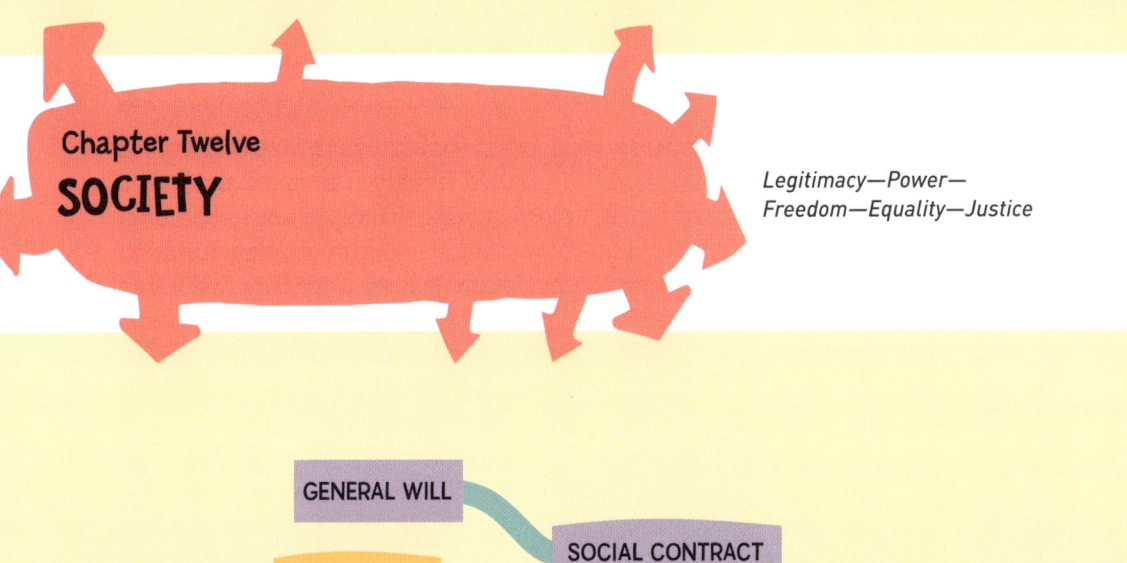

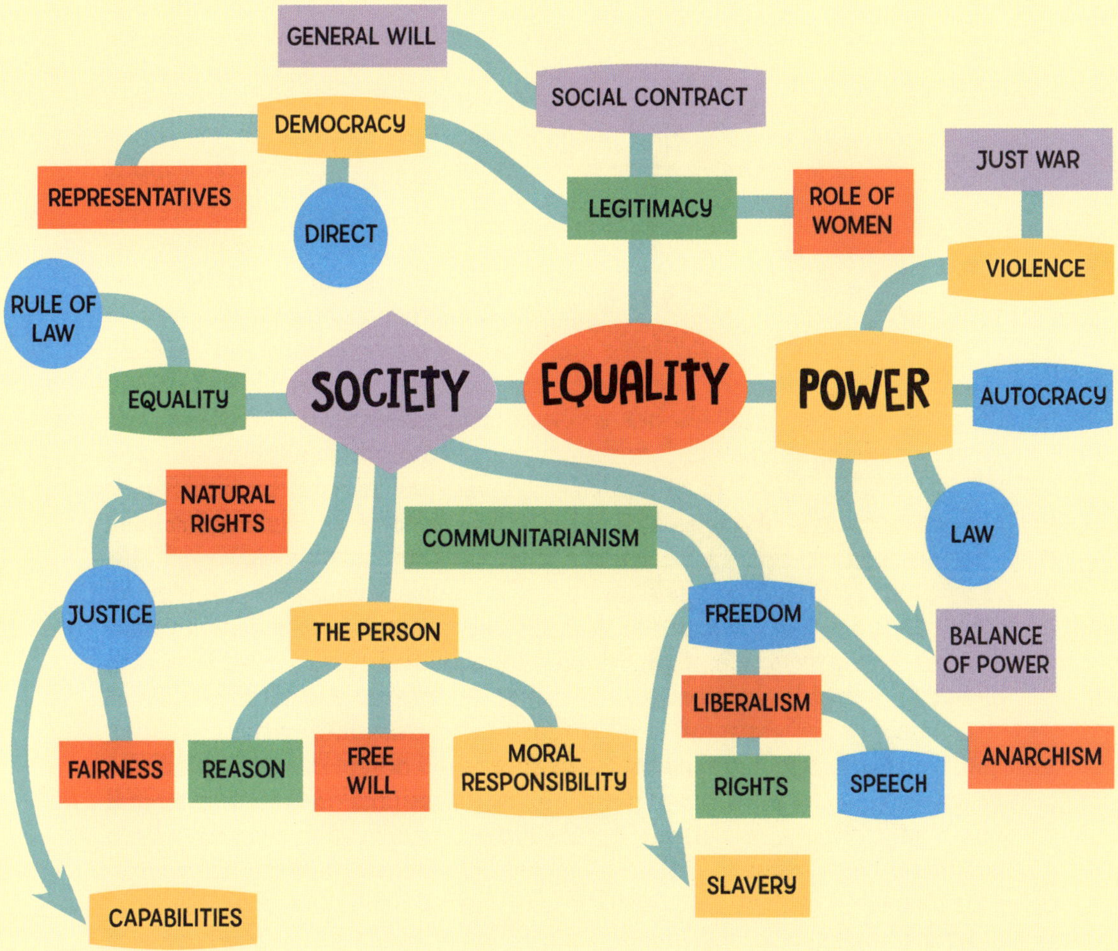

CHAPTER 12

LEGITIMACY

Humans are a sociable species who started out in tribal groups bound together by their teamwork. More stable societies formed when "a people" settled in one place, united around a territory, a language, and rituals. Societies became "states" when they developed borders, institutions, and the centralization of law and warfare. Political philosophy studies the best principles for organizing such a state.

The ideal starting point would be an agreement about the purpose of a state. If we decided that efficiency was the main aim, we might think that extensive slavery would be good, or even that robots would be better than people as citizens. If military conquest was the purpose of the state, then communal life would focus wholly on fighting (as happened in ancient Sparta). Such views are no longer popular, and the normal assumption is that a state aims to make its citizens happy. This theoretically could be achieved by a benevolent form of slavery, but most people see freedom as essential for the good life. They may also want some control over the state itself, as well as over their personal lives.

John Locke introduced the idea of tacit assent.

The Legitimacy of Government

> **SOCIAL CONTRACT** ▶ *The agreement to be governed between the people and their rulers.*

Modern political philosophy begins with the question of the legitimacy of a government. What entitles some people to rule over others? Thomas Hobbes proposed the idea of a *social contract*, which says people can only be legitimately governed if they agree to it. Since actual social contracts are almost unknown, Locke introduced the idea of *tacit assent*—that if you use a country's roads, for example, you accept the authority of the government that built them. Rousseau added the ideal picture of an assembly in which the people reach a consensus (expressing the *general will*) and appoint a government.

> **GENERAL WILL** ▶ *The consensus of the people.*

John Rawls brought objectivity to this approach, by proposing an imagined *initial position* from which a large group of people choose their preferred society. They start behind a *veil of ignorance*—meaning they will belong to the new society, but do not know what social position they will occupy. If people in this impartial position reach a consensus about the structure of their society, then this consensus is the basis for legitimate government—and for the main direction of its policies, which Rawls thought would include some welfare for the most disadvantaged citizens.

Jean-Jacques Rousseau added the idea of the general will to the social contract model.

Democracies

Democratic legitimacy arises from the direct choices of the citizens. However, democracy is not the decision of the whole people, because the majority get their way, and the minority become spectators. Rousseau wanted the General Will to be unanimous, rather than a majority choice. So is a government legitimate if a large minority do not accept its right to rule? The government undermines its own authority if it persecutes minorities, so what principles can bind a minority into the unified state? The inclusive attitude might involve increased toleration of life in sub-cultures, or respect for the political system itself, ensuring acceptance of democratic votes and good representation for minorities.

Small democracies can make direct decisions after discussion in an assembly. In modern large democracies, decisions are made by *representatives*, rather than the direct will of the people.

In a democracy, decisions can be made after discussion in an assembly.

Two Types of Elected Representatives
Delegate ▶ *Instructed to present the people's views.*
Trustee ▶ *An admired person expected to think for themselves.*

If the representative is a member of a political party, this may increase their legitimacy, because the people endorse a party manifesto, which is essentially a promise to act in certain ways, but at the risk of divided loyalty, with the representative torn between party and constituents. However, both delegates and trustees may fail to represent minorities, because they either speak only for the majority or are a typical member of the majority. So a good electoral system must find representatives who "mirror" the whole population, and are accountable to the people between elections.

The Representation of Women

An obvious modern concern is to ensure that women are fully represented. Virtually all civilizations have been wholly dominated by men until recent times. This imbalance can be rectified by equal rights to vote, and equal opportunities in education and the workplace, but feminist political philosophers argue that the problem runs deeper. Even when equal representation is achieved, the institutions of government and assumptions of the culture (including family life) remain masculine creations, so the language, rituals, and procedures of society need a profound rethink. The very idea of "gender" seems to be created as much by social conventions as by biology.

Though women did achieve equal representation in the early 20th century, culture and the institutions of government are still masculine creations.

Individuals and Legitimacy

This idea that people choose how they are governed relies on the idea of a "person" as a separate self, with powers of reason and free will, and capable of taking moral responsibility. Deriving legitimacy from this individualistic starting point implies a *liberal* society. The essential presumption is that citizens are free, as long as they do not harm other citizens. Liberal philosophers then focus on the extent to which individuals should maintain their presumed separation, or should choose to combine their efforts for community projects.

> **Critics of Liberalism**
>
> Left-wing critics ▶ *The freedom to make contracts means that citizens in a weak position (such as manual workers) can too easily be exploited.*
>
> The communitarian critics ▶ *Liberal freedom makes it too easy to opt out of society, when people are essentially social rather than solitary and can only flourish within a community.*

POWER

Given that a government is reasonably legitimate, the next question is how much power it should have over its citizens. These powers might be broad in scope (covering most aspects of life) but with weak penalties to enforce them, or they could be limited in scope but very strong. Should a government be able to decide its own powers, or should this be firmly restricted? Governments must have power, but maybe citizens should also have their own powers over government. And should government power be concentrated in a few hands, or spread more widely? One familiar modern idea is the *separation of powers*, where the government has no power over the legal system, which can therefore enforce the constitution in a more neutral way. According to this idea, the three branches of government (the executive, the judiciary, and the legislature) must remain entirely independent. Today, while most states subscribe to this ideal in theory, it is rarely followed absolutely. For example, in the United States, the justices of the Supreme Court (the judiciary) are nominated by the President (the executive), and approved by the Senate (the legislature).

In traditional autocracies, land-owning aristocrats were bound to the ruler's power by patronage.

	AUTOCRACY	**TECHNOCRACY**	**DEMOCRACY**
Type	Government by one	Government by experts	Government by many
Advantages	Swift decisions	Welfare—protecting those who need help	Restrains excessive powers
Disadvantages	Bad life for the people	Taxes	Slow decisions

Ancient philosophers thought a benign *autocracy* (rule by one person) was the ideal system, but the dangers of corruption are obvious. Traditional autocrats were surrounded by a land-owning aristocracy, which spread the power, and the state was bound together by the protection and patronage of the ruler. Powerful autocracy at least produces swift decisions (often delegated to a chief adviser) and may produce memorable achievements, but rarely results in a good life for the people. If there is no autocrat, the state may still be run by an elite group, with an authority that is military, aristocratic, or economic authority.

Plato dreamed of a state run by leading philosophers, distinguished by their wisdom, and the modern equivalent is a *technocracy*, in which a group of experts have the greatest influence. The main debate in liberal philosophy concerns the justification of "welfare," since this values individuals who need help, but at the expense of those who can afford to pay for the help. The modern power of governments to tax the rich at a higher rate is now generally accepted, but the three great political ideas of *freedom*, *equality,* and *justice* are in tension.

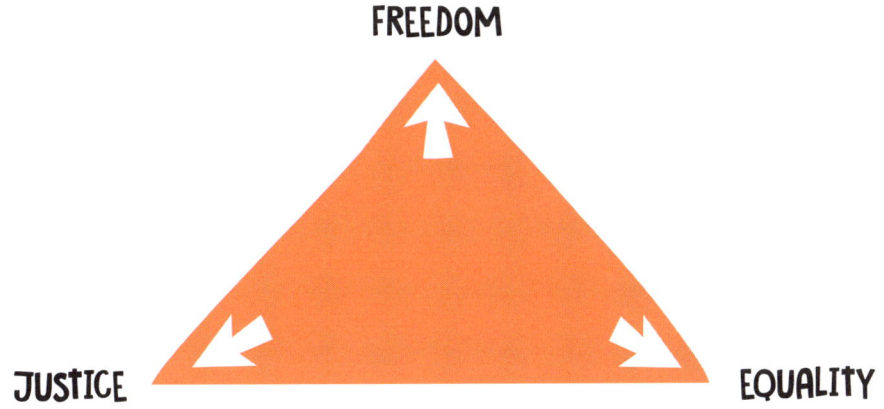

CHAPTER 12

Do the rich have the freedom to retain what they have earned? Do the poor have equal rights to expensive health treatments? Is there a basic injustice if many people are excluded from the benefits of a society?

In theory, a victory in a democratic election gives a government full powers, but one aim of **democracy** is to restrain excessive powers, so where is the balance? The key power which all democrats want is to get rid of bad leaders. If democracy is a mere technique for choosing leaders, that gives the leaders a fairly free hand, but the broader concept of democracy includes public discussion and involvement in decision-making, and can be extended into the workplace and even into family life. Government in democracies is a frustrating activity, because decisions are slow and can be blocked by objectors, and long-term policies are disrupted by repeated elections. So should we just follow democratic procedures, or should good citizens have democratic virtues, seeking to be involved, and to include the people around them in civic processes?

The Use of Force

Governments have the right to enforce the law, by violence if necessary. But is the power to punish justified as retribution, as deterrent, as prevention, as reparation, or as reform? That is, are **punishments** inflicted because they are deserved, or to scare other people, or to put a stop to the crimes, or to put things right, or to change the character of the culprit? But what punishment does a blackmailer deserve? Won't punishing an innocent person scare people? Punishment comes too late if we just want to stop crime. We can restore lost property, but not a lost life. And changing character is rather hopeless for older culprits. We could try to eliminate crime by ruthless social control, but this would conflict with the basic liberal ideals of freedom and autonomy.

A government can try to eliminate crime through ruthless social control, but it comes at the cost of freedom.

The greatest power of a government is to declare war on another state, but when should this happen? The theory of a *just war* has been developed, which says war is permissible if it resists aggression, has a genuine reason, is proportionate, is a last resort, is not futile, and has the full authority of the state. Modern wars have become so horrific that even these cautious principles are thrown into doubt, since the destruction in a large war probably exceeds anything which is appropriate and justified. Standard principles have also been developed about the conduct of any war, saying force must not be excessive, targets must be legitimate, prohibited weapons must not be used, prisoners must be protected, and reprisals are wrong. But how is the justice of the war to be balanced against justice to those involved? How do we balance the value of each life lost against the value of an uncertain future after the war?

Just War
- Has a genuine reason
- Resists aggression
- Proportionate
- Last resort
- Has a chance of success
- Has the authority of the state

Modern wars have thrown the principles of the "just war" into doubt.

CHAPTER 12

FREEDOM

In modern democracies and liberal societies, freedom is one of the most cherished values. We all now despise slavery, which is total denial of freedom, but what is actually wrong about it? It can't merely be the suffering involved, because slavery still seems wrong if the slaves are happy. One possibility is that all human beings have "self-ownership," so the claim to "own" a slave is simply the crime of theft (or purchasing stolen goods). It seems reasonable that you own yourself (if anyone does), but this would mean that selling your own kidney when you need money would have to be legal, and that women can rent out their wombs for surrogate babies. If we are wary about these consequences, a better concept is *autonomy*—the basic capacity of each person to be responsible for themselves.

AUTONOMY ▶
The capacity of each person to be responsible for themselves.

If people should be in charge of their own lives, then enslaving someone does not just deprive them of a right, but partly destroys an essential feature of their existence. This implies that the autonomy of each individual must be protected (even in a society where slavery is illegal), and is a basis for asserting the full equality of women.

Slavery is now universally despised—even if the slaves are happy.

Anarchism

> **ANARCHISM** ▶ *The state has no right to exist and no legitimate power.*

Anarchism claims that a state has no legitimate power, because it has no right even to exist. This gives freedom and autonomy the highest possible value, because just as destroying autonomy by enslavement is wrong, so giving up your freedom in a social contract is also impermissible. Given a person's normal right to become a monk or nun, this claim is unpersuasive, but each loss of a freedom needs to be justified in a modern society. Anarchism can still be defended if humans flourish much better with a high degree of autonomy, implying that the making of a social contract is permissible but a mistake. Critics say that anarchism can work well when there is peace and plenty, but central organization is needed when a crisis occurs.

Anarchism rejects the idea of the social contract and a central authority entirely.

CHAPTER 12

Conflicting Freedoms

We all want freedom for ourselves, but are nervous about freedom for other people:

- It is nice to choose where you will live, but most states restrict immigration.
- Free speech is good, but freedom to insult people creates misery.
- Freedom to own fierce dogs or dangerous weapons is very threatening, even if no actual harm is done.
- A capitalist economy needs a free market, but ruthlessly destroying a rival small business seems wrong.

So some freedoms clash with others, and our love of freedom can conflict with our other values. If you grant the majority a lot of freedom, they may use it to unjustly persecute a minority. Complete freedom in the market may well result in huge inequalities in wealth. If we grant people various rights, these often imply duties from fellow citizens—such as walking around a large property to avoid trespassing. The challenge is to find the right balance and priorities among these competing values.

Freedom of speech is of great importance in a democracy, though freedom to spread lies is an obvious danger. *Freedom of belief* is even more basic, and a liberal society is impossible without it. We may see freedom of belief as absolute, but some problem cases must be considered. Intense loyalty to a religion may override a citizen's loyalty to the state, and a minority religious group may have more sympathy with a wartime enemy than with their home country. Other beliefs may be supportive of major violence, even if the violence is not enacted. Such beliefs cannot be eradicated, but how far should a state go with persuasion and propaganda to confront such problems?

Most states can tolerate a large variety of *sub-cultures*, but there may be traditional activities (such as drug-taking) which are illegal in the host state. Such a situation is a problem for both democracy and the ideal of freedom—which may give different answers. Democrats can justify suppressing such things in the name of the majority, but the violation of the minority's freedom may need a different justification.

One possibility is the *Utilitarian approach*, which says right actions are those which result in maximum benefits. This approach has been very influential in political decision-making (such as spending on health services). So we might justify suppressing the freedom of a minority if the total overall happiness of the state is increased. However, the notorious problem with this Utilitarian view is that it has no qualms about being massively unfair as long as the consequences turn out for the best. Hence a small minority can easily be suppressed for the greater happiness of all, but a larger minority may feel too much distress if its freedom is curtailed.

EQUALITY

In the sense of being identical, people are clearly not "equal." The idea that people should be viewed as equal in some respects is not, however, a new one. In a hierarchical society, persons of the same rank (such as two sergeants in an army) expect to be treated as equals, and slaves of similar status would hope to be treated equally. The modern idea is that in some respects *all* the citizens of a state, and even all human beings, should be considered as equals. But in what respects? And is it just a matter of having equal rights, or should people *actually* be equal in some ways?

The social contract and Rawls's "initial position" both assume that the people making the choices have an equal voice. The society they choose is likely to be unequal, but justice seems to need an initial state of equality. The assumption is that people are politically equal unless a reason can be given for their inequality.

> In democracies, it has been suggested that superior voters should have more than one vote, but in practice all qualified citizens get one equal vote.

> The Utilitarian approach to government, despite its tolerance of unfair distributions, starts from the assumption that each citizen's happiness is equally valuable.

Equality is most obvious in the "rule of law." In traditional societies it was common for aristocrats to get away with a crime, but in stricter systems everyone is equal before the law, and even heads of state can end up in jail. True equality before the law concerns not only the status of the accused in court, but also who gets charged in the first place, and who gets the best defense lawyers.

Two officers of the same rank in the army expect to be treated as equals.

CHAPTER 12

In ordinary life, we accept many inequalities without argument. The coach of a sports team can overrule the other players, and the founder of a business is assumed to be its manager. It is also normal to accept considerable inequality in wealth, and people with great talent or energy are assumed to deserve their larger rewards. But what are the acceptable limits of such inequality? In a capitalist society, "wealth breeds wealth," so a person who has deserved a large reward can use the money to increase their advantage, creating very large inequalities.

The desire that people should be equal is driven by our sense of fairness and justice. But there is nothing good about making all the people equally poor, and we approve of large rewards if they are an incentive to valuable achievements—so mere equality is not an important ideal. People want shares to be fair in benefits such as wealth, education, and health care—and, as Rawls pointed out, we are particularly concerned for the least advantaged members of the community, who may suffer real hardship because of their inequality.

Inequality is often accepted in ordinary life, for example when a coach overrules his players.

JUSTICE

We would all prefer a society where justice can be taken for granted, so one aim of political philosophy is to design a perfectly just *constitution*. The first assumption is equality, since favoring one group for no reason is obviously unjust. Some inequalities are then acceptable, but how are they justified?

Rawls's idea of justice	Utilitarian idea of justice	Robert Nozick's concept of justice	Martha Nussbaum's view of justice
Fairness, which concerns what people deserve, their opportunities, and needs.	Produces the maximum benefits.	What you are entitled to.	People fulfilling their individual capabilities.

However we assess justice, it is implemented in a society by giving people *rights*. This starts from the idea of "natural" rights (to food, water, shelter, and self-defense), but mainly concerns legal rights. The simplest enforceable right is the keeping of contracts, which is your right to receive what has been legally agreed with you.

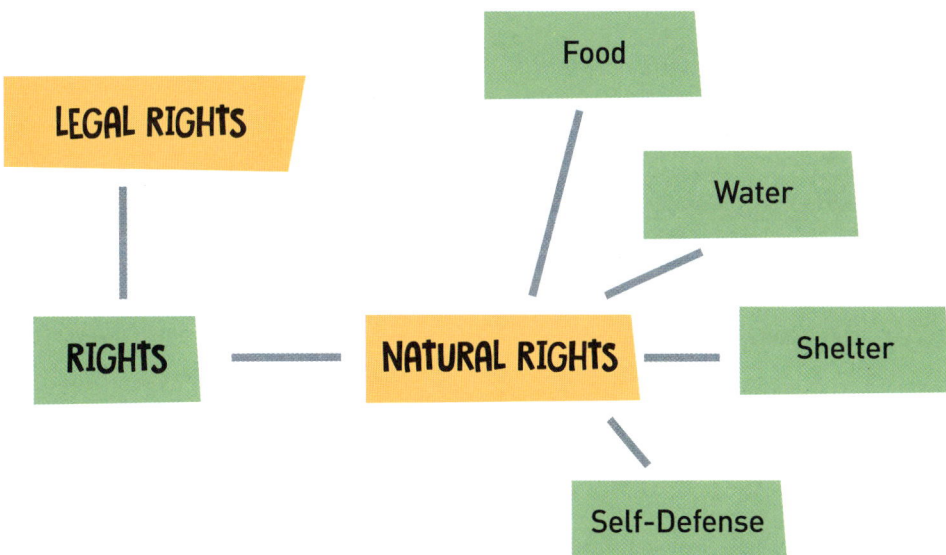

CHAPTER 12

For Nozick, this is virtually all that is required for justice. The preliminary assumptions are individual freedom and autonomy, and the initial just ownership of property. All that is then needed is the keeping of just contracts. If you become wealthy and others become poor in this way, there is no just way to intervene, and whether or not to be charitable is the choice of the individual.

Nozick gives a famous example of a champion basketball player, who gets very rich by charging extra admission just to see him play. It seems unfair that he earns vastly more than the rest of the team, but what is wrong, if everyone agreed to it? This is the **libertarian** view of justice, where individual freedom is the highest value, and any resulting unfairness is irrelevant.

Most criticisms of Nozick concern the dubious justice of "original ownership," given the historical facts about how property has actually been acquired. Not only may land have been stolen long ago, but it may have been a gift from a tyrannical ruler, or it may have been legally purchased with money that was illegally or immorally acquired. Subsequent just transactions cannot erase such facts.

Rawls agrees that we start as free and equal individuals living autonomous lives, and any subsequent inequalities must be justified. His test is what is acceptable to the people, when they see society from an objective and impersonal viewpoint. Justice will then focus on the position of the most disadvantaged, who therefore need *basic goods*—the normal crucial supports for life—plus equal opportunities to make their way in society. This needs redistribution by a taxation system, rather than personal charity, but we should all see the justice of this if we take a broader view of the whole society.

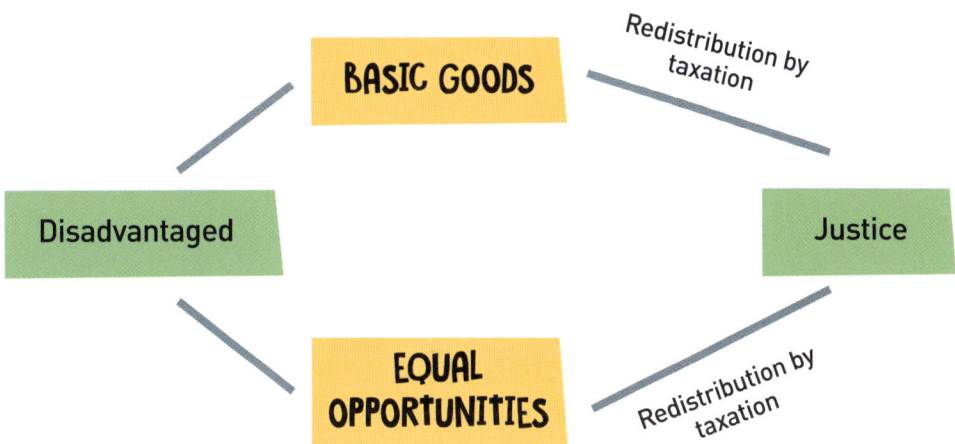

Amartya Sen sand Martha Nussbaum say justice is less a matter of rights, opportunities, and contracts, and more a matter of whether people are actually able to live decent lives (defined as reasonably fulfilling their capabilities). They are less concerned with the just institution that Rawls tries to design, because injustices like slavery, domestic abuse, and lack of food are just obvious to everyone.

Theoretical opportunities are no help if practical circumstances thwart people's hopes, and it is a poor justice that leaves some people with nothing more than "basic goods." They particularly focus on disability, since disabled people are often unable to express their capabilities without help. This is the most practical view of justice, since it requires not only the creation of opportunities (such as ramps for wheelchairs) but also the addressing of prejudices that limit fulfilling activities (such as the denial of education for girls).

CHAPTER 12

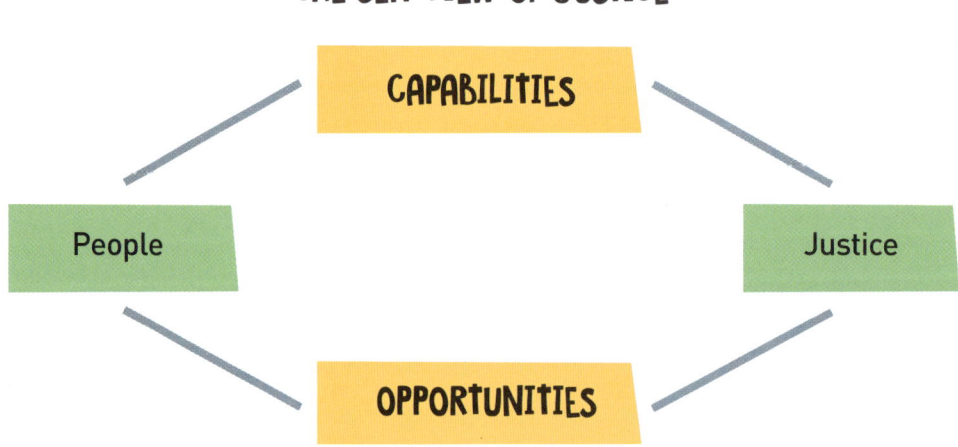

Amartya Sen views justice as a matter of allowing people to live good lives.

THE SEN VIEW OF JUSTICE

- CAPABILITIES
- People
- Justice
- OPPORTUNITIES

Chapter Thirteen
NATURE

Causation—Laws of Nature—Physicalism—Time—Life

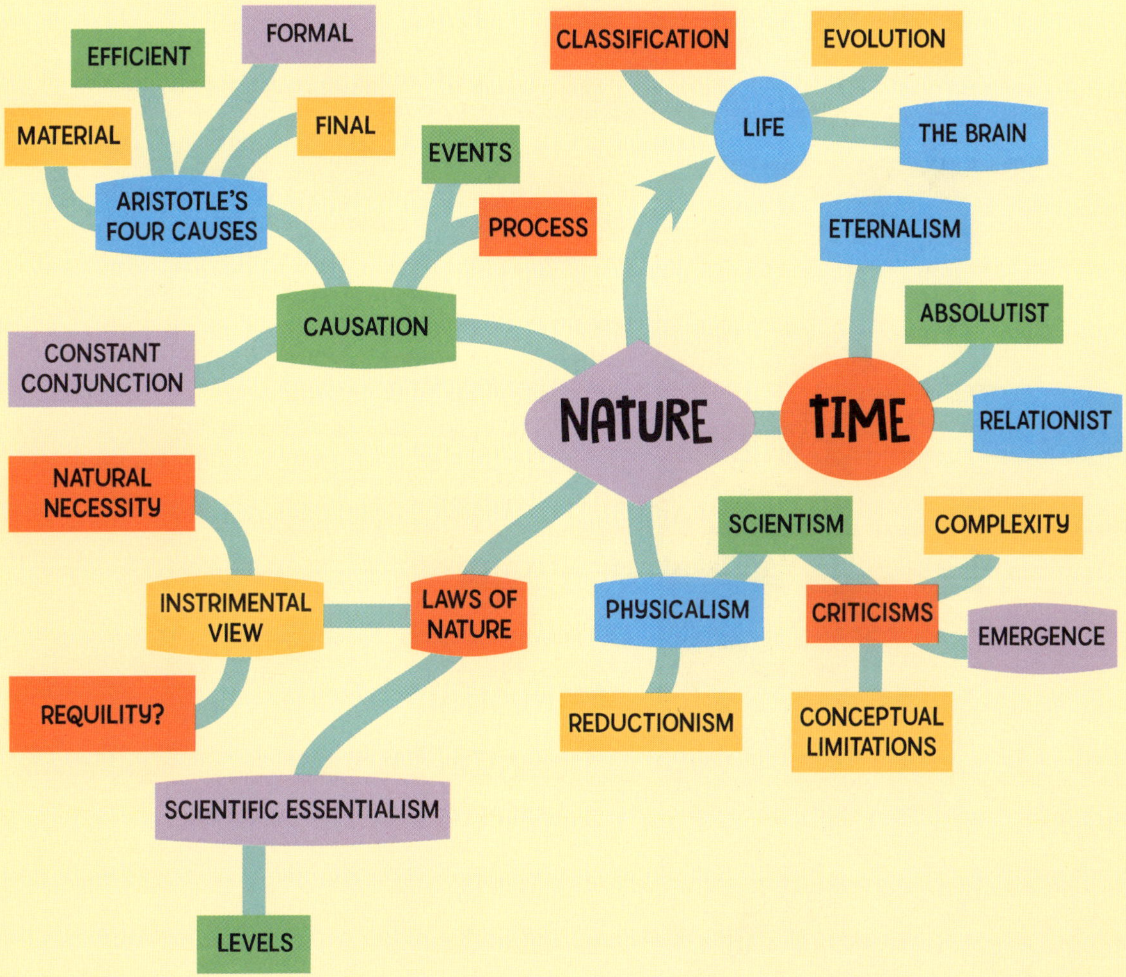

CHAPTER 13

CAUSATION

Philosophy is about the real world. Some philosophers lose touch with that fact, but many great philosophers have also been great scientists and mathematicians, and most modern philosophers pay careful attention to the findings of science. The secure findings of science form the bedrock of any good philosophy.

Philosophers, however, have different interests from scientists, and focus on facts and concepts that the scientists themselves may take for granted. A good example is the concept of *causation*. In ordinary life we talk of "one thing leading to another" (when a raindrop moves a leaf), and we explain events by what preceded them and made them unavoidable. Hence we generalize, and talk of "the causes" of actions and events.

But when empiricists (notably David Hume) looked at causation from a more scientific viewpoint, they had doubts. When the drop moves the leaf,

we see the first followed by the second, but no extra ingredient called the cause can be observed at the moment of impact. All we see is the regularity of one happening following another (what Hume called a *constant conjunction*). Since it always happens, we assume it must happen, and we imagine an entity called a "cause" that makes it happen—but science depends on observations, and the cause is never actually observed. Modern science produces precise equations that describe the regular patterns of the "conjunctions," but the word "cause" rarely appears in physics books, and it has been suggested that science could drop the whole idea.

CONSTANT CONJUNCTION ▶ *One happening following another.*

When the raindrop moves a leaf, it is not possible to see "the cause" at the moment of impact.

NATURE

If the tomato falls in half when it is cut, you are the efficient *cause (see page 190).*

CHAPTER 13

A few philosophers have tried to describe nature in this non-causal way, by giving general description of the patterns of our experiences, but for most philosophers the idea of causation won't go away.

Most modern discussion focuses on the "efficient" cause, where one thing makes another thing happen. But what exactly are the things that can be causes and effects? The standard view calls them "events" (rather than "facts" or "states of affairs"), but that is a fairly vague word, given that we talk of a whole ice age as an "event." An ice age can cause an extinction, but it is more precise to talk about the causal effects of a temperature on an animal. If a cause needs to be even more precise, then we must focus on the interactions of specific properties, rather than events. Talk of causes and effects implies one thing and then another, but a ball denting a pillow or sugar dissolving in tea are simultaneous, and it may be better to talk about causal "processes" rather than more static components.

LAWS OF NATURE

The idea that there are "laws" of nature arose at the time of the birth of modern science. It is particularly connected to the application of mathematics to nature, because equations such as Newton's inverse square law (giving the strength of attraction between two objects a given distance apart) seemed to be very simple, unchangingly true, and "obeyed" by all physical objects. Modern physics is dominated by such mathematical methods, and the great equations of the subject are known as its "laws." It is sometimes thought that science is entirely concerned with discovering laws, but this neglects great discoveries such as the existence of galaxies or the electrochemical mechanisms operating in brain neurons.

Isaac Newton's discoveries confirmed the idea that nature has mathematical laws.

Hume's view of causation led to a related view that laws are no more than regular patterns in natural activity. Just as we observe no causation making a stone fall when we drop it, so we see nothing more in frequent droppings of various objects than *regularities*, which seem to fit Newton's equation.

> **INSTRUMENTAL VIEW** ▶ *The laws are mathematical descriptions of scientific measurements.*

This implies an *instrumental* view of the laws—that laws are no more than mathematical descriptions of measurements made by scientific instruments. Such laws are strong on prediction, but weak on explanation. Quantum theory, for example, is mathematically secure, and exceptionally successful at prediction, but physicists often admit to not really understanding what is actually happening.

We sense a *natural necessity* in law-like behavior, but the regularity view only says that some behavior never changes, without showing us that it couldn't possibly change. This leads to a common Humean view that the laws could change, so that we can speculate about universes that have identical contents to ours, but with the activities of the contents controlled by quite different laws.

> **REGULARITY** ▶ *Laws are descriptions of regularities.*
> **NATURAL NECESSITY** ▶ *Laws are a description of a controlling authority in nature.*

Laws seem to be either descriptions of regularities, or some controlling authority in nature. The first view seems safe but superficial, and the second gives a puzzling view of laws. It seems that they must be *super*-natural, if they stand outside the natural world and tell it what to do. This implies that if the universe vanished, the laws would still exist, waiting for another universe to come along, but nothing in science supports such a view.

CHAPTER 13

> **SCIENTIFIC ESSENTIALISM** ▶ *Laws arise from the contents of the universe.*

A more recent view (*scientific essentialism*) sees the laws as arising from the contents of our universe, rather than being imposed on it. The behavior of things results from the active "dispositions" or *powers* of matter, rather than from abstract laws. This suggests where laws come from, confines them within the nature that is familiar to us, and also suggests that they are necessarily true, because they are part of what nature is, rather than an added ingredient. The laws could be different only if the contents of the universe were different. The idea that our universe could have different laws is rejected, because we can't assume that gravity could be weaker or light slower simply because we can imagine things that way.

Followers of Hume say this goes beyond what can actually be observed, and that not everything can be a collection of "powers," because something more *fundamental* must have the powers. The prospects of finding what is actually fundamental are not promising.

- How could we know whether our deepest level of explanation is fundamental?
- How can we know whether something at a deeper level may be forever hidden?

Our enquiries involve the idea of *levels* because the building blocks formed at one level create structures at the next level. Thus, the main particles of the standard model of physics (electrons and quarks) compose the 92 naturally occurring types of atom. This takes us from the physics level to the periodic table of the chemistry level, where the atoms can compose molecules. That takes us to the biological level, where molecules compose life forms—and so on. Explanations can at least work at each level, even if things get murky down at the bottom.

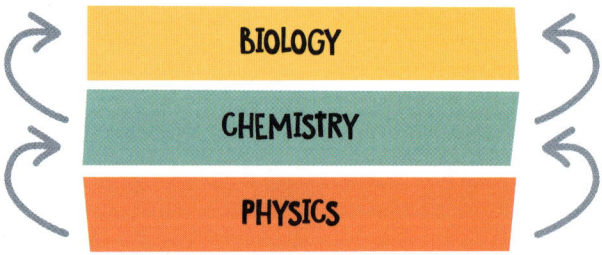

PHYSICALISM

> **REDUCTIONISM** ▶ *Each level contains the potential for the higher level.*

We might explain physics, then chemistry, then biology, and then psychology, then economics, and so on, exploring each level, but without a picture of the whole. But a unified picture appears if all the levels are connected, and each higher level can be deduced from or explained by the level beneath it. This is the reductionist view of nature, that the entire potential for each higher level is contained in, and explained by, the level beneath it. *Reductionism* is supported by the modern claim that the causal explanations of the physical sciences are closed, meaning that no other types of successful explanation seem possible.

> **SCIENTISM** ▶ *Every possible good explanation will eventually be a scientific one.*

If our lowest known level is entirely physical, and each level explains the one above it, then this not only implies *Physicalism* (the view that only physical things exist), but also *Scientism* (the view that every possible good explanation will eventually be a scientific explanation, and most of our current explanations will drop by the wayside). The idea that the low levels of physics might explain the upper levels of human culture sounds initially attractive (to Physicalists), but the idea that economics might be explained entirely in terms of low-level physics is absurd. It might be imaginable for some god-like intellect, but human minds would struggle to grasp such a picture. This is frustrating, if our theory is that economics consists entirely of fundamental physics in action.

CHAPTER 13

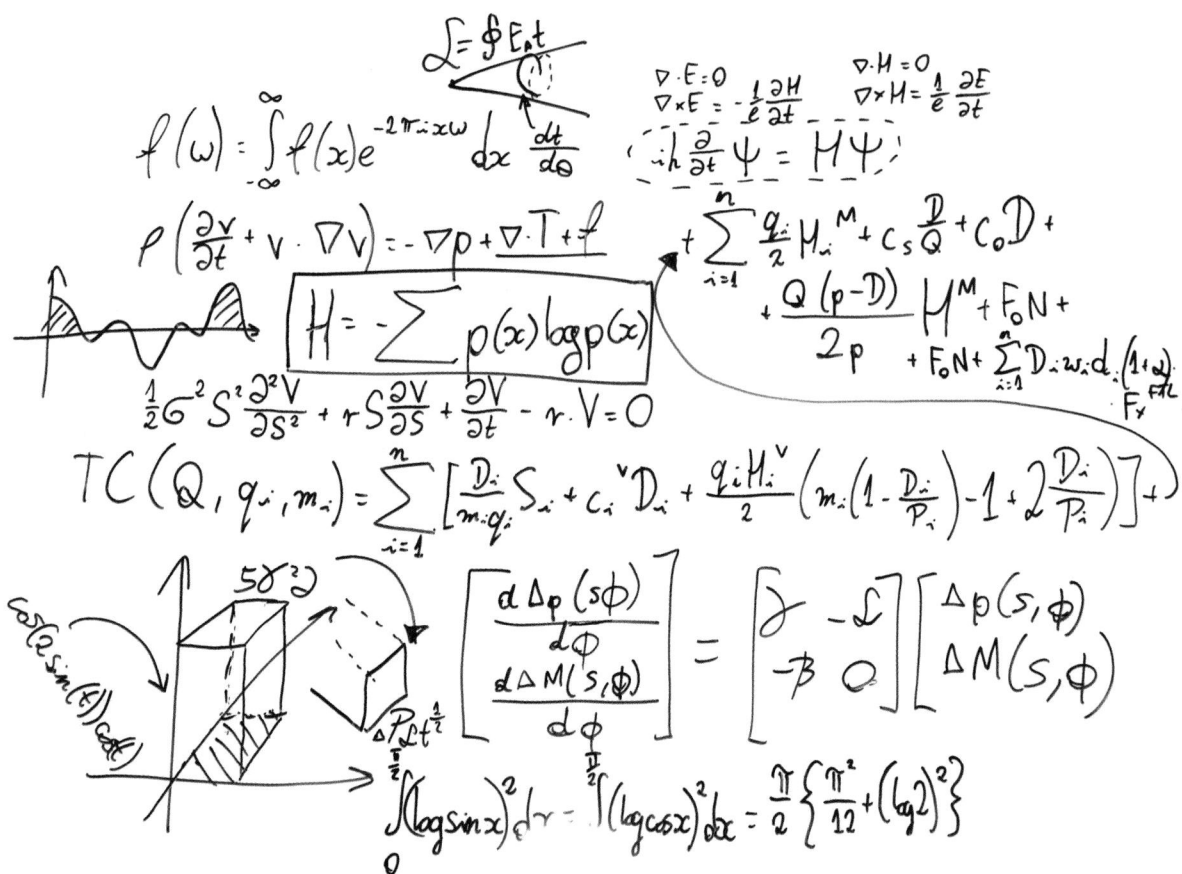

Regular patterns in nature can be presented as mathematical equations, but there are limits to what they can explain.

Science aims to discover the patterns of natural existence, from the smallest to the largest. The most regular patterns can be presented as mathematical equations, and we can also identify recurrent mechanisms and structures. Despite this, there are three primary reasons physics can't explain economics:

COMPLEXITY

There are limits, because of the sheer complexity involved. Even with the most powerful computers we are never going to forecast the weather on a given day ten years hence, or predict the exact shape of the next wave that hits the beach. So economics may be like that—rising through the causal links between levels, but becoming so complex in the process that it moves beyond our grasp.

CONCEPTUAL LIMITATIONS

A second difficulty is the limitations of even our best imaginable conceptual scheme. Economists have created a system of concepts ("credit," "debt," "inflation," "profit," and so on) to explain their subject, each picking out something in the pattern of human economic activity. Accountants try to pin down the financial facts, mathematics is employed where possible, and the relations between the concepts are explained in textbooks. But this can never achieve the precision of physics, because the concepts used embrace groups of diverse facts (just as the word "cloud" embraces an endless number of shapes).

EMERGENCE

A third problem that seems to block explanatory reduction between levels is the possibility of emergence. A property can "emerge" when a group of ingredients are put together, as when enough grass is assembled to become a lawn. That is just a new descriptive term, but a new feature could also emerge, such as being a "plush" lawn. The interesting question is whether the emergent features can be predicted from the ingredients, which is possible in both of these examples.

We could take an *eliminativist* view of lawns, if we say that lawns don't exist as distinct entities because they are just grass. The lawn and the grass do not both exist. But could what emerges be *more than the sum of its parts*? If so, then both reduction and elimination of what emerged would be impossible. The best-known candidate for such strong emergence is the mind, which appears to contain much more than the sum of the edible gray matter inside our skulls. The hallmark of a strong emergent feature is that it has its own causal powers, which are not predictable from or entirely composed of the causal powers of the ingredients. Thus, if minds are strongly emergent, and economics involves minds, then economics will not be reducible.

According to the eliminativist view, a lawn does not exist, because it is just grass.

CHAPTER 13

A commitment to Physicalism can only be a metaphysical theory, a presupposition of our view of nature, with no chance of being proved by showing precise reductive links between the levels. Of course strong emergence may be impossible, our grasp of complexities in nature may continually advance (with successful month-long weather forecasts), and we may find ways to enlarge and focus our conceptual scheme.

There remains one other barrier, though, to modern hopes of establishing that "everything is physical," which is that the physical matter upon which hopes are being pinned has to exist in space and time. In ordinary conversation we take these two background features for granted, as the containers for physical matter. Physicists see space and time as part of the physical world, but they seem to exist, so any theory of Physicalism must accommodate them.

TIME

The first dispute about both space and time is the "absolutist" versus the "relativist" views. Isaac Newton took space to be ***absolute***—a fixed background of places where objects can be located. Einstein saw both space and time as ***relative***, being a matter of relationships between their contents, and only measurable within a frame of reference. His theories referred to a single space-time. Quantum theory talks of processes, where waves "collapse" and quantum particles "leap," which requires real time. So the question of whether time is relative or absolute has not been settled by science.

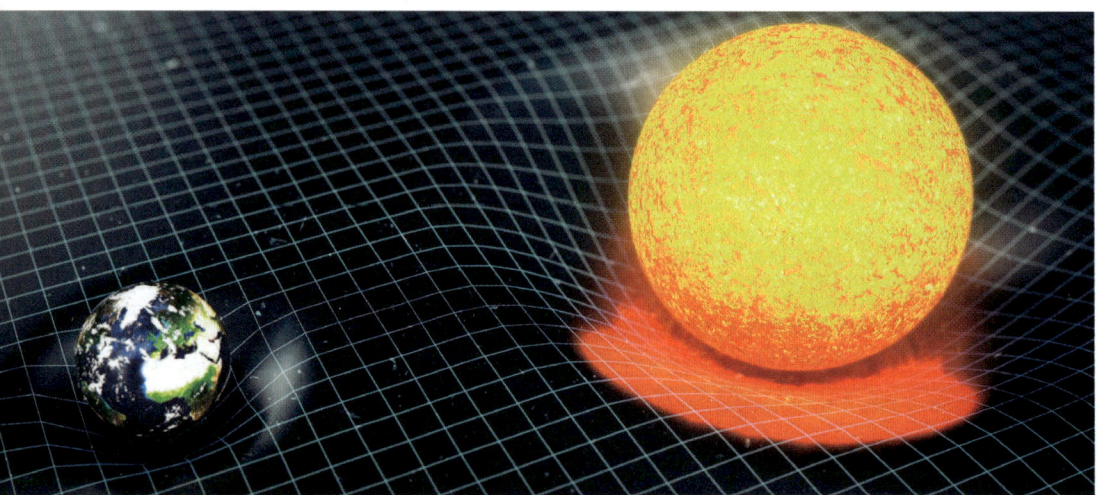

Einstein's theories referred to the concept of a single "space-time."

NEWTON	EINSTEIN	QUANTUM THEORY
Absolutist	*Relative*	*Absolutist*
Space and time are fixed.	Space and time are measurable only within a frame of reference.	Processes occur in real time.

Doubts about the existence of time were raised by the earliest philosophers. The present moment doesn't exist, being merely where past meets future; the past has ceased to exist; and the future hasn't arrived yet—so there is no time! If the present moment does exist, how can a year exist, if its moments don't exist together? But there are reasons to believe in time. We say that dinosaurs have ceased to exist, implying that their time has gone, and yet the sentence "dinosaurs once existed" is true. Its truthmaker must be the long-dead dinosaurs, which must therefore have some sort of reality.

The present moment may be impossible to pin down, but present experience is far more vivid than memories or imagination. And denying that the future exists is equivalent to saying "we have no future," which seems wrong. The view that past, present, and future equally exist is *eternalism*, which says all time co-exists, and the "present moment" is not a special part of reality.

ETERNALISM ▶ *Past, present, and future exist equally.*

Scientists favor *eternalism*, and physics only concerns general sequences of events, rather than particular moments. For the rest of us, however, life makes no sense if the present moment is unimportant, and past and future have equal status. We have bitter regrets about the past, and desperate hopes for the future. We can never believe the present moment is unreal when we are racing to catch a train.

We can both recognize that dinosaurs no longer exist and that they once existed.

A distinction is made between the "***A Series***" and the "***B Series***" of time. The ***A Series*** is a tensed view of time, because "she ran," "she is running," and "she will run" express three different objective facts. Time is seen from the present viewpoint, and the truth of the three sentences changes as time passes. The ***B Series*** of time talks only of "before" and "after" (the ***untensed*** view) of time, with no importance for the present moment, and no sense that time passes. Ordinary conversation favors the A Series (where time passes), and science tends to favor the B Series (where events just have an order).

In favor of the A Series view is that we remember the past but not the future, and dread or plan for the future but not the past. In favor of the B Series is that the present moment is irrelevant to the great truths of physics, and that all times must have equal existence because we can make true statements about all of them. The common-sense A Series may imply that both past and future are utterly non-existent. If the present moment has no duration, this implication may induce a feeling of panic. Time seems uncontroversial in the B series view, but in the A series view our experience of time becomes baffling, because each instant is gone before you can grasp it.

NATURE

"A" SERIES	"B" SERIES
Tensed	Untensed
"She ran," "she is running," and "she will run"	Only "before" and "after"
Ordinary conversation	Scientific discourse

Even eternalists concede that time has a direction, but see it as an aspect of causal relations, or arising out of entropy (the universal dispersal of energy). But this can be expressed by using the before and after of the B Series, along with giving a name to the time of each event in the sequence, such as "August 4, 1914," the date on which Great Britain declared war on Germany. We only have a concept of time because things change, so maybe we can just describe the changes and drop the fiction of "time."

We only understand the idea of time because things change.

CHAPTER 13

LIFE

In addition to exploring the way we think, philosophers also need a picture of our biology and our place in Earth's ecosystem. A lot depends, for example, on how fundamentally different from other animals we seem to be. The most influential biological theory is the natural selection view of evolution, which may explain how we think as well as why we are here. We can also now have an ecological perspective on life, which places humanity in a much wider context.

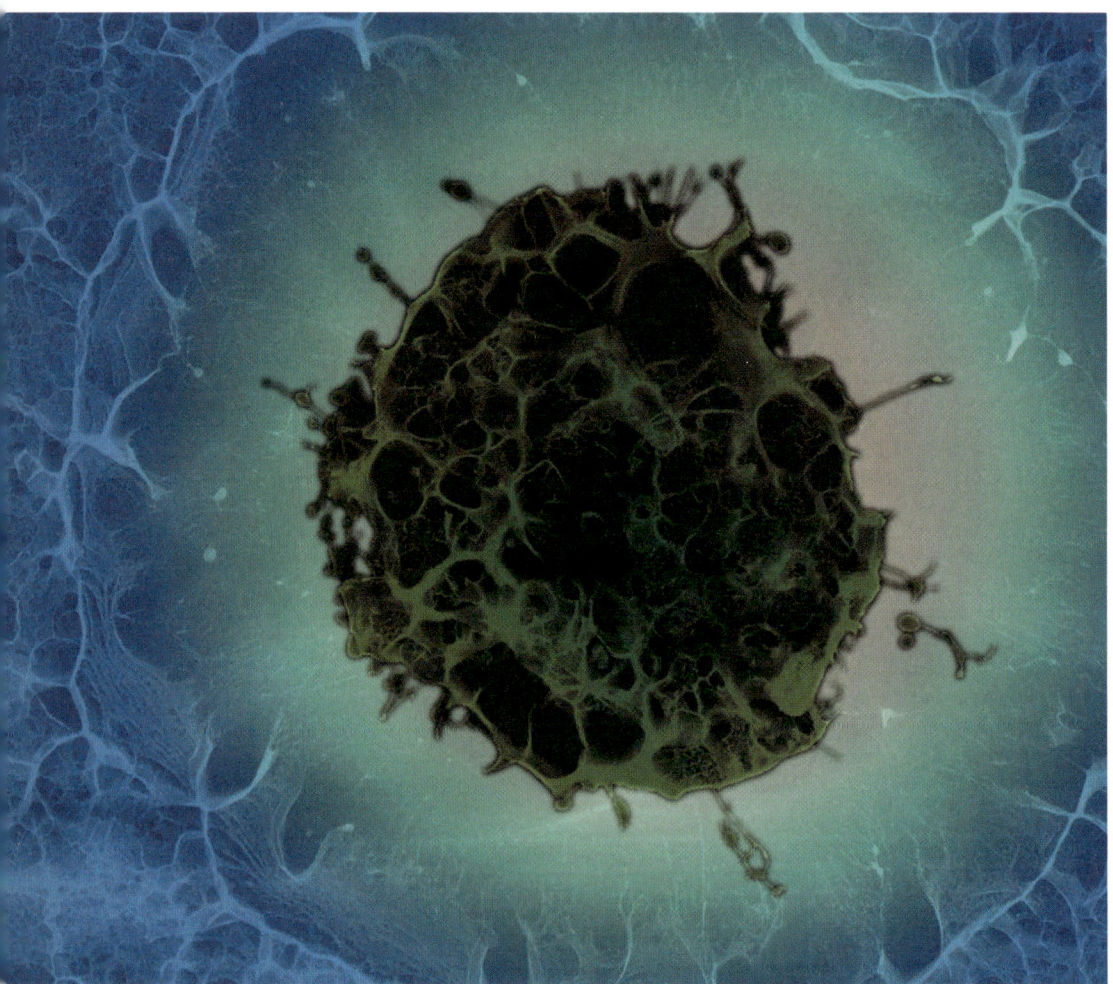

Science has changed our concept of life, as modern microbiology has shown that life can be reduced to physical events.

SCIENTIFIC CHALLENGES TO THE SOUL

> Chemicals in our bodies can be synthesized in a test tube.

> The law of conservation of energy suggested there could be no further energy source outside of physics.

> Modern microbiology found no signs of any extra forces at the level of cells or biochemistry.

Science has strikingly changed our modern concept of *life*. It was assumed that to be alive needs some extra ingredient—such as a type of fire, or a spiritual soul, or an extra natural force, or a special life substance.

These developments strongly imply that physics is "closed" (requiring no external explanations) and also that life is reducible to physical events. Nowadays, most of us accept that the life of a plant is essentially chemistry. Since the most important aspect of DNA is the information it carries, life is now sometimes defined in terms of information rather than chemistry.

Classifying Nature

Aristotle was the first person to propose categories in biology, and classifying nature has always interested philosophers.

Modern methods of classification are controversial. Originally this was just done by external features such as stripes and shells. Nowadays, we have evolutionary heredity and genetic analysis to consider. There are four main methods of classification:
- by features, internal as well as external
- by being in an isolated breeding group
- by occupying an environmental niche
- by the history and division points in their lineage.

Scientists prefer classifying things by their relationships, rather than by their essential nature, because that places them accurately within a system. Philosophers are divided between skeptics about classification, seeing it as a mere convention (like convenient names for stretches of land), and those who say names of animals relate to their essential nature. Kripke argues that the word "tiger" must originally name one particular animal, and other animals are tigers because they share the essential nature of the first one (such as its typical DNA).

Aristotle was the first philosopher to categorize nature.

Philosophers have been slow to address the implications of Charles Darwin's theory of natural selection.

Philosophy and Evolution

Darwin's theory of *natural selection* (that the traits of living creatures all result from earlier success in breeding) offered a good explanation of natural variety, and modern genetics has made it a secure part of modern biology. Philosophers have been slow to address the implications of evolution. While being bipeds with opposable thumbs may be an obvious result of natural selection, the idea that the workings of our brains and hence our thinking may also result from this process is harder to digest.

In ethical philosophy, the unpopular contractarian view of morality (that it is a strategy for selfish people to get assistance from others) has gained in support.

CHAPTER 13

Genetics has strongly confirmed our close relationship to apes such as the chimpanzee and bonobo, and even bananas seem to be our very distant cousins. This has greatly strengthened the picture of humanity as integrated into the environment, and produced the science of Ecology, encouraging us to live within nature rather than detaching ourselves from nature and ruthlessly exploiting it. All of these biological developments are crucial to philosophy, because the way we see the human race has significantly changed, and all our theories in philosophy arise partly from how we see ourselves.

Genetics has confirmed that humans are closely related to chimpanzees.

Chapter Fourteen
TRANSCENDENCE

Beyond Nature—The Existence of God—The Nature of God

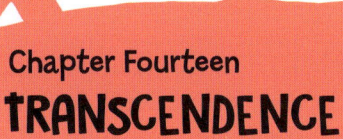

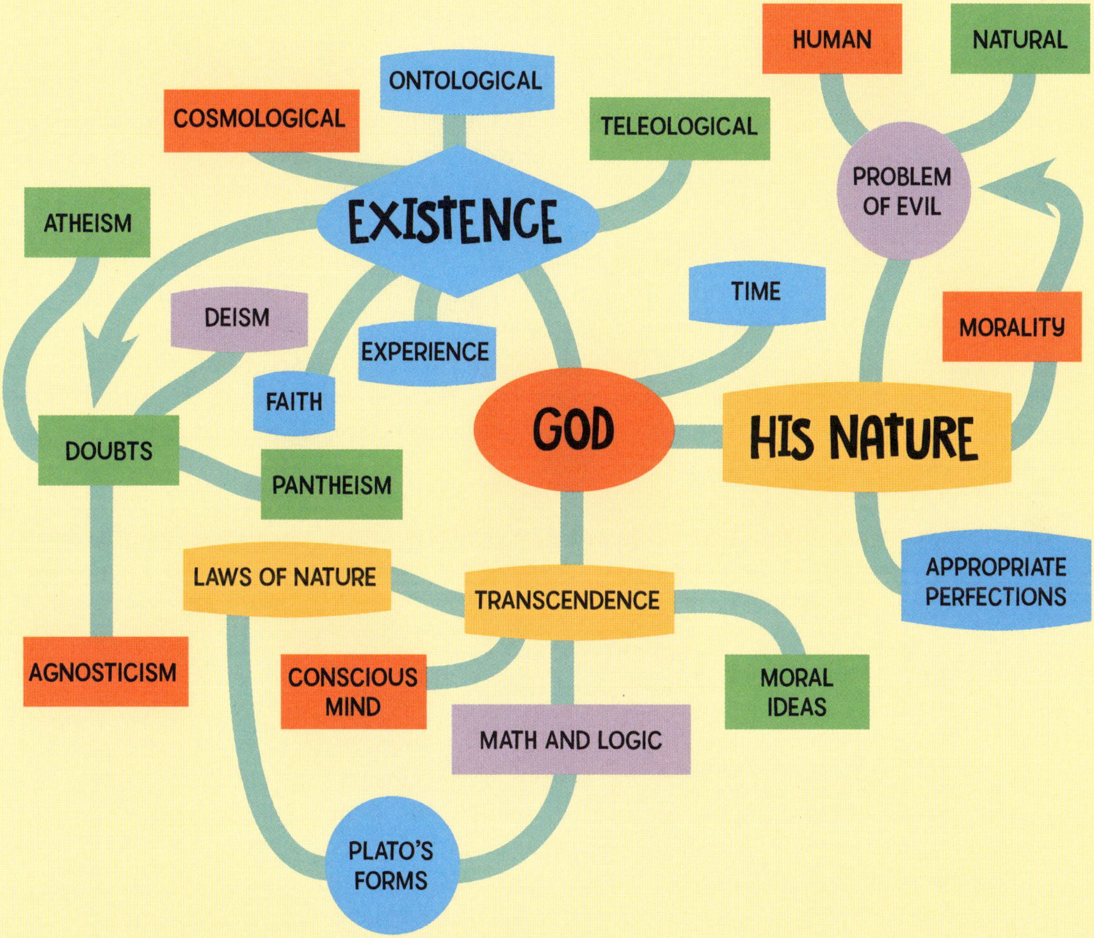

CHAPTER 14

BEYOND NATURE

Does anything exist which transcends nature (lies beyond it)? The most obvious transcendent beliefs are religious. These assert the existence of spiritual minds (notably God), which are not subject to our laws of nature. There are four categories of phenomenon which may also transcend the merely physical:
- consciousness
- mathematics and logic
- the laws and ideas that control nature
- moral ideals.

We can consider all four of these to be non-physical features within nature, or to be lying beyond nature in a "super-natural" realm.

Of these four possibilities, the conscious mind is the most important, because we could have no knowledge of the other three if our mind is unable to bridge the gap between our physical brain and these non-physical phenomena. We have discussed these issues earlier in the book (see chapter six). The mind is physical, or it is weakly emergent (resulting from brain events), strongly emergent (having some causal power over brain events), or a non-physical substance.

Strong emergence still places the mind within nature, but **substance dualism** (see page 88) places the mind at least partly in the super-natural world. The implication of strong emergence is that nature is profoundly different from the picture offered by physics. We may think that physics is closed (and can thus explain everything), but actually this is not so, because events are also caused by emergent mental powers, most obviously when humans make conscious decisions. Substance dualism takes us beyond nature, because it involves the existence of a different mode of reality—the spiritual realm. We don't detect any mechanisms in the physical brain that can bridge the gap to this mental/spiritual world, so the capacity to reach out to the physical world must be an aspect of the mental substance.

The Super-natural Mind

If the mind has a super-natural mode of existence, this opens the possibility that logic, the laws of nature, and moral ideals (with which the mind is acquainted) might also transcend nature, having eternal and necessary existence yet having some powers that influence nature. Plato's Forms (idealized concepts that guide both thought and reality) have just such an eternal status, and many logicians and mathematicians see in their subjects truths that exist quite independently from human thoughts about them. Evidence for the influence of this transcendent realm on nature is seen in the precise mathematical patterns found in the structures of plants and chemicals, and the fact that nature must conform to logical laws such as non-contradiction. Some actions, such as cruelty to the innocent, seem so self-evidently wicked to everyone that the only explanation is the existence of transcendent moral values.

This train of thought, starting with Physicalism, can gradually lead us toward religion—but the history of our cultures goes the other way, because religious beliefs were a universal assumption long before a few thinkers suggested Physicalism. Science largely works with an assumption of Physicalism, and Theology assumes the existence of God (and aims to develop consistent doctrines). Philosophy prides itself on its minimal assumptions, so we will consider religious belief from as neutral a view as possible.

THE EXISTENCE OF GOD

Most modern religious beliefs center on the existence of God, a single supreme spiritual being, combining powers and perfections in such a way that God dominates nature and has a status of ultimate importance. Belief in the existence of such a supreme being is based on five main grounds: the mere existence of nature; the order within nature; the self-evident necessity of such a being; personal experiences; and intuition or faith. Of these five, the first three are the most important: the Cosmological Argument, the Teleological Argument, and the Ontological Argument.

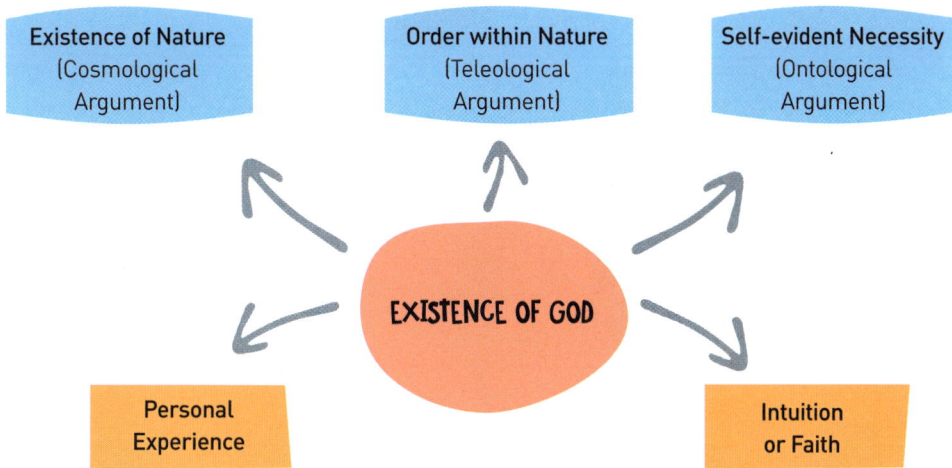

CHAPTER 14

Cosmological Argument

The *Cosmological Argument* claims that the very existence of the cosmos implies the existence of God—as its starting point and source. In nature we assume that every event has a cause, which implies a chain of caused events leading back in time, either to a first event or to eternity. If every event has a cause, how can there be a first event? The first event has to be an exception to the rule—something which is *self-caused*. Everything within nature seems to be caused, so this **First Cause** must be outside of nature, and only a mind could have such an ability—resembling our own ability to make free choices. But what if the chain of events has no beginning? Then we need an explanation of why the chain has persisted instead of fizzling out, and why the chain took the direction it did, rather than something different. So there must still be an external cause to sustain and direct what exists. In both cases (with or without the assumption of a beginning), the only conceivable external cause of the cosmos is a supreme mind that can initiate events.

The Cosmological Argument suggests that the existence of the universe itself provides evidence of a Creator.

Teleological Argument

The Greek word *telos* means "purpose," and the *Teleological* or *Design Argument* says the ordered structure of nature implies the role of an ordered and purposeful mind. The argument usually assumes that without an organizer, nature would be a chaotic mess. The idea that nature should have its intricate and beautiful structure by pure chance is ridiculous (like letters thrown onto the floor forming a perfect poem). The argument is sometimes spelled out as an analogy. If we see a group of people well organized, or a machine with a successful function, we assume someone is in charge of the group, or someone has planned and made the machine. But we see just such organization and functioning in nature, so we must equally assume a controlling mind.

Ontological Argument

The first two arguments refer to evidence: of the existence of nature or of its orderliness. The *Ontological Argument* relies on pure a *priori* thought, about the concept of this supreme being. The concept we all have of God is of a "supremely perfect being," or a being "than which none greater can be conceived." In either case, we then consider what attributes such a concept must necessarily have, in order to fit the agreed description. These must include the greatest possible power, knowledge, and moral goodness. But we also see that a crucial attribute is existence, without which no other perfections are possible. So existence is the first perfection, and God must necessarily exist, because the very concept requires it, in the same way that a triangle necessarily has three sides.

Faith and Experience

Many people have personal experiences that seem to involve direct awareness of or communication with God, and groups of people have experienced miracles, which appear to be direct intervention by God in human affairs. Philosophers usually give less weight to these as arguments for God's existence (in comparison with the first three arguments), because they are far less universal in their application, and depend on trusting the testimony of other people, sometimes from the distant past. They can be very powerful reasons for the people who had the experiences, but they are usually single events that cannot be repeated for a new audience. The same can be said of faith or intuition, which may dominate the mind of a believer but be less persuasive for a skeptic, especially as the approach gives no way to arbitrate between rival faiths, or rival intuitions about conflicting versions of the truth.

Chapter 14

Evaluating the Arguments

The three main arguments for God's existence have each been criticized by doubters. The Cosmological Argument has the obvious difficulty of assuming that everything has a cause, and then inferring that something doesn't have a cause. If something can be "self-caused," why does that have to be God, rather than an unusual first event? Each of the arguments for God has implications about the nature of God, but this argument merely implies a mind that gives a first push to causation, which is not the being worshipped in most religions.

The Design Argument is probably the one favored by most believers. We live in a world that functions exquisitely and looks awesomely beautiful. This not only seems to imply a designer, but also a being who commands our worship. Critics respond that the world also has a bad side, of malfunctions and ugliness, so we cannot infer a perfect designer. Hume said that if the argument is an analogy, then the creator of the universe might well be a team of gods, or a god who makes mistakes. The biggest challenge to the argument is the claim that nature might have developed its beautiful order by natural selection, without super-natural help. This may explain living things, but the harmonic motions of the cosmos and the powerful simplicity of the laws of nature remain unexplained.

Hume argued that the creator of the universe might be a team of Gods who made mistakes as they designed the world.

The Design Argument has been strengthened in modern times by the realization that the *cosmological constants* (the basic values of physics, such as the strength of gravity or the mass of the electron) seem to be fine-tuned to make life possible. Computer modelling shows that almost any small deviation from the current set of constants would make life impossible. This suggests that the values were set by a designer, for a purpose. This remarkable fact would be less surprising, though, if there were a multitude of varied universes, rather than merely the one we find ourselves in.

Few people have accepted God's existence simply because of the Ontological Argument, which looks ingenious rather than persuasive, but it appeals to anyone who feels that there *must* be a God (rather than God being a promising theory). If the argument is invalid, it is a great challenge to say what is wrong with it. The argument relies on existence being one of the attributes of God (or of anything that exists). So three features of your shoe are its having a sole, it being foot-shaped, and it existing. Kant said this is a misunderstanding, because existence is a presupposition of discussing your shoe, not one of its features. In modern logic, existence is treated as a quantifier, specifying what exists in a sentence, rather than being an ingredient of the sentence. But Kant's objection may be wrong, and contemplation of the concept of God may still lead a sympathetic thinker to the inescapability of God's existence.

DEISM ▶ *God exists, but has no involvement in human affairs.*

Doubts about religion come in varying degrees. Deism accepts God's existence because of the Cosmological Argument (that the foundation of nature must be a spiritual mind), but sees no sign of God's involvement in human affairs, and views God as very remote and unresponsive to prayer (a view sometimes called "the God of the philosophers"). Spinoza proposed *Pantheism*, which has a *naturalistic* view of the mind and sees no reason to believe in spiritual substances, but is impressed by the awesome character of the

Spinoza wrote extensively on the subject of God, but many commentators claim he was close to atheism.

natural world and so identifies God and nature as a single substance. Spinoza's writings continually talk of "God," but some commentators say he was close to atheism.

> **PANTHEISM** ▶ *God and Nature are one and the same.*

The *agnostic* position gives priority to direct evidence, and concludes that there is little evidence either way, so that no firm opinion about God's existence can be formed. Atheists commit themselves to the view that God does not exist. The main grounds for atheism are the weaknesses seen in the three main arguments for God's existence, the lack of evidence for the existence of a soul and immortality, and scientific explanations of the existence and character of the human race. *Atheists* are also inclined to doubt the occurrence of miracles, and they deny the sacred status of major religious texts.

> **AGNOSTICISM** ▶ *There is not enough evidence to form an opinion about God's existence.*

The *logical positivists* (a modern empiricist movement) also raised an important challenge to the meaningfulness of much *religious language*, by asking what evidence could count for or against its truth. If believers do not vary the strength of their convictions according to the evidence, then has anything worthwhile actually been proposed?

THE NATURE OF GOD

When God's existence is discussed, there must be some idea of what is meant by "God," even if such a being is also mysterious. The reasons for believing in God help to clarify what the concept means, since we infer that God loves beauty and order from the Teleological Argument, and that God has all possible perfections from the Ontological Argument.

If the arguments are accepted, and God is presumed to exist, then further clarifications are possible, by considering what is likely given the evidence, what is necessarily true, and what is impossible. Thus, it seems likely that God loves order, it seems necessary that God exists eternally, and it seems impossible that God could prove that God does not exist.

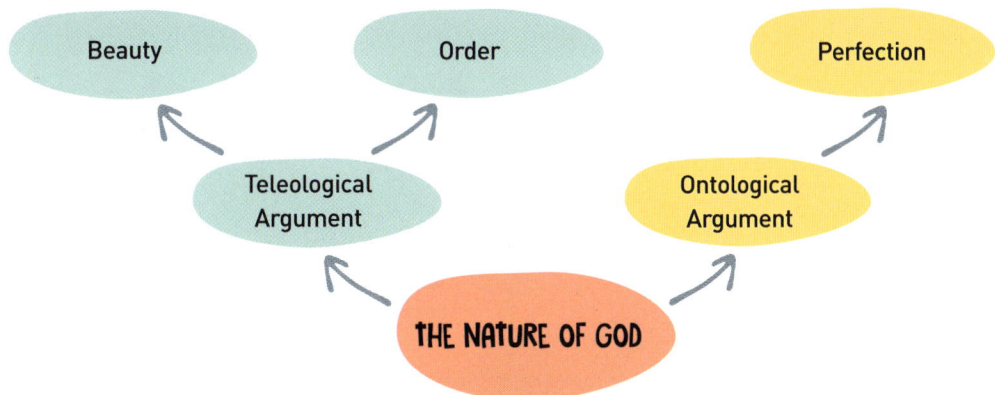

One version of the Ontological Argument says God is "supremely perfect," so we can ask what those *perfections* might be, and whether they can be consistent. Some perfections are trivial, such as making a perfect cake, so we must say that God has "appropriate perfections." An all-powerful being could not create something over which it had no power, so we must also restrict the perfections to what is possible. These tend to be the most admired human virtues—such as knowledge, power, wisdom, and benevolence—but that indicates the difficulty of using human concepts to think about God. Possible contradictions among the perfections include having both knowledge of the future and free will, since the future needs to be fixed in order to be known, and so it can't be chosen.

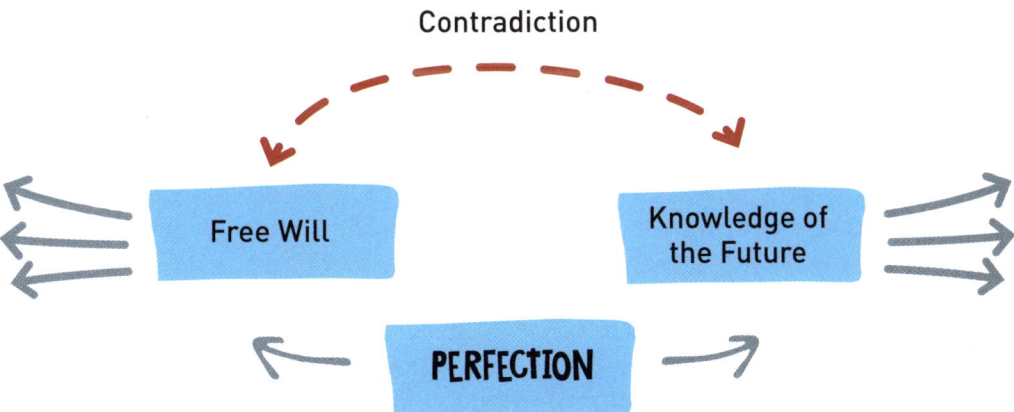

CHAPTER 14

If God created the cosmos, does God exist outside time entirely?

This difficulty raises the interesting question of *how God relates to time*. If God is presumed to create the cosmos, and occasionally intervene in its workings, these are actions which take place in time, implying that God has an unchangeable past and an unknowable future, just as we do. Such limitations are normally rejected in favor of God existing either at no time, or at all times. If God is wholly outside time, that makes the creation and interventions perplexing, so the best account says God exists at all moments, just as we exist in one present moment. This fits with the perfections of omniscience and omnipotence (because all events can be both known together and controlled), but gives God a mode of temporal existence which for us is unimaginable.

God and Morality

Most discussions of the nature of God focus on morality. Plato raised the problem (his ***Euthyphro Question***) of which has priority, morality or God? That is, is God very wise and therefore understands what is virtuous, or are the virtues those qualities that God prefers?

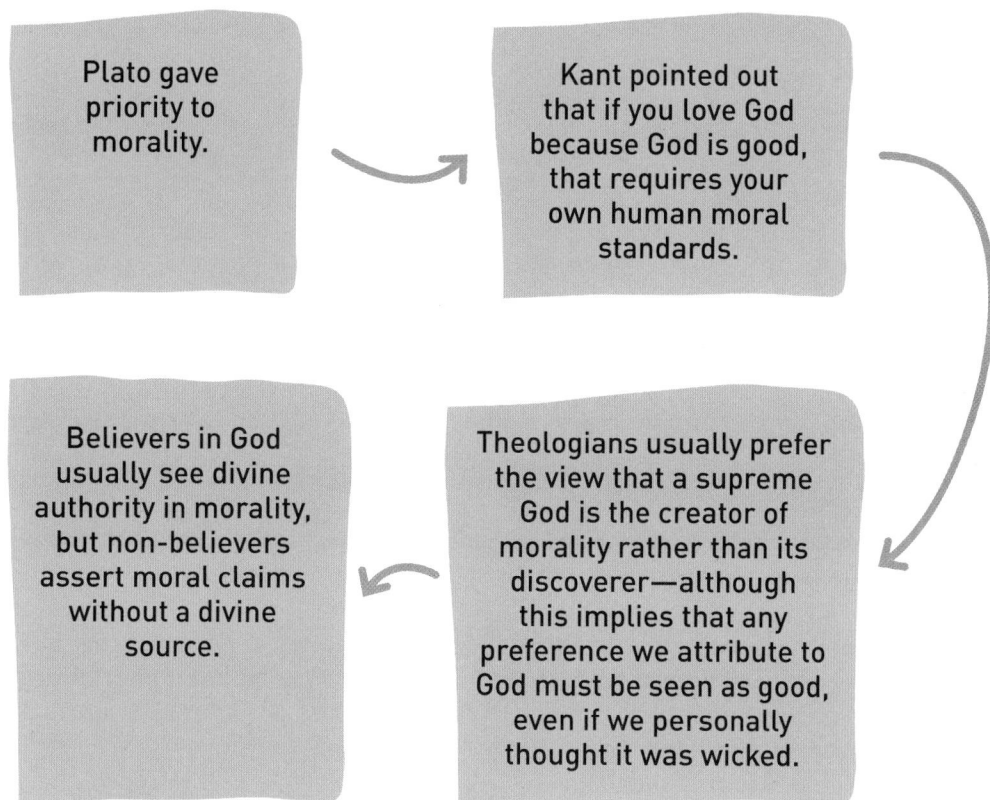

The Problem of Evil

It is normally assumed that benevolence is one of the perfections of God, even though in the past God has been seen as angry, jealous, or vengeful. This leads to the ***problem of evil***—that there is a contradiction if a benevolent being fails to control evil when they have both the power and the knowledge to do so.

Different problems arise for "human evil" (such as genocide) and "natural evil" (such as an earthquake). A response to the first case is to urge the importance of human free will. The key fact about humans is said to be their autonomy, their full control over their own lives. Since evil deeds are possible in any world, people are therefore free to be evil, and they will inevitably do so—but this is better than a world where people lack such freedom. It can still be replied that the freedom to commit genocide is too much freedom, but life would be greatly diminished if evil were impossible.

CHAPTER 14

Natural disasters such as earthquakes suggest that a benevolent God does not exist.

Natural evil is the bigger problem, because humanity is powerless against such things, and God appears to be fully responsible. Non-believers cite natural evil as important evidence that a benevolent God does not exist. The normal defenses against this charge are:

- Such evil is unavoidable.
- Evils are good in the long run.
- Evil is only apparent and not real.

Leibniz argued that a perfect God has created a perfect universe, and we only doubt that because we don't understand the unavoidable trade-offs involved in such a creation. It is impossible to make a planet, for example, without regular earthquakes. The second defense says we need to see God's greater plan before we condemn natural disasters, since suffering may be an unavoidable step toward human salvation or moral improvement. The third defense suggests that we exaggerate the evil in physical pain and bereavement because our view is too narrowly human. Thus, an earthquake is a good event—for the planet, rather than for us.

Leibniz argued that we fail to realize that the world God created is perfect, because we don't understand the trade-offs involved.

GLOSSARY

"A" and "B" Series Time can be seen in two ways. For the A Series view, the present moment is crucial, the past is gone, and the future yet to come. In the B Series view, there is no present moment, and events are ordered as before or after one another. In the A series an event moves through time, but in the B series it has a fixed temporal location. Talk of past and future is meaningless in the B series.

A Priori/A Posteriori Knowledge is a priori if it can be learned by mere thought, via direct insights and unpacking concepts; it is a posteriori if its truth depends on experience. Possible all truths about ideas are revealed a priori, and all truths about the world are revealed a posteriori.

Agent Causation A different kind of causation may be involved when the decisions of a mind (an "agent") cause events, rather than causation by previous physical events. This aims to explain free will.

Agrippa's Trilemma Knowledge must be justified, but the justification also needs to be known—which needs another justification. Does this go on forever, or end in unjustified knowledge, or do the justifications go around in a circle? In all cases the desire for a foundation is frustrated.

Akrasia [Gk] Lack of control over one's actions, also called "weakness of will," when we judge that we should do one thing, but do another because of temptation (such as breaking a diet). Are actions controlled by reason, or by desires?

Analytic/Synthetic Sentences are analytically true because of the words involved, or synthetically true because of external facts. The first type may be knowable by thought, and the second by experience. The distinction is criticized as arbitrary.

Attributes/Substrate Objects have attributes (or properties, or qualities) but what are they attributes *of*? We can think of an underlying "substrate" which has all the attributes, but that is a very puzzling entity.

Autonomy A person is autonomous if they are capable of making totally independent and free decisions.

Behaviorism There is nothing more to a conscious mind than its observable or potential behavior.

Categorical Imperative Kant's claim that each action follows a principle, and that our moral duty is to obey the principle which everyone ought to follow in such circumstances.

Circularity Two explanations or definitions are useless if they depend on one another. Descartes said it is true that God exists, and truth is reliable because God guarantees it. This is logically valid, but not helpful.

Coherentism Justification of a belief is successful if it is fully coherent, meaning its ingredients are relevant, connected and consistent, and form a convincing picture.

Compatibilism An account of human action is compatibilist if it finds some compromise between full free will and rigid determinism, perhaps by saying reason or mental causation or emergent mental properties make a different type of causation possible.

Constant Conjunction Hume's view that causation is nothing more than what can be observed, which is just pairs of events of a certain type always occurring together.

Contextualism Whether a person knows something is not a fact, but depends largely on the context, which can be either relaxed or very demanding.

Contractarianism The only basis for ethics is agreements between people, which creates an obligation to return a favor.

Correspondence Theory A thought or sentence is true when its ingredients match up with features of the world in the correct arrangement.

Cosmological Argument God must exist, to explain either the existence of the cosmos, or its existence in this particular form.

Deflationary Theory Truth is not a robust concept about the connection between mind and world, but a mere endorsement that the sentence expressing it is acceptable and may be asserted.

Deontology Morality consists entirely of duties to perform actions which seem to be right.

Design Argument God must exist, as the only plausible explanation of the order and beauty found in the cosmos.

Dialectic Approaching the truth by a sequence of proposals and objections; or approaching the truth by seeing how one concept leads to another.

Downward Causation The mind can exert downward causation on the brain if it has independent causal powers, which are not just generated by brain activity.

Dualism Mind and brain are different types of thing. If the mind is entirely non-physical, that is Substance Dualism. If the mind is the unique properties of a physical substance, able to have their own causal powers, that is Property Dualism.

Empiricism and Rationalism Empiricists say only experience gives knowledge of the world, but rationalists say such knowledge results from judgments, and involves direct insights of reason.

Essence We understand a thing if we know its indispensable features, and what causes it to be the type of thing it is, and to behave in certain ways.

Eudaimonia [Gk] A life is *eudaimon* if it is a flourishing example of its kind, which we would consider successful and admirable. Sometimes translated as "happy."

Existentialism The key fact about humanity is our freedom, not only to act, but to remake ourselves into something new. Choice is the central fact of our lives.

Expressivism Value judgments appear to be stating facts, but are really emotional expressions of preferences or dislikes.

Externalism and Internalism Internalists say meanings occur entirely inside minds, but externalists say they are partly social conventions or features of the world. These views may imply that the mind itself is either wholly within the brain, or extends out into the world.

Fact-Value Distinction Most empiricists say that experience may reveal facts, but can't reveal values, so facts cannot imply values (and what "is" the case does not entail what "ought" to be the case). Critics reply that some human facts necessarily involve values.

Fallibilism It is possible to know something, despite a faint possibility that it is false.

Foundationalism Justification can only ensure knowledge if it has a secure foundation, either in self-evident rational truths, or undisputed empirical evidence.

GLOSSARY

Functionalism The mind is a structure of interconnected functions (rather than the brain that performs the functions), and each part of the mind should be understood by its role in the system.

Gettier Problem A relevant supporting truth may not be enough to justify knowledge, if the truth was learned in a way that involved luck or misunderstanding.

Idealism Reality exists entirely as ideas within minds, because any knowledge of reality beyond mental experience is impossible. C.f. Phenomenalism.

Induction Learning from experience, by inferring general truths from patterns in experience. Critics say it is not logical, or even rational.

Infinite Regress When the explanation of something always requires a further similar explanation to support it, resulting in an unending chain.

Intentionality The capacity of mental events to have content, and to be about something.

Metaethics Study of underlying assumptions and justifications that support theories about correct moral behavior.

Modality Concerning the way in which something is true, usually about whether it is necessarily or possibly true. Modal logic is its system of formal reasoning.

Natural Necessity A universal and unvarying truth about nature (though we can imagine it being false in a different reality).

Naturalism There can be no meaningful discussion of the existence of anything that is not part of the natural universe we inhabit.

Non-Contradiction A statement and its negation cannot simultaneously be true, so that at least one of them has to be false.

Normative Ethics Moral theories which lay down norms or guidelines for ethical behavior. Distinct from metaethics (the pure theory) and applied ethics (the practice).

Ontological Argument God must exist, because we have a concept of a supreme being, and examining this concept shows that it involves necessary existence.

Ontology Study of the basic ingredients and relationships of existence.

Phenomenalism Physical objects consist entirely of the actual and possible experiences which they can give us. Unlike idealism, the existence of an external world may be accepted.

Phronesis [Gk] Practical reason, or common sense. Said to be the most important faculty if we wish to live virtuous lives, because it judges how to apply virtues in practical situations.

Physicalism Everything that exists is physical, including minds and their ideas.

Pragmatism Truth and knowledge should focus on future success, rather than past evidence.

Predicate The part of a sentence which gives information about its subject. Sometimes identified with a property of the specified object.

Primary/Secondary Qualities Primary qualities accurately reveal reality, as agreed by different types of experience. Secondary qualities are confined to one type of experience (such as color vision), and are more dependent on the responses of the observer.

Private Language Argument Claim that a language which only exists within a single mind, to describe its experiences, is logically impossible, because the rule-following needs a whole community.

Proposition A complete unambiguous idea which can be true or false, expressible in various sentences and languages.

Propositional Attitudes Mental states seeing a proposition in a particular way, such as doubt, fear, belief, or hope.

Qualia A quale is the raw quality of an experience, such as the redness of a rose, or the loudness of a sound. It is said to be particularly hard to explain in physical terms.

Realism/Anti-Realism Realists are committed to the existence of an external world which does not depend on how we experience it. Anti-realists say either that for us only the experiences exist, or that detailed knowledge of any reality is impossible.

Reductionism Reductionism says that something (such as the mind, or biology) can in principle be completely explained by some lower level (such as the brain, or chemistry).

Relativism A truth is relative if it is in relation to something else (such as being "rich" or "poor"). It is claimed that all truths are relative, and that there are no facts or correct beliefs, but merely many points of view. In effect, there is no truth.

Reliabilism The main version of the view that justification is external, and not in the knower's mind, says that knowledge is good if arrived at by a reliable process, such as seeing clearly in bright light.

Representative Realism Our experience reveals the real world to us, but via representations in the mind (e.g. sense-data), which contain accurate information. Others say our experience of reality is "direct."

Sense/Reference The phrase "the inventor of the light bulb" has a sense or meaning (whoever achieved that) and a reference (Thomas Edison). Reference may be fixed by the sense, or by more direct contact with the person.

Social Contract A ruler or government only has legitimate power if there is an actual or theoretical agreement by the people who are to be ruled.

Solipsism Extreme idealism, saying that not even other minds can be known, so that nothing exists apart from the contents of the thinker's mind. Implausible, but hard to disprove.

Theory of Forms Plato's claim that important key ideas and ideals do not just exist in the mind, but are a basic feature of reality, existing independently from thinkers.

Truthmaker Claim that nothing can be true unless something makes it true. This seems right for simple truths, but controversial for complex or general truths.

Universal A single idea, word, or phrase which can be applied with the same meaning to many different things. The problem is to explain how they are the same yet different.

Utilitarianism Theory that moral choices should be made and judged by their increase in "utility," which is the welfare, benefits, and preferences of those involved.

Verificationism Empiricist claim that a sentence is only meaningful if there is some possible way of establishing whether it is true. It is used to dismiss the bolder claims of metaphysics as meaningless.

SUGGESTED READING

1. WHAT IS PHILOSOPHY?
Plato *Gorgias*. Dialogue in which Socrates defends philosophy, first against Gorgias, who rejects truth, and then against Callicles, who despises philosophers for their irresponsibility.
Thomas Mautner (ed.) *The Penguin Dictionary of Philosophy*. An excellent way to achieve a quick grasp of almost any topic in philosophy. Also explains thinking techniques.
Simon Blackburn *Think*. Guide to the main topics, written for beginners by a prominent thinker.
Thomas Nagel *What Does It All Mean?* Short and straightforward book by a leading philosopher, showing how philosophy relates to what most concerns us.
Roger Scruton *Modern Philosophy*. An exceptionally clear and well written survey of philosophy since about 1880.
Alison Stone *An Introduction to Feminist Philosophy*. Focuses on gender issues, rather than the full range of philosophy, but a clear survey of this modern approach.
Simon Critchley *Continental Philosophy: A Very Short Introduction*. Clear and readable survey of the German and French traditions since 1790.
Stanford Online Encyclopaedia of Philosophy (plato.stanford.edu). Not easy reading, but a wonderfully thorough and free resource, giving an overview of almost every topic, with extensive guides to further reading.

2. TRUTH
Pascal Engel *Truth*. Very good survey, also covering the anti-realism debate.
Chase Wrenn *Truth*. Clear expansion of the topic, leading into related areas.
Bertrand Russell *The Problems of Philosophy*. A classic introduction to the subject, focusing on knowledge and metaphysics. Ch. 12 defends the correspondence theory.
Paul Boghossian *Fear of Knowledge*. Short book by a leading philosopher, defending a robust view of truth and knowledge, against widespread modern relativism.

3. REASONING
Plato *Meno*. Short dialogue illustrating Socrates's approach to reasoning, while trying to define virtue. Includes a famous defense of a slave boy's innate knowledge of geometry.
Robert Fogelin *Walking the Tightrope of Reason*. Excellent modern account of reasoning, confronting how difficult it is for us to be completely rational.
Graham Priest *Logic: A Very Short Introduction to Logic (2nd edn)*. Readable account which is not excessively technical, but delves into some very interesting background.
E.J. Lemmon *Beginning Logic*. Classic introduction to sentential and predicate logic, famous for its clarity, and for spelling out each step in detail. With exercises.
Volker Halbach *The Logic Manual*. A recent short survey of all the main techniques.

4. EXISTENCE
Robin Waterfield *The First Philosophers*. Excellent survey of the earliest Greek philosophers, including a comprehensive chapter on Parmenides.
Plato *Republic*. One of the great works. His main ideas about Forms and reality are found in sections 474b–521b [in the standard numbering used in modern editions].
Gottfried Leibniz *Monadology*. His short summary of his whole system of metaphysics.
Immanuel Kant *Prolegomena to Any Future Metaphysics*. The shorter version of his basic ideas. Not an easy read, but one of the major landmarks in philosophy.
Stephen Mumford *Metaphysics: A Very Short Introduction*. Compact and clear survey of the main topics.
Edward Conee and Ted Sider *The Riddles of Existence*. A short and readable introduction to the problems of metaphysics.
Cynthia MacDonald *The Varieties of Things*. An excellent survey of modern metaphysics.
Kathrin Koslicki *The Structure of Objects*. A good example of modern metaphysics, discussing how parts can compose whole objects, and what unites them.

5. KNOWLEDGE
Sextus Empiricus *Outlines of Pyrrhonism*. Fascinating ancient text by a thorough skeptic about almost everything. Full of inventive and enduring arguments.
René Descartes *Meditations I and II*. The first two meditations contain the famous Cogito Ergo Sum argument, and a rationalist attempt to find foundations for knowledge.
George Berkeley *Three Dialogues between Hylas and Philonous*. Intriguing discussion of the idealist interpretation of empiricism (that experience *is* reality).
Linda Zagzebski *On Epistemology*. Short and accessible modern survey of the topic, by a leading theorist.
Laurence Bonjour *In Defense of Pure Reason*. Spirited modern defense of rationalism.

6. MIND
René Descartes *Meditations V and VI*. Offers arguments for the substance dualism theory of mind. He then offers qualifications of his theory, because mind and body are so close.
Ian Ravenscroft *Philosophy of Mind: A Beginner's Guide*. Excellent concise guide to the whole topic, covering most of the major issues.
David Papineau *Thinking About Consciousness*. Clear defense of the physicalist view of mind, including an appendix on the closure of physics.
David Chalmers *The Conscious Mind*. Best-known attack on the failure of physicalism to answer the "hard question" of why we *experience* what we think. Challenging but rewarding.
William G. Lycan *Consciousness*. Attempt to explain the nature of consciousness, by refining the functionalist theory of mind.

7. PERSONS
John Perry (ed.) *Personal Identity (2nd edn)*. Excellent anthology which includes classic extracts from Locke, Butler, Hume, and Reid, and good modern articles.
Thomas Pink *Free Will: A Very Short Introduction*. Concise and clear modern summary of the issues.
Baruch de Spinoza *Ethics*. His great work on metaphysics. Not easy reading. He defends determinism and mind-brain unity.
Peter van Inwagen *An Essay on Free Will*. A sustained modern defense of free will.

8. THOUGHT
Tim Bayne *Thought: A Very Short Introduction*. A nice overview of current thinking.
Jerry A. Fodor *LOT2*. The title means "language of thought version 2." The inventor of the theory that the mind uses an inner language develops his idea further.
Jerry A. Fodor *The Elm and the Expert*. Four lectures about the way our concepts reflect the internal and external views of thought.
François Recanati *Mental Files*. Examination by a leading philosopher of language of the recent idea that the mind is built up of labeled files.
Gregory L. Murphy *The Big Book of Concepts*. Splendidly thorough survey of the essential nature of our concepts, avoiding unnecessary technical language.

219

SUGGESTED READING

Rowland Stout *Action*. He proposes a personal theory of action, but gives a good concise account of modern discussions.

9. LANGUAGE

William G. Lycan *Philosophy of Language: A Contemporary Introduction (2nd edn)*. Well organized and thorough survey of all the main topics.

Michael Morris *An Introduction to the Philosophy of Language*. A historical approach, exploring the ideas of the main thinkers on the subject.

Colin McGinn *Philosophy of Language: The Classics Explained*. Covers each of the major modern theories of language, with clear explanations.

A.J. Ayer *Language, Truth and Logic*. A famous defense of the empiricist view that meaning depends on verifiability. A good example of the wide implications of theories about meaning. Includes a chapter arguing that moral statements merely express emotion.

Saul Kripke *Naming and Necessity*. Influential classic lectures, focusing on direct theories of reference, but with important implications about the nature of necessity.

10. VALUES

Aristotle *Ethics*. One of the great works, on the virtues. It focuses on *eudaimonia* (flourishing), and explores the basis for morality in human nature. The style is compressed but readable.

W.D. Ross *The Right and the Good*. Classic very clear discussion of moral principles, placing confidence in our intuitions about moral truths.

Stephen Davies *The Philosophy of Art (2nd edn)*. Good approachable survey of all the main topics in modern aesthetics.

Roger Scruton *Beauty: A Very Short Introduction*. Thoughtful account of one of the central concepts of aesthetics.

Francesco Orsi *Value Theory*. Excellent compact discussion of all the current theories.

John Kekes *The Human Condition*. Clear and well written analysis of the different types of basic moral value.

11. ETHICS

Thomas Hobbes *Leviathan*. Great work of politic philosophy, introducing the social contract. Book One gives an account of morality in terms of agreements between people. Readable, once you tune in to an older prose style.

Immanuel Kant *Groundwork of the Metaphysic of Morals*. Summarizes his account of morality in terms of rational principles and duties.

John Stuart Mill *Utilitarianism*. The classic summary of the view that morality concerns achieving the best consequences.

John Deigh *An Introduction to Ethics*. Clear and thorough introduction to each of the major theories.

Rosalind Hursthouse *On Virtue Ethics*. Excellent modern account of Aristotelian virtue theory, exploring some of the practical issues.

Murdoch, Iris *The Sovereignty of Good*. Well written account of the modern platonist approach to ethics, presenting goodness as the great ideal.

Jean-Paul Sartre *Existentialism is a Humanism*. A famous lecture summarizing the existentialist approach to living, which inspired a generation.

David E. Cooper *Existentialism: A Reconstruction*. Excellent discussion of existentialist theories, including its background in phenomenology.

Peter Singer *Practical Ethics*. Sustained argument that we should live by utilitarian principles, and aim to increase happiness, especially among animals.

Jonathan Glover *Causing Death and Saving Lives*. Clear discussion of most of the major dilemmas of applied ethics.

12. SOCIETY

Jean-Jacques Rousseau *The Social Contract*. Classic proposal for how to implement a social contract, so that the people sustain the legitimacy of their government.

John Stuart Mill *On Liberty*. Famous text defending the supremacy of the liberal ideal of freedom of the individual, as long as others are not harmed.

Karl Marx and Friedrich Engels *The Communist Manifesto*. Influential analysis of the role of economic power in human life, and how things can be improved.

Andrew Shorten *Contemporary Political Theory*. Excellent survey of all the major concepts involved in debates about political justice and legitimacy.

Jonathan Wolff *An Introduction to Political Philosophy (3rd edn)*. Readable and well balanced survey of the main issues in democratic politics.

John Rawls *A Theory of Justice (2nd edn)*. A long book, but his famous modern defense of liberalism is found in Chapters I–III.

Michael J. Sandel *Justice: What is the Right Thing to Do?* Popular series of lectures exploring where morality and politics meet, in the concept of civic duty, with very good examples.

Martha C. Nussbaum *Creating Capabilities*. Detailed proposals for how liberalism can focus on achieving good lives for people, rather than just freedom and opportunities.

13. NATURE

Lucretius *On The Nature of Things*. Wonderful ancient text presenting the atomistic science of the Epicurean school. Contains many remarkably modern ideas.

David Hume *Enquiries Concerning Human Understanding*. Sections II–VII expound empiricism, and consequent doubts about knowing causation, inductive truths, and necessary laws of nature.

Stephen Mumford and Rani Lill Anjum *Causation: A Very Short Introduction*. Concise approach to the nature of causation, and Hume's doubts about it.

Brian Ellis *The Philosophy of Nature*. Clear and interesting argument in favor of the Aristotelian essentialist approach to modern science.

Daniel Dennett *Darwin's Dangerous Idea*. Argues that our whole world view should be shaped by the idea of natural selection. Explores some of its implications for philosophy.

Eric R. Scerri *The Periodic Table*. Excellent example of a philosopher looking at the history of a major scientific idea, and the principles behind its discovery.

14. TRANSCENDENCE

Plato *Phaedrus*. Dialogue containing an inspiring vision of a world of truth and beauty that extends beyond the natural world.

Michèle Friend *Introducing Philosophy of Mathematics*. Good beginner's introduction to a difficult topic. The status of mathematics is a key question in the study of existence.

Cicero *On the Nature of the Gods*. The best discussion surviving from the ancient world of the basic questions of religion. Contains the earliest versions of many of the major arguments concerning God's existence.

Peter Cole *Philosophy of Religion*. Compact and clear survey of all the main issues.

Brian Davies (ed.) *Philosophy of Religion: A Guide and Anthology*. Extensive collection of classic statements of the main arguments, and modern papers exploring them.

INDEX

a posteriori knowledge 77
a priori knowledge 76–7
abortion 189
actions
  intentions 134–5
  judgments and desires 136
  performance 133
  willed 137
ad hominem fallacy 52
aesthetic values 161–4
agent causation 119
agnosticism 241
Agrippa's Trilemma 83–4
American Pragmatism 32–3
analytical ideas of language 153
analytic necessities 66, 67
analytic school 10, 15, 48, 153
anarchism 204
animal rights 191
anti-realism 65
applied ethics 175
Aquinas, Thomas 17
Aristotle
  and causation 217
  and classifications of nature 229
  and existence 59
  and formal logic 15
  influence on Christianity 18
  life of 43
  and reasoning 43
  and syllogisms 44, 45
  and values 171
  and virtue theory 178–9
art 164–6
artificial intelligence 105
autocracies 200
autonomy 203

Bacon, Francis 19
begging the question 52
Behaviorism 102
Being 58
beliefs
  knowledge 71–2
  mind 95
Bentham, Jeremy 183
Berkeley, George 13
blindsight 97
body/mind 99–100
Boole, George 46
brain in a vat thought experiment 88, 89
Buddhism 110, 112

casual chains in language 146
Categorical Imperative 181–2
categories of existence 62–3
category mistake 52
causation 215–17, 218
changes in existence 63–4
Christianity 17, 18
circularity 52
classical logic 48
Coherence Theory 30–1
coherentism 85
communication 154–7
compatibilism 119
compositional sentences 145
concepts in thought 130–2
consequentialism 168
consciousness 97, 99, 110
constant conjunction 215
content of thoughts 130
contextualism 87
continental school 10, 58
contractarianism 186, 188
contradictory propositions 76
conversational implicature 157
Correspondence Theory 31–2
counterexamples 52

Darwin, Charles 230
dasein 58
death 105
Deflationary Theory 36
democracy 197, 201, 205, 206
Democritus 100
deontology 175, 181–2
Descartes, René
  as Enlightenment philosopher 13
  and knowledge 82, 84
  and mind 100–1
  and rationalism 81
determinism 121
dialectic 41–2
Dialogues (Plato) 42
direct realism 75
double effect 189
downward causation 103
dualism 100–3, 105

economics 220–2
Einstein, Albert 223, 224
elenchus 42
eliminative physicalism 100
empiricism 82, 84, 215
Enlightenment
  description of 12
  philosophers of 13
  and rationalism 82
  truth in 29
  and values 170
Epicureans 171
epistemology 71–2
equality 206–7
essence of objects 59–60
eternalism 224–6
ethics
  abortion 189
  animal rights 191
  applied 188–91
  Categorical Imperative 181–2
  contractarianism 186, 188
  deontology 175, 181–2
  euthanasia 190
  feminism in 21
  normative 175
  scale of virtue 177–8
  utilitarianism 183–5
  values 176–8
  varieties of 175–81
eudaimonia 171, 176, 177
euthanasia 190
evidence in philosophy 20, 49–50
evil 244–5
evolution 230–1
existence
  anti-realism 65
  Being 58
  categories of 62–3
  changes in 63–4
  direct realism 75
  idealism 74
  knowledge of 74–5
  metaphysics 57
  modal profile 66
  naturalism 65
  necessities 66–7
  objects 58–63, 66
  ontology 57–8
  phenomenalism 75
  physicalism 65
  realism 65
  representative realism 74
  solipsism 74
  Theory of Forms 61–2
existentialism 114, 115
expressivism 168–9
extension of concepts 131
extreme relativism 29

fallacies in reasoning 52
fallibilism 77
fatalism 121

feminism 16, 21
Fodor, Jerry 127
Form of the Good 170
formal logic 15, 43
frame problem 129
free will 118–21
freedom 203–5
Frege, Gottlob 47, 141, 171
Functionalism 102–3

Game Theory 188
games 131
general will 196
Gettier Problem 83
God
  agnosticism 241
  Cosmological Argument for 237, 239–41
  experience of 238
  morality 243–5
  nature of 241–3
  Ontological Argument for 238, 239–41, 242
  problem of evil 244–5
  Teleological Argument for 238, 239–41
  and time 243
Greece, Ancient
  consciousness 97
  language in 154
  method of study in 15, 42–3
  reasoning in 42–3
  religion in 17, 18
  values 170–1, 179
Grice, Paul 157hard problem 99
heap paradox 51
hedonism 171
Hegel, Georg Friedrich 114
Heidegger, Martin 58
Heraclitus 13
Hobbes, Thomas 13, 186, 196
Hume, David
  and actions 136
  and causation 215, 218
  as Enlightenment philosopher 12, 13
  and induction 50
  and knowledge 82
  and self 112, 113
  and values 168
Hypatia of Alexandria 14

idealism 74
ideas
  innate 76–7
  and philosophy 11
indexical words 150

INDEX

induction 50
infinite regress 52, 83
intension of concepts 131
intention to act 134–5
intentionality 95–7
internalism 85
inverted qualia 97
Islam 17, 18

jargon 22
Judaism 17
just war 202
justice 208–11
justification 83–4

Kant, Immanuel
  and analytic school 153
  as Enlightenment
    philosopher 12, 13
  and Categorical
    Imperative 181–2
  and categories of
    existence 63
  and self 112
  and thought 126
Kierkegaard, Søren 18
knowledge
  a posteriori 77
  a priori 76–7
  brain in a vat thought
    experiment 88, 89
  coherentism 85
  contextualism 87
  contradictory
    propositions 76
  belief 71–2
  empiricism 82, 84
  epistemology 71–2
  existence 74–5
  fallibilism 77
  innate ideas 76–7
  internalism 85
  justification 83–4
  nature of 71–3
  objectivity 86
  perception 78–80
  prejudices 96
  rationalism 80–1, 82, 84
  reliablism 85
  skepticism 88
  understanding 73
Kripke, Saul 146, 229

language
  analytical ideas 153
  communication 154–7
  meaning 141–4
  propositions 151–2
  reference 144–6
  semantics 147–50
  synthetic ideas 153
legitimacy 195–9
Leibniz, Gottfried

as Enlightenment
  philosopher 13
and existence 58
and God 245
and knowledge 82
liars paradox 51
liberalism 199
linguistics 33–4
Locke, John
  as Enlightenment
    philosopher 13
  and knowledge 82
  and legitimacy 195
  and memories 116, 117
  and personhood 109
  and truth 29
logic see also formal logic
  classical logic 48
  modal logic 48–9
  predicate logic 47–8
  propositional logic 46–7
  reasoning 44–9
  syllogisms 44–5
  truth 35–6
  truth tables 46–7
  validity 45
logical necessities 66
logical positivism 241
lottery paradox 51

Maimonides 17
Marx, Karl 114, 115
meaning
  approaches to 141
  reference 144–6
  speakers' intentions 143
  truth-conditions 142
  usage 144
  verificationism 143
memories 116–17
meta-language 34
metaethics 175
metaphysical necessities 66
metaphysics 57
methods of study 15, see
    also reasoning
mind
  beliefs 95
  body 99–100
  consciousness 97, 99
  dualism 100–3, 105
  Functionalism 102–3
  intentionality 95–7
  nature of 93
  physicalism 104–5
  purpose of 94
  qualia 95–7
Minimalist Theory 36
modal logic 48–9
modal profile 66
modular mind 127–8
Moore, G.E. 84
moral luck 168, 169

morality
  in age of Enlightenment
    12
  feminism in 21
  God 243–5
  values 167–9

natural necessities 66
naturalism 65
nature
  causation 215–17
  classifications 229
  evolution 230–1
  laws of 217–23
  life 227–31
  time 223–6
neuroscience 112, 113, 120
Newton, Isaac
  as Enlightenment
    philosopher 12
  laws of nature 217
  and time 223, 224
Nietzsche, Friedrich
  and self 112, 113
  and truth 28
non-contradictions 41
normative ethics 175
Nozick, Robert 208, 209
Nussbaum, Martha 208,
    210

object language 34
objectivity 86
objects 58–63, 66
ontology 57–8, 63

Pantheism 240–1
paradoxes 51
Parmenides 57
particularism 181
perception
  and knowledge 78–80
  primary qualities 79–80
  secondary qualities 79–80
personhood
  consciousness 110
  continuity of 116
  free will 118–21
  idea of 109
  memories 116–17
  self 110–15, 117
  self-awareness 111–12
phenomenalism 75
philosophy
  critics of 16–23
  and ideas 11
  jargon 22
  methods of study 15
  poetry 16, 21
  practicality of 16, 23
  purpose of 9–10, 11
  questions for 10
  religion 16, 17–18

science 16, 19–20
  in universities 14
  women in 14, 16, 21
physicalism 65, 100, 104–5,
    220, 223, 236
Plato
  and beauty 162
  and existence 61
  morality of God 243
  political philosophy 200
  and reasoning 42
  Theory of Forms 61–2
  and truth 28
  and values 170
poetry 16, 21
political philosophy
  democracy 197, 201,
    205, 206
  equality 206–7
  force 201
  freedom 203–5
  just war 202
  justice 208–11
  legitimacy 195–9
  liberalism 199
  powers 199–202
possible worlds semantics
    149
postmodernism 114, 115
practicality of philosophy
    16, 23
precision in philosophy 20
predicate logic 47–8
predictions 50–1
prejudices 96
prior intentions 135
private language argument
    156
progress in philosophy 20
properties of objects 61–2
property dualism 103
propositional logic 46–7
propositions 125–6, 151–2
Protagoras 28–9
psuché 97
purpose of philosophy
    9–10, 11
Putnam, Hilary 52
Pythagoras 29

qualia 95–7
quantum theory 224
Quine, Willard 67, 153,
    157

Ramsey, Frank 33
rationalism 80–1, 82, 84
Rawls, John 208, 210
realism 65
reality see existence
reasoning
  in age of Enlightenment
    12

in Ancient Greece 42–3
counterexamples 52
dialectic 41–2
elenchus 42
evidence evaluation 49–50
fallacies 52
induction 50
logic 44–9
paradoxes 51–2
predictions 50–1
thought 126
thought experiments 52
truth 41
reductionism 220
reductive physicalism 100
Redundancy Theory 33
reference 144–6
Reid, Thomas 117
relativism
extreme 29
science 30
truth 28–31
reliablism 85
religion *see also* transcendence
philosophy 16, 17–18
science 18
values 170
representative realism 74
Romanticism 12, 170
Rousseau, Jean-Jacques 13, 196
Russell, Bertrand 148, 152, 171

science
classifications of nature 229
evolution 230–1
laws of nature 217–23
life 227–8
method of study 15
philosophy 16, 19–20
relativism 30
and self 112, 113, 117
scientific essentialism 219
scientism 220
self 110–15, 117
semantics
description of 147
indexical words 150
possible worlds 149
subject-predicate form 147–8
Sen, Amartya 210–11
Seneca 28
Ship of Theseus 64
skepticism 88
social contract 196
Socrates
and reasoning 42
and truth 28

and virtue 177, 178
solipsism 74
speakers' intentions 143
Spinoza, Baruch
and free will 120
and God 240
and knowledge 82
and truth 28, 29
substance dualism 101
substrates 61
sustained intentions 135
syllogisms 44–5
synthetic ideas of language 153

tabula rasa 77
Tarski, Alfred 34, 36, 51
technocracies 200
Theory of Forms 61–2
Theory-Theory of Concepts 132
thought
action 133–7
concepts 130–2
content 130
frame problem 129
mechanics 126–9
modular mind 127–8
propositions 125–6
reasoning 126
types of 125–6
thought experiments 52, 64, 88–9
time 223–6
transcendence *see also* religion
existence of God 236–41
forms of 235
nature of God 241–3
super-naturalism 235–6
values of God 243–5
truth
American Pragmatism 32–3
Coherence Theory 30–1
Correspondence Theory 31–2
Deflationary Theory 36
definition of 27–8
importance of 27
linguistics 33–4
logic 35–6
reasoning 41
relativism 28–31
Redundancy Theory 33
truthmakers 37
validity 45
values 168–9
truth-conditions 142
truthmakers 37

understanding 73
universities 14, 15

utilitarianism 175, 183–5, 205, 206, 208

validity 45
values
aesthetics 161–4
ethics 176–8
God 243–5
identifying 170–1
moral 167–9
truths 168–9
types of 161
verificationism 143
virtue theory 178–9, 181
volitionism 137

whole sentences 145
willed actions 137
Wittgenstein, Ludwig 131, 156, 171
women *see also* feminism
in philosophy 14, 16, 21
political representation 198

PICTURE CREDITS

Alamy: 60 (Geoff A. Howard), 73 (Pictorial Press Ltd), 145 (DC Premiumstock)

Getty Images: 21 (top—The Age/Fairfax Media), 26 (Heritage Images/Hulton Fine Art Collection), 129 (Peter Stackpole/The LIFE Picture Collection)

Library of Congress: 28, 109

Met Museum: 37

Science Photo Library: 41

Shutterstock: 8, 15 (x6), 17, 21 (bottom), 22, 25, 31, 32, 33, 34, 44, 45, 46 (x2), 48, 52, 53 (x2), 54, 57 (x3), 63, 65 (x2), 67, 69, 70, 71, 76, 82, 84, 85, 92, 95 (x2), 96, 100, 101, 102, 103, 106, 111 (x2), 112, 113 (x2), 114, 115, 116, 117, 118, 119, 120, 123, 124, 126, 128, 130, 133, 136, 143 (Igor Bulgarin), 152, 153, 157, 161, 164, 166, 167, 172, 173, 174, 176 (Chad Zuber), 177 (Everett Historical), 178, 179, 182 (Maxisport), 188, 189, 194, 195, 196, 198, 199, 204, 210, 214, 216 (top—think4photop), 216 (bottom)

Wellcome Collection: 12 (x8), 18, 80, 86, 94, 154, 155, 160, 168, 170, 171, 181, 190, 200, 203, 211

Wikimedia Commons: 11, 14, 16, 20, 27, 30, 38, 50, 51, 56, 62, 64, 78, 98, 99, 105, 122, 125, 127, 137, 141, 142, 144, 156, 159, 186, 202, 208

Yale Center for British Art: 13 (Paul Mellon Collection)